£15.99

UNIONISM IN MODERN IRELAND

D0452878

PMA

Also by Richard English

RADICALS AND THE REPUBLIC: Socialist Republicanism in the Irish Free State, 1925–1937

Also by Graham Walker

THE POLITICS OF FRUSTRATION: Harry Midgley and the Failure of Labour in Northern Ireland
SCOTTISH SPORT IN THE MAKING OF THE NATION (*co-editor*)
SERMONS AND BATTLE HYMNS (*co-editor*)
THOMAS JOHNSTON
INTIMATE STRANGERS: Political and Cultural Interaction between Scotland and Ulster in Modern Times

Unionism in Modern Ireland

New Perspectives on Politics and Culture

Edited by

Richard English
Reader in Politics
The Queen's University, Belfast

and

Graham Walker
Reader in Politics
The Queen's University, Belfast

First published in Great Britain 1996 by
MACMILLAN PRESS LTD
Houndmills, Basingstoke, Hampshire RG21 6XS
and London
Companies and representatives
throughout the world

A catalogue record for this book is available
from the British Library.

ISBN 0–333–64672–X hardcover
ISBN 0–333–64673–8 paperback

First published in the United States of America 1996 by
ST. MARTIN'S PRESS, INC.,
Scholarly and Reference Division,
175 Fifth Avenue,
New York, N.Y. 10010

ISBN 0–312–15979–X

Library of Congress Cataloging-in-Publication Data
Unionism in modern Ireland : new perspectives on politics and culture
/ edited by Richard English and Graham Walker.
p.   cm.
Includes bibliographical references and index.
ISBN 0–312–15979–X
1. Trade-unions—Ireland—Political activity—History.   2. Trade
-unions–Northern Ireland—Political activity—History.   3. Trade
-unions—Ireland—History.   4. Trade-unions—Northern Ireland–
–History.   I. English, Richard, 1963–   . II. Walker, Graham S.
HD6670.3.Z65U55   1996
322'.2'09417—dc20   96–10387
                                                CIP

10   9   8   7   6   5   4   3   2   1
05   04   03   02   01   00   99   98   97   96

Printed and bound in Great Britain by
Antony Rowe Ltd, Chippenham, Wiltshire

Contents

Acknowledgements   vii

Notes on the Contributors   viii

Introduction
Graham Walker/Richard English   ix

1   Ulster and the British Problem
    Ian McBride   1

2   Thomas Sinclair: Presbyterian Liberal Unionist
    Graham Walker   19

3   The Modernisation of Unionism, 1892–1914?
    David Burnett   41

4   Ulstermen of Letters: The Unionism of Frank
    Frankfort Moore, Shan Bullock, and St John Ervine
    Patrick Maume   63

5   The Protestant Experience of Revolution
    in Southern Ireland
    Peter Hart   81

6   The Twinge of Memory: Armistice Day and
    Remembrance Sunday in Dublin since 1919
    Jane Leonard   99

7   Ulster Unionism and Loyalty to the Crown of the United
    Kingdom, 1912–74
    Thomas Hennessey   115

8   In Search of Order, Permanence and Stability: Building
    Stormont, 1921–32
    David Officer   130

9   'Meddling at the Crossroads': The Decline and
    Fall of Terence O'Neill within the Unionist
    Community
    Feargal Cochrane   148

Contents

10   Direct Rule and the Unionist Middle Classes   169
     Colin Coulter

11   17 November 1993 – A Night to Remember?   192
     Scott Harvie

12   The Same People with Different Relatives?
     Modern Scholarship, Unionists and the Irish Nation   220
     Richard English

Index   236

Acknowledgements

Most of the contributors to this book are, or have been, associated with the Department of Politics at Queen's University, Belfast. Professor Bob Eccleshall, the Head of Department, provided vital support for the project; the editors would also like to acknowledge the backing of the Department's Centre for Irish Politics. Betty Donnelly, Eileen Maguire and Vincent Geoghegan were tremendously helpful in the production of the manuscript, while Fergal Tobin (Gill and Macmillan) and Gráinne Twomey (Macmillan) provided fine editorial advice and support.

RICHARD ENGLISH
GRAHAM WALKER

Notes on the Contributors

David Burnett is a PhD student in the School of Modern History, Queen's University, Belfast.

Feargal Cochrane is a Fellow of the Centre for Irish Politics, Department of Politics, Queen's University, Belfast; he is the author of 'Any Takers? The Isolation of Northern Ireland', *Political Studies* (1994).

Colin Coulter is a Lecturer in the Department of Sociology, Maynooth College; he is the author of 'The Character of Unionism', *Irish Political Studies* (1994).

Richard English is a Reader in the Department of Politics, Queen's University, Belfast; he is the author of *Radicals and the Republic: Socialist Republicanism in the Irish Free State 1925–1937* (1994).

Peter Hart is an Assistant Professor in the Department of History, Memorial University, Newfoundland; he is the author of *The Irish Republican Army and its Enemies: Violence and Community in County Cork 1916–1923* (1996).

Scott Harvie works in the School of Education, Queen's University, Belfast; he completed a PhD in the Department of Politics, Queen's University, Belfast.

Thomas Hennessey works at the Centre for the Study of Conflict, University of Ulster, Coleraine; he is the author of 'Ulster Unionist Territorial and National Identities', *Irish Political Studies* (1993).

Jane Leonard teaches at the Institute of Irish Studies, Queen's University, Belfast.

Patrick Maume is a Post-Doctoral Fellow in the Centre for Irish Politics, Department of Politics, Queen's University, Belfast; he is the author of *D. P. Moran* (1995).

Ian McBride is a Junior Research Fellow in Corpus Christi College, Cambridge.

David Officer is a PhD student in the Department of Politics, Queen's University, Belfast.

Graham Walker is a Reader in the Department of Politics, Queen's University, Belfast; he is the author of *Intimate Strangers: Political and Cultural Interaction between Scotland and Ulster in Modern Times* (1995).

Introduction
Graham Walker and Richard English

This is a book about a tradition which has often been disparaged and has
lent itself easily to caricature and misrepresentation. Valuable scholarly
studies of Unionism, across disciplines, have appeared since the 1970s,
but it is a topic around which the mists have yet to clear. Fundamental
disagreements over whether to approach Unionism on the same terms,
using the same concepts, as Irish Nationalism, remain unresolved. Inherent
in the study of Unionism are ambiguities surrounding the co-existence of
political strategies and objectives with questions of identity and allegiance.

The essays in this collection all attempt to build on the important and
influential treatments of Unionism which have emerged, particularly in the
last twenty years, while at the same time signalling aspects of the movement which have been neglected and which might point to new ways of
viewing, or approaching, the subject. They range over a broad canvas:
there is discussion and critical interrogation of 'high' Unionist politics,
the significance of certain individuals, Unionist political ideology, the role
of literary figures from a Unionist background, Unionism in the South of
Ireland, class relations within Unionism, the uses of particular imagery
and symbolism, and manifestations of Loyalist popular culture. This range
of topics is matched by the broad spectrum of opinions on Unionism
which is in evidence here. The volume is not as a whole intended to
present any one line of argument; the most that might be said is that all the
contributions attempt to transcend a well-documented tendency to reduce
Unionism to a particular quality or theme, usually for the purposes of
unfavourable categorisation.

Unionism in Ireland[1] emerged as a response to the perceived threat of
Home Rule; it became a mass movement in the heavily Protestant counties
of the North, and proclaimed its loyalty to the Union with Britain as the
source of all progress and guarantee of security against Catholic
Nationalist domination. Beyond this it was a movement riddled with tensions of a political, cultural, class, regional and denominational nature.
The scholarly task of 'unpacking' Unionism in this crucial formative era,
so impressively undertaken recently by Alvin Jackson, is continued here
by David Burnett, while Patrick Maume investigates the trenchant con-

temporary perspectives on the movement and the constitutional crises held by respected men of letters from Irish Unionist backgrounds of contrasting characters. It may always have been likely that Unionism would become reliant on its populist Protestant base in Ulster, but the 'Ulsterisation' of the opposition to Home Rule helped to produce a more intense and intractable conflict than many anticipated. Along with loyalty to Britain went, increasingly, a celebration of 'Ulsterness'. In some ways this in turn merely reflected the deeply ambiguous nature of the concept of 'Britishness', a theme considered here by Ian McBride in relation to recent seminal work such as that of Linda Colley. Indeed, one of the most important aspects of the study of modern Irish Unionism is that it be appreciated within a British Isles, rather than an insular Irish, framework; this has implications for our understanding both of Britain and of Ireland (see the chapter by Richard English).

The relationship of the Ulster Unionists to Britain and 'Britishness' was further called into question by the granting of devolution to the six-county 'Northern Ireland' state in accordance with the terms of the Government of Ireland Act of 1920. The Unionists from the time of the State's inception were preoccupied above all with its security and with the maintenance of the British link. They continued fulsomely to stress their loyalty to Crown and Empire but, increasingly, this only served to set them apart from a rapidly changing British society, especially when considered along with their exclusion from the mainstream of British politics. The anomalous circumstances of Northern Ireland as a devolved unit within the 'UK' but set apart from 'Britain', stunted the development of much of the Unionist political thought forged in the Home Rule era, and intensified the cultivation of an Ulster Protestant ethnic identity around ideas of polit-ical self-preservation and cultural defiance. Unionist politics in the 1921–72 devolution period were shaped less by a coherent political philos-ophy than by reactions to pressures concerned with the defence of posi-tion, territory and pan-Protestant unity. It was a politics reducible to tests of loyalty (see Thomas Hennessey's chapter) and capable of delusions of grandeur fed by an uninterrupted diet of local power (see David Officer's essay). It was also a politics arguably incapable of renewal within the context of Stormont: when in the 1960s Terence O'Neill attempted to give the outside world the impression of a modern, forward-looking state moving beyond the shibboleths of religious sectarianism and class, he neglected fatally the populist imperatives which had sustained his prede-cessors (see the chapter by Feargal Cochrane).

The outbreak of the contemporary 'Troubles' in Northern Ireland in 1969 traumatised and fragmented Unionism. Put on the defensive over the issues of civil rights, which triggered upheaval, Unionists of all kinds struggled to put their case coherently and in terms likely to win them a sympathetic hearing from outsiders. The prorogation of Stormont in 1972 intensified divisions over political goals: some pursued the option of complete political integration with the rest of the UK; others hankered after the restoration of devolution; those most disillusioned and resentful even contemplated ditching the Union, in favour of an independent Ulster. Paramilitaries, distinguished as 'loyalist' to convey notions of extremism and social deprivation, denounced bitterly the 'betrayals' of British governments and their own political leaders. Unionism/Loyalism collapsed into a cacophony of angry voices. Self-confidence and intellectual argument were at a premium. The Protestant middle class to a great extent opted out of politics and failed to argue purposefully enough the integrationist/equal citizenship case likeliest to lend a cogent civic and liberal colouring to the Unionist cause (see the chapter by Colin Coulter). The Protestant working class became more 'alienated' and tended either to be comprehensively dismissed by commentators as bigoted, or naively celebrated as proto-republicans by those who misinterpreted their frustrations and resentments (see Scott Harvie's essay). The Unionist case – or at any rate persuasive refutations of the claims of Irish Nationalism and Republicanism – were put best by intellectuals of a non-Ulster Unionist background such as Conor Cruise O'Brien, and English Conservatives who largely took up where Dicey and Balfour had left off.[2]

The Republican and Loyalist paramilitary ceasefires of 1994 have opened up a new political context. On the evidence of the 'Framework Document' agreed between the British and Irish governments in February 1995, it is a problematic context for Unionists in relation to their overriding objective of securing and strengthening the Union. Nevertheless the period since the ceasefires has witnessed the emergence of new Unionist and Loyalist voices, and has given indications of a fruitful process of re-thinking and re-evaluation within Unionism. There seems now to be a deeper appreciation of how well placed Unionists are to take advantage of the current political emphasis on civic values and the language of citizenship, much of it Euro-inspired.[3] Surprisingly, some of the strongest arguments in favour of cultural pluralism and citizens' rights as central to political progress in Northern Ireland have come from figures such as David Ervine and Gary McMichael, respective leaders of the small, community-based loyalist parties, the Progressive Unionist Party (PUP), and the Ulster Democratic Party (UDP).[4] Both have emerged from backgrounds steeped in a profoundly ethnically-conscious Loyalism which has drawn heavily upon folk history to support assertions of distinctive identity; and both have signalled a break with much traditional Unionist and Loyalist rhetoric. It remains to be seen if they, and others in the more mainstream Unionist parties, can resolve the tensions between 'secular' Unionist politics and exclusivist Loyalist 'identity politics' – a significant theme in this book[5] (see, in particular, Graham Walker's chapter).

Unionism must also define more clearly its relationship to Orangeism. The latter is still central to Ulster Protestant culture, although its political clout has waned rapidly since the imposition of Direct Rule in 1972. The Orange Order still awaits a full scholarly treatment, and assessment of its historical significance can only at this stage be hazy. Nonetheless, it might be hazarded that the extent to which Unionism can separate itself from it will be an index of progress towards civic and pluralist goals.

This volume, therefore, offers exciting, fresh and wide-ranging work by young scholars at an early stage in their careers. It aims to build on the foundations laid in the field by figures such as Steve Bruce, Alvin Jackson, Arthur Aughey, Paul Bew, Henry Patterson, Jennifer Todd and Peter Gibbon. Drawing on different disciplines, it addresses often neglected aspects of Unionism and takes in much material (literary, political, cultural, intellectual) which has previously been ignored. Using new and extensive sources, the contributors examine important features of modern Irish Unionism and do so in ways that challenge much previous thinking about the subject. The book will, it is hoped, be of value to scholars working on any aspect of modern Ireland, and also to students and a wider public with an interest in Irish history, politics, culture and society.

NOTES

1. It is important not to confine our understanding of Unionism to Ulster; see in particular the chapters by Peter Hart and Jane Leonard.
2. In the contemporary period there have been attempts by intellectuals from a diversity of backgrounds to present the Unionist case in reasoned, indeed reasonable, terms; see, for example, J. W. Foster (ed.), *The Idea of the Union* (Vancouver, 1995).
3. See Gavin Adams, 'The Blue Skies of Europe', *Fortnight* (June 1995).
4. See J. McAuley, 'The Changing Face of New Loyalism', *Parliamentary Brief* (Spring 1995) and G. McMichael, 'Engaging Interpretation', *Fortnight* (June 1995).
5. See also T. Nairn, 'On the Threshold', *London Review of Books*, 23 March 1995.

1 Ulster and the British Problem[1]

Ian McBride

Ulster Unionism is commonly portrayed as irrational, backward and deviant. While Unionists have resisted any accommodation with Irish nationalism, the argument runs, their conditional loyalty to the Crown has obstructed the emergence of a genuine sense of Britishness. The Union is usually interpreted as a tactical alliance designed to maintain colonial privileges rather than a *bona fide* expression of emotional commitment to British culture and values. At the same time, loyalists have failed to invent their own distinctive Ulster nationality; consequently they are unable to articulate their political demands in the respectable language of self-determination. Instead Ulster Protestants seem trapped within religious and political attitudes derived from the seventeenth century: one historian has written that the sense of community shared by Ulster Protestants is best seen as 'an arrested development towards modern nationalism'.[2]

It is undeniable, of course, that Unionist political culture contains sectarian and atavistic elements. What I would like to query in this essay is the view that this regression is a unique product of Protestant Ulster's siege mentality. It will be suggested below that Unionists possess a multi-layered identity of the kind generated by the composite states of early modern Europe. The argument entails a rejection of the single and unitary sense of belonging fostered, but seldom realised, during the heyday of the nation-state. According to an alternative view, it is not unusual to find examples of ethnic allegiances co-existing in concentric circles, with different patterns emerging in different contexts – politics, economics, religion, literature or sport.[3] A number of recent studies, reviewed below, have demonstrated the persistence of such concentric loyalties within the United Kingdom. The literature of loyalism, examined in this light, suggests that Ulster's apparent backwardness cannot be explained by reference to the peculiar development of the six counties alone, but that the problem lies partly within the unresolved nature of Britishness itself.

'To a large majority in Northern Ireland', wrote the New Ulster Movement in 1972, 'British nationality seems as natural as the air they breathe.'[4] Most outside commentators, however, have treated such claims with suspicion. Tom Nairn, presenting a stereotypical view of Ulster Protestant culture as an unsavoury mixture of 'the Orange Order, Calvinist bigotry and Kiplingesque empire', has drawn the conclusion that Britishness in this context is merely an assertion of ascendancy over the native Irish, a regressive alternative to an authentic sense of nationality. If Unionism can be dismissed as some sort of false consciousness, then it follows that Protestants must wake up to their true identity as members of an Irish (or more rarely, an Ulster) nation. In *The Break-Up of Britain* Nairn describes Protestantism and imperialism as 'aberrant substitutes' for the construction of a separate Ulster consciousness; nationalism is the only way Protestants have of ceasing to be 'backward, religion-ridden, lunatic reactionaries'.[5]

Nairn's neo-Marxist reading of the Northern Ireland conflict is unusual in several respects, but there are similarities with the most sophisticated and influential analysis of Ulster loyalism, David Miller's *Queen's Rebels* (1978). Stressing the confusion and haziness of Unionist thinking on issues of identity, Miller argues that northern loyalists do not think in terms of nationhood at all. Ideologically, they can be seen as a relic from a former age when loyalty rested on dynastic legitimacy and confessional identification rather than the principle of nationality. Unionists thus subscribe to a contractual interpretation of their relationship with the crown which is best summed up by Thomas MacKnight, editor of the *Northern Whig* at the time of the first Home Rule bill:

> When the Ulster settlements were made, there was an implied compact that they who crossed the Irish Sea on what was believed to be a great colonising mission should not in themselves, nor in their descendants, be abandoned to those who regarded them as intruders, and as enemies.[6]

Loyalism, Miller concludes, is not rooted in 'a wholehearted sense of incorporation into the British *nation*', but in 'an external relationship to the British *state*'.[7]

What is missing from this discussion, as with so much writing on the subject, is any consideration of 'the British nation' itself. Since the publication of Miller's book, and particularly in the last five years or so, Britishness has been pushed to the centre of historical debate. Much of the inspiration has come from a series of articles by Professor John Pocock, who was the first to propose that an aggregate account of British history should be written.[8] Its primary theme would be the creation and interaction of a variety of cultures and sub-cultures in what he has called the 'Atlantic archipelago', and it would include not only the four component parts of the United Kingdom but also the related cultures reproduced in the colonies. While recognising that the central dynamic in this process was the growth of English political and cultural hegemony, this multicultural and plural account of the British past would show how the various communities of these islands have 'interacted so as to modify the conditions of one another's existence'.[9]

It is no coincidence that Pocock is a New Zealander, the product of a culture which he defines as neither English nor Scottish but British. He is clearly disillusioned with the UK's drift away from the Commonwealth towards the European Community, lamenting at one point that 'in the 20th century we fought a series of wars, half a world away, for the maintenance of our place in an empire which in the end was dismantled by others'.[10] Pocock's complaint is that the anglocentric arrangement of a common history has marginalised the experience of other cultures shaped by the British experience. There is a sense of unrequited loyalty here which will be instantly recognisable to observers of Ulster Protestant politics.

This wider British history, sometimes labelled 'Britannic' in deference to Irish sensitivities, has become increasingly fashionable.[11] It has an obvious appeal for many Scottish, Irish and Welsh scholars as a means of subverting the old Whiggish approach in which the 'United Kingdom' was simply regarded as an extension of 'England'. Over the last decade, however, a growing number of English historians have also been converted to an 'archipelagic' framework. In part, this is a consequence of a shift away from older liberal or Marxist orthodoxies. During the academic boom of the 1960s and 1970s the version of the past served up in UK universities continued to be 'the old Whig history of Britain's unique and privileged development dressed up in Butskellite guise'.[12] (For Britain, of course, read England.) But the long process of economic decline, the threat posed to British sovereignty by European integration and, not least, the contraction of public spending on higher education, have encouraged a reaction against the old success story of English exceptionalism. One by one the great historical landmarks – the Tudor revolution in government, the social upheavals of the Civil War, the triumph of constitutional monarchy in 1688 and the Industrial Revolution – have been 'demythologised' by new generations of professional historians.

As the Whig interpretation has been progressively undermined, modern historians have come to recognise that the nations and sub-nations of these islands cannot be treated as self-contained units without distorting their histories. The most spectacular developments in recent years have come from historians of the seventeenth century, where revisionist assaults on Whig history have been most successful. It is now accepted that the convulsions of the 1640s and 1650s are only explicable in the context of the British problem, that is, the turbulent relationship between the three kingdoms yoked together under the Stuart crown. The English Civil War has consequently been rewritten as what the Belfast historian J. C. Beckett long ago called 'the War of the Three Kingdoms'.[13] Much of this new work might be described, in terms borrowed from feminist historians, as additive rather than substitutive, since the Celtic fringe is often treated as a source for footnotes to the main text. But John Morrill has called for a more thoroughgoing, 'holistic' approach to the British past which comes closer to Pocock's original project, and to what Northern Irish politicians sometimes refer to as 'the totality of relationships' within these islands.[14] Viewed from this perspective, the construction of the British state can be understood as the rise of a multiple or composite monarchy rather like France or Spain, bringing together a number of kingdoms and cultures.[15] In early-modern Europe these composite structures became dominant, engendering a variety of dual loyalties which can still be detected in the periodic resurgence of ethnic and regional tensions.

The most recent historian to establish her Britannic credentials is Linda Colley. In her widely acclaimed *Britons* (1992), which charts the development of the United Kingdom between the Anglo-Scottish Union of 1707 and the accession of Queen Victoria, she explicitly avoids an anglocentric angle on the past. She claims that the emergence of Great Britain cannot be explained as the imposition of English cultural and political hegemony over a defenceless Celtic fringe, nor as a hybrid of the older national cultures contained within its boundaries. Instead Britishness should be regarded as an overarching identity which developed alongside existing allegiances to kingdom, county or village. It was forged during a series of wars fought against Catholic, absolutist France between 1689 and 1815, and by imperial expansion overseas. The raw materials were provided by the religious inheritance shared by England, Scotland and Wales; 'Protestantism', she establishes, 'was the foundation that made the invention of Great Britain possible.'[16]

Regrettably, Colley does not extend her discussion to John Bull's other island,[17] despite the obvious parallels, but there are clear implications here for students of Northern Irish politics. Firstly, militant Protestantism and imperialism, far from being 'aberrant substitutes' are seen as central to the construction of the United Kingdom. Secondly, Colley recognises that identities within the UK are stratified: Britishness did not replace more traditional regional and local ties but was superimposed on top of them.

Thirdly, although she highlights the artificial and manufactured character of Britishness, she also discusses its relationship to broader social and cultural forces. Commercial and industrial growth, the revolution in communications, the spread of literacy, and the emergence of a 'warfare state' all contributed to closer integration in the two islands, while a shared history rooted in the break with Rome, and sustained by more recent confrontations with Catholic enemies, laid the basis for a common self-understanding.[18] Finally, this process should not be seen as the subjugation of the Celtic periphery by the metropolitan core: on the contrary, the idea of Britain was imposed upon the English by their northern neighbours.

Britishness, as many recent historians have confirmed, is primarily a Scottish invention. In the seventeenth century, military and economic inferiority had forced the Scots to imagine their future within the geopolitical framework of the three kingdoms. Following the union of the crowns of England and Scotland in 1603, James I and VI had adopted a policy of integration, taking the title of 'Emperor of the whole island of Britain'.[19] His attempts to promote a new British imagery and terminology met with little enthusiasm in his English kingdom. North of the border, however, the notion eventually did catch on; the Scots (and their brethren in Ulster) welcomed the creation of a new imperial stage on which to act out their apocalyptic vision of the battle against popery. The most dramatic testimony to this Presbyterian enthusiasm was the Solemn League and Covenant of 1643, which called for a federal union of the three kingdoms and their three churches.[20]

The same pattern was repeated after the parliamentary union of 1707. Once more it was the Scots who most enthusiastically embraced the name of 'Briton'. It was the son of a Scottish Presbyterian minister who wrote 'Rule Britannia', Scotsmen like John Arbuthnot, David Hume and Tobias Smollett who popularised the character of John Bull, and the philosophers of the Scottish Enlightenment who sought to rescue the British constitution from the vulgar whiggism of the 'barbarians who inhabit the Banks of the Thames' by setting it upon new scientific foundations.[21] Above all, it was the Scottish influx into the military and the colonial administration which ensured that the army and the empire would be genuinely *British*. This brand of Britishness was not an engine of anglicisation; for the Scots it was a device for circumventing the unalterable fact of England's economic, political and cultural predominance in these islands. For similar reasons the name of Briton was adopted by Ulster Presbyterians in the early eighteenth century as a way of asserting their equality with members of the established Church of Ireland.[22]

The sacrifice of political sovereignty was the price paid for the preservation of a Scottish identity, embodied in distinctive systems of law, education and religion. Their conception of the Union was thus thoroughly contractual and conditional: in return for Scottish support London guaranteed the protection of their customs and institutions and promised them equal access to the liberty and prosperity enjoyed by Englishmen. A new Britain, in which the two old kingdoms would become equal partners, was the only alternative to the incorporation of Scotland into a Greater England. In the eighteenth century calls for the dissolution of the Union therefore gave way to demands for its 'completion', meaning the extension of civil freedom and economic opportunity north of the border. Of course the 'North British' identity of Scottish unionists was not incompatible with the survival of Scottish patriotism, periodically renewed by examples of metropolitan partiality.[23]

The crucial problem was that the English never learned to think of themselves as South Britons. For the metropolitan elite, the Union of 1707 (like that of 1801) was the product of military necessity; it had nothing to do with the birth of a new nation. The traditional English attitude to the idea of a union was one of indifference, and there was a conspicuous lack of enthusiasm for the new United Kingdom. The outburst of vicious anti-Scottish invective which followed the appointment of Lord Bute as George III's prime minister demonstrated that, half a century after its enactment, the English still refused to consider the Union as an equal partnership. Reared on images of Scotland as backward and barbarous, eighteenth-century Englishmen remained convinced Britosceptics. Even parliamentary reformers combined their opposition to political corruption with fervent chauvinism: the radical clergyman Horne Tooke denounced the notion that the Englishman should be 'melted down into Briton', while John Wilkes refused to use the term 'Great Britain'.[24] Over a century later, in 1887, the constitutional expert James Bryce noted the contrast between the dual allegiance of the Scots and the unitary identity which prevailed south of the border. 'An Englishman has but one patriotism', he wrote, 'because England and the United Kingdom are to him practically the same thing.'[25] By this stage, of course, Scotland's position within the Union was apparently secure. It was Ireland which now presented the British state with its greatest challenge, as Westminster politicians were confronted by the rise of Catholic nationalism, and the beginnings of a loyalist reaction in Bryce's own native Ulster.

The orthodox view has always been that Ulster Unionism ought not to be classed as a local variety of nationalism. 'They had resisted home rule for

Ireland', comments J. C. Beckett, 'but had never demanded home rule for themselves.'[26] Partition was not the result of a movement for an independent Ulster; it was taken up at Westminster as a way of reconciling two conflicting ideas about the government of Ireland. The most notable exception to this consensus is Peter Gibbon, who regards the emergence of a political, territorial and cultural Ulster identity as the creation of a type of nationalism.[27] Gibbon has found little support from other scholars, however, and a judicious survey of the field has recently concluded that 'loyalism was ultimately tailored to a negative end, the defeat of Home Rule, rather than to the positive expression of an identity'.[28]

Unfortunately the debate over the *status* of Ulster Protestant identity has tended to deflect attention away from its *substance*.[29] The reluctance of Unionists to resort to the language of nationality should not be allowed to obscure the fact that the Home Rule crises saw the crystallisation of a provincial *mentalité* which drew upon a distinctive Protestant culture sharpened by recent bursts of evangelicalism.[30] Attempts to construct the stereotypical 'Ulsterman' produced a stream of new books such as James Barkley Woodburn's *The Ulster Scot* (1914), F. F. Moore's *The Truth about Ulster* (1914), Ernest Hamilton's *The Soul of Ulster* (1917), H. M. Pim's *Unconquerable Ulster* (1919), and James Logan's *Ulster in the X-Rays* (1923).[31] The Ulster 'character' which emerged was dour but hospitable, shrewd, self-reliant, steadfast and industrious, blunt of speech, and gifted with the capacity to govern less fortunate peoples. These sterling qualities had been demonstrated in the colonisation and civilisation of the northern province, in the struggle for constitutional freedom in both Ireland (1688–90) and America (1776), in resistance to religious persecution and participation in the great enterprise of empire. For the historian of ideas, the invention of 'Ulster' as a separate entity, endowed with particular characteristics and virtues, constitutes one of the central themes of the period.

The conventional justification for Protestant Ascendancy in the nineteenth century can be found in Edward Saunderson's 1884 pamphlet *Two Irelands, or Loyalty versus Treason*.[32] Saunderson's idea of 'loyal Ireland' was defined in ethical rather than ethnic terms, evoking an older colonial discourse in which Protestant settlers were portrayed as bearers of civilisation, law and religion in a barbarous land. But as Thomas Macknight, editor of the *Northern Whig*, later pointed out, the thirty-two-county loyalism of Saunderson and other Orange leaders was not shared by the commercial classes in the north-east.[33] Within the northern liberal tradition, which MacKnight represented, the idea of a separate Ulster solution had been received with some favour. In *From Liberal Ulster to England*

(1886) it was suggested that Ulster might be established as a 'sovereign area' as the lesser of two evils.[34] A later Liberal pamphlet, *Ulster on its Own* (1912) argued the case for self-government for the five counties (Fermanagh was excluded) around Lough Neagh.[35] Confronted with the ideological demands of Irish nationalism, it was not surprising that some northern Protestants were driven to assert their own rival claim to self-determination.[36] By 1912 Saunderson's brand of Unionism had been superseded by what some contemporaries referred to simply as 'the Ulster movement'.

Some attempt was made to supply a cultural basis for this muted nationalism with the creation of an 'Ulster Scot' mythology. The groundwork for this development had been laid by the pioneering research on the plantation carried out by the Rev. George Hill, librarian at Queen's College and a Unitarian clergyman.[37] There was also a robust tradition of Presbyterian historiography based on the authoritative scholarship of James Seaton Reid.[38] A Presbyterian Historical Society was founded in 1908 by a group of local historians including W. T. Latimer, J. W. Kernohan, R. M. Young, and the Liberal Unionist leader Thomas Sinclair, and further interest was stimulated by the tercentenary of the Irish Presbyterian Church in 1913.[39] But support was also forthcoming from an unexpected quarter. In the United States the second half of the nineteenth century had witnessed a revival of interest in 'Scotch-Irish' history, as Americans of Ulster descent sought to distance themselves from the waves of Catholic immigrants arriving from Ireland. A fresh burst of historical research was stimulated by the foundation of the Scotch-Irish Society of America in 1889, culminating in Charles Hanna's two volume epic, *The Scotch-Irish, or The Scot in North-Britain, North Ireland and North America* (1902).[40] This work was well received in the north of Ireland, and it is from this period that the familiar roll of US Presidents, frontiersmen and millionaires became a stock feature of Unionist apologetics.

The myth of the Ulster Scot played a valuable part in the propaganda campaign against Home Rule.[41] It is true that parallels can be found in the antiquarian studies so fashionable in Victorian and Edwardian Britain, but this process of self-definition represents more than local pride in Ulster's provincial characteristics: the cultural construction of the Ulsterman was an overtly political project. John Harrison's *The Scot in Ulster* (1888) begins with a declaration that the plantation origins of Ulster Protestants gave them 'an inalienable right' to oppose the dissolution of the Union, while Woodburn's book was written under the 'dark cloud' of the third Home Rule bill.[42] Like their nationalist opponents, Unionists were seeking to bolster their ideological position by appealing to racial theories. This mythology not only highlighted the separateness of the north; it also appealed to a Scottish audience by invoking historical ties. It was entirely appropriate, then, that in their attempts to publicise the campaign against Home Rule, Unionists should have adopted the model of the Solemn League and Covenant, the seventeenth-century Scottish document which had enshrined the first great vision of a pan-Britannic community embracing all three kingdoms.

Finally, it is worth noting the versatility of the Ulster Scot idea. Many Unionists, eager to distinguish themselves from the native stock of the degenerate south, depicted the archetypal Ulsterman as an Anglo-Saxon, the embodiment of the industrious virtues celebrated in the Victorian literature of self-help.[43] But the Ulster Scot thesis was sometimes given an unexpected Celtic gloss. By demonstrating the racial and cultural similarities between Planter and Gael, writers like Thomas Johnstone found it possible to appropriate elements of Ulster's ancient past for the loyalist cause. Cuchulainn and the Red Branch Knights were recruited to show that the north had always maintained its isolation and independence from the other provinces.[44] Johnstone's contention that Ulster was 'the most typically Irish of all the provinces' was not an expression of fellow feeling with Catholic Ireland; rather he was concerned to dissociate the pure Celtic stock of the north-east from the mixture of Gaelic, Spanish and Anglo-Norman blood characteristic of the south.[45] This alternative approach also enabled Unionists to exploit the topography of the north in aid of a more organic Ulster separatism. Woodburn made much of the province's distinctive climate and geography, drawing attention to the line of hills and mountains which guarded the north like 'sentinels'.[46]

Alongside the development of a specifically Ulster heritage there remained a profound and enduring identification with the island of Ireland. Throughout the Home Rule debates, Protestant spokesmen insisted on their devotion to their country, their pride in its traditions and affection for its landscape; even after 1922 it was possible for Unionists to speak of 'our common land'.[47] Declarations of Irishness were often defensive in tone, however, taking care to distinguish Protestant patriotism from Catholic nationalism. Thus the local historian W. T. Latimer, who took pride in the fact that the Ulster Scots had resisted absorption by the 'Keltic Irish', nevertheless insisted that Presbyterians were 'as good Irishmen as the descendants of the Milesians or any of the other tribes by whom the country was colonised'.[48] Similarly, Robert Lynd attacked the racial exclusivity behind the slogan 'Ireland for the Irish', protesting that 'We, too, are Irish. We love Ireland with as pure a patriotism as any. It is our own and our fathers' native land; we have no other.'[49] In dwelling on their ancestral ties with Ulster, their contribution to agricultural and industrial improvement and their close identification with the landscape, Unionists were addressing the central contradiction of a nationalist ideology which insisted that, if all Irishmen were Irish, some were certainly more Irish than others.[50]

To complete their trinity of allegiances, Unionists highlighted their racial, religious and cultural connections with the peoples of Great Britain, and expressed their attachment to the empire both as an expression of Britain's international influence and as a great civilising, moral force which stood for progress, liberty and individualism.[51] Thus Robert Lynd, quoted above, insisted that a feeling of Irishness was perfectly compatible with devotion to the empire, which for him signified military power, freedom, Christianity and economic opportunity.[52] In 1913 the members of the Presbyterian General Assembly declared that they were not ashamed to call themselves 'Britons'; despite past quarrels with government policy their pride in the imperial inheritance was unshaken.[53] Liberal writers pointed to the positive benefits of the Union, including land reform, educational expansion, the disestablishment of the Church of Ireland and growing prosperity.[54] Although geared towards the defeat of Catholic nationalism, it would be wrong to see Ulster Unionism as an entirely negative creed: like the eighteenth-century Scots, if for very different reasons, Ulster Protestants were asserting their right to a share of imperial patrimony. The role of Irishmen in the army and the administration was consequently emphasised to show that the 'British Empire is ours as well as England's'.[55]

A survey of Unionist propaganda during the Home Rule crises uncovers levels of loyalty to Ulster, Ireland, and the British empire. These references to national identity have often been interpreted as signs of ideological confusion, but they might also be read as an expression of the multi-layered allegiances created by the interaction of cultures within the British Isles.[56] A common thread in the literature of loyalism is the conviction that there are several degrees of political and cultural allegiance, which might be ordered differently depending on the context. The Rev. Thomas Johnstone described one such hierarchy of identities when he explained that 'If in one sense, Ulstermen are Irishmen first and Britishers afterwards, in another sense they are Ulstermen first and Irishmen afterwards.'[57] The Scottish sociologist Sarah Nelson has drawn similar conclusions from interviews carried out in the 1970s. 'Most loyalists have complex and ambivalent feelings of identity', she writes; 'in different situations, a sense of "Ulsterness", "Britishness" or even "Irishness" may dominate'.[58] By breaking up nationality into a series of different fields –

political, economic and cultural – it is possible that future research will build up a more nuanced picture of Ulster Protestant *mentalités*.

There is not enough space here to trace the trajectories of Protestant cultural identities since partition, but two complementary trends may be sketched out: the gradual relegation of the Irish component, accompanied by a more entrenched attachment to the six-county unit. After 1921 Stormont, rather than Westminster, became the focal point of Protestant allegiance; the existence of local institutions inspired what J. C. Beckett has described as a kind of 'Ulster patriotism' or 'embryonic nationalism', revealed in Brookeborough's attempts to have the name 'Northern Ireland' changed to 'Ulster' and in the promotion of the six-county flag.[59] More important, however, was the emergence of a new regime in the south which institutionalised the Gaelic and Catholic ethos of nationalism. In the decades after partition the northern papers reported on the persecution of southern loyalists, the introduction of compulsory Gaelic in southern schools and the eradication of British symbols from public life. The codification of Catholic social teaching in the 1937 constitution and the policy of neutrality maintained during the Second World War completed the northern image of the Free State as alien, church-dominated and implacably hostile to British culture. Unionists now found themselves fighting a rearguard action against the monopolisation of Irishness by the Free State; as late as 1956 one Stormont minister admitted the 'sentimental appeal' of a common Irish identity but lamented the fact that it had become incompatible with 'being at the same time British'.[60]

Unionist propaganda after 1921 presents the historian with a curious paradox. The battle for a distinctive Ulster entity had apparently been won, and Protestant apologists were now eager to demonstrate that partition rested on ideological, historical and ethnic foundations.[61] Yet there was no cultural policy of Ulsterisation pursued under the new six-county government. Part of the explanation no doubt lies in the continuing siege mentality institutionalised in the structures of the Stormont regime. But it is also necessary to note the final eclipse of those Liberals (often Presbyterian clergymen) who had been foremost in the invention of 'Ulster'. Under Stormont there was no longer a need to explain Protestant culture to the outside world; the main task now was to maximise the Unionist turn-out within the six counties by appealing to sectarian slogans. Dissenting voices were occasionally raised on the literary left in the journals *Lagan* and *Northman*. Inspired by the Scottish literary renaissance of Hugh MacDiarmid and Lewis Grassic Gibbon, the socialist poet John Hewitt called for the creation of an Ulster regional culture which would flesh out the province's political existence.[62] But even these tentative moves towards cultural autonomy, although clearly rooted in a Planter tradition, were too much for the Minister of Education, who retorted that 'Northern Ireland [is] as much a part of the United Kingdom as Yorkshire'.[63]

It took the imposition of direct rule in 1972 and the Anglo-Irish Agreement to produce further lurches towards Ulster separatism. One response to the shock of 1985 was the formation of the Ulster Society, dedicated to the promotion of 'Ulster-British heritage and culture' and the publication of its journal *New Ulster*, a fairly predictable mixture of Orange folkculture, military history and Ulster–American links. Early in 1986 a symposium organised by this body asserted a claim for nationhood on grounds of ethnicity, dialect and religion, but ultimately foundered on the old problem of whether Ulsterness constituted 'an independent entity' or 'an element within British culture generally'.[64] Much of the impetus behind Ulster nationalism has come from the paramilitaries rather than official Unionism, however. In 1974 the idea of negotiated independence was floated by Glenn Barr, vice-chairman of Vanguard and chairman of the Ulster workers' strike committee, although it is clear that other loyalist leaders regarded the formation of a provisional government as part of a doomsday scenario.[65] Tentative arguments for independence had already been advanced in a series of slim pamphlets published by Vanguard in 1972–73. Although these continued to define the loyalist cause as 'the preservation of a British tradition and heritage', they accepted that the maintenance of this 'distinct way of life' might require a secession from the Union.[66] Significantly, disillusionment with Westminster was fuelled not only by traditional distrust of the British government but also diverging social attitudes: 'Both in terms of permissiveness and in attitudes to religion, urbanised society in Great Britain is far out of step with Ulster.'[67] Increasing secularisation across the water was particularly disturbing for evangelicals who opposed the spread of 'the Republican Sunday' and the liberalisation of legislation against homosexuality.[68] On another level, however, Vanguard recognised a common interest between the people of Great Britain, Ulster and Eire, and proposed a federal constitution for the British Isles; a remarkable peroration called on the Ulster people 'like Finn MacCool of old [to] build a new Causeway to join all the people of these islands in a new community of spirit and endeavour'.[69]

Barr later resurfaced in the New Ulster Political Research Group, whose *Beyond the Religious Divide* (1978) proposed the creation of a self-governing Ulster within the European Community. The conversion of the UDA to separatism has been accompanied by the appearance of an innovative version of the Ulster Scot thesis, popularised by Ian Adamson's *The*

Cruithin (1974) and *The Identity of Ulster* (1982). Adamson draws inspiration from a bewildering variety of sources ranging from the *Tain Bo Cuailgne* to the Ulster-Scottish philosopher Francis Hutcheson to Kropotkin and Bakunin. His central argument, however, is that both communities in the north are descended from the Cruithin, a Pictish people who flourished in pre-Gaelic Ulster. When these aboriginal inhabitants were driven out of Ireland they sought refuge in those parts of Scotland which centuries later provided the colonists for the plantation. The result is a loyalist counter-mythology which replicates the republican narrative of golden age, dispossession, and rebirth. Such novel ideas have been slow to catch on among the rank and file, but they are clearly indicative of profound dissatisfaction with the direction of British government policy. Since the end of Stormont, and more particularly since 1985, there has been a marked shift in Unionist symbolism away from the Union Jack in favour of the Northern Ireland flag. Significantly, the latter has also appeared in de-anglicised forms, with the crown removed and the cross of St George replaced by that of St Patrick.[70]

The more extreme and exotic fringes of loyalism – Free Presbyterianism, Orangeism, the Protestant paramilitaries – have attracted a fair amount of attention. Much less research has been done on the survival of a wider British identity in Northern Ireland, although an important article by Jennifer Todd has recently done something to redress the balance.[71] This neglected strand of Unionism, represented by liberals like St John Ervine, Charles Brett, John Oliver and Robert McCartney, has always been strongest among intellectuals and the professional middle classes. Their primary allegiance is to London rather than Belfast, and they have a patriotic attachment to British ideals and institutions. Often the accent is on economic policies and the achievements of the welfare state, but there is also a continuing belief in Britain's international role as a progressive force. Many of these themes were to be found in the Ulster celebrations for the Festival of Britain in 1951 which profited from the renewal of national pride after the Second World War, and focused on the centrality of democracy, technology and modernity to the British way of life.[72] In the era of the cold war, however, Unionists were faced with the problem that Northern Ireland no longer occupied the strategic position which it had before 1945. Stormont ministers, who tended to rank Republican Ireland along with the USSR as a threat to the free world, were driven to the rather desperate ploy of portraying their corrupt sub-state as a bastion of democracy and individualism.[73]

As the empire – and the sense of common purpose it provided – has faded from memory, Protestant Ulster has been deprived of its traditional role in the wider British world. While this crisis of identity is rooted in peculiarly Irish conditions it also returns us to the wider British problem. Linda Colley has argued that the rather haphazard, artificial construction of the United Kingdom bears some responsibility for the doubts and divisions which currently afflict its inhabitants. As she points out, Protestantism is now a residual part of their culture, they are now part of the European community, and the empire has gone. The foundations of Britishness have been slowly eroded, hence the reassertion of subordinate nationalities.[74] As a direct product of British expansion, Ulster loyalism has experienced a particularly virulent form of disorientation; while Scotland retained its educational, legal and ecclesiastical institutions, and Wales preserved its language, Protestant Ulster was a seventeenth-century creation. This weakness helps to explain the inhibited and impoverished nature of Ulster nationalism and the continuing fidelity to a Britishness which has largely ceased to serve its function elsewhere.

While Ulster Unionism is in many ways anomalous, it also reveals, in heightened form, problematic questions about nationality and sovereignty which are rooted in the structure of the United Kingdom itself. The apparent paradox of rebellious loyalism is better understood if Britishness is viewed not as a single, homogenous entity, but as a plurality of identities brought together by common historical experience yet retaining distinctive characteristics. In the wake of the Anglo-Irish Agreement the historian A. T. Q. Stewart insisted that Britishness is not simply Englishness writ large: 'Nothing irritates an Ulsterman more than the assumption that the United Kingdom exists for the comfort and security of England and the English.'[75] The rebellion of 1985, like those of 1912 and 1974, thus reveals the clash of rival conceptions of Britishness. While the Scots and the Irish have often been forced to think of their destinies in wider, Britannic terms, the English have continued to regard the Union as a strategic arrangement; emotional commitment to the idea of a wider British community has always been weakest at the centre.

It is perhaps not surprising that an understanding of the different strata contained within Ulster Unionism, and in particular its British dimension, has been noticeably absent from recent government pronouncements on Northern Ireland. The language of the Downing Street Declaration and the Framework Document, like that of the SDLP, pushes the Northern Ireland debate into a one-island context. The central issue now becomes the relationship between northern Protestants and the rest of the island; the British state appears as an external player, mediating between two antagonists in an essentially Irish dispute. As this insular (in both senses) approach gains ground, it is worth remembering the three-dimensional perspectives recommended by historians of the 'Atlantic archipelago'. Ulster is a British problem too.

NOTES

1. I am indebted to both Colin Kidd of Glasgow University and John Morrill of Selwyn College, Cambridge, for sharing their thoughts on Britishness, and and for allowing me to read copies of forthcoming articles on the subject.
2. Charles Townshend, *Political Violence in Ireland: Government and Resistance since 1848* (Oxford, 1983), p. 342.
3. Anthony D. Smith, *National Identity* (London, 1991), p. 24.
4. New Ulster Movement, *Two Irelands or One?* (Belfast, 1972), p. 5.
5. Tom Nairn, *The Break-Up of Britain: Crisis and Neo-Nationalism* (London, 1977), pp. 236, 243, 245.
6. Thomas MacKnight, *Ulster as it is, or Twenty-Eight Years' Experience as an Irish Editor* (London, 1896), II, 379. Another good example is the Rev. William McKean's Ulster Day sermon, *Belfast Newsletter*, 30 Sept. 1912.
7. D. W. Miller, *Queen's Rebels: Ulster Loyalism in Historical Perspective* (Dublin, 1978), p. 120 (my italics).
8. J. G. A. Pocock, 'British History: A Plea for a New Subject', *Journal of Modern History*, XLVII (1975), 601–21; idem, 'The Limits and Divisions of British History: In Search of the Unknown Subject', *American Historical Review*, LXXXVII (1982), 311–36.
9. Ibid., 317.
10. J. G. A. Pocock, 'Between God and Magog: the Republican Thesis and the Ideologia Americana', *Journal of the History of Ideas*, XLVIII (1987), 333.
11. Richard S. Thompson, *The Atlantic Archipelago: A Political History of the British Isles* (Lewiston, New York, 1986); Hugh Kearney, *The British Isles: A History of Four Nations* (Cambridge, 1989); D. G. Boyce, 'Brahmins and Carnivores: The Irish Historian in Great Britain', *Irish Historical Studies*, XXV, no. 99 (May 1987), 225–35; J. C. D. Clark, 'England's Forgotten Context: Scotland, Ireland, Wales', *Historical Journal*, XXXII (1989), 211–28.
12. David Cannadine, 'British History: Past, Present – and Future?', *Past and Present*, 116 (Aug. 1987), 173.
13. See Conrad Russell, 'The British Problem and the English Civil War', *History*, LXXII (1987), 395–415; *The Causes of the English Civil War* (Oxford, 1990).
14. John Morrill, 'The Causes of Britain's Civil Wars', in *The Nature of the English Revolution* (London, 1993), p. 258.
15. J. H. Elliott, 'A Europe of Composite Monarchies', *Past and Present*, 137 (November 1992), 48–71.

16.   Linda Colley, *Britons: Forging the Nation 1707–1837* (London, 1992), pp. 6, 18, 54.
17.   Though see her 'Britishness and Otherness: An Argument', *Journal of British Studies*, XXXI (1992), 309–29.
18.   These themes can be pursued into a later period in Keith Robbins, *Nineteenth-Century Britain: Integration and Diversity* (Oxford, 1988).
19.   Keith M. Brown, 'The Vanishing Emperor: British Kingship and its Decline 1603–1707', in Roger A. Mason (ed.), *Scots and Britons: Scottish Political Thought and the Union of 1603* (Cambridge, 1994), p. 79.
20.   John Morrill, 'The Fashioning of Britain', in S. G. Ellis and S. Barber (eds), *Conquest and Union: Fashioning the British State 1485–1725* (forthcoming); Arthur H. Williamson, 'Scotland, Antichrist and the Invention of Great Britain', in John Dwyer *et al.* (eds), *New Perspectives on the Politics and Culture of Early Modern Scotland* (Edinburgh, 1982), pp. 34–58.
21.   Colley, *Britons*, p. 11; Miles Taylor, 'John Bull and the Iconography of Public Opinion in England *c.* 1712–1929', *Past and Present*, 134 (Feb. 1992), 101; Colin Kidd, 'North Britishness and the Nature of Eighteenth-Century Patriotisms', *Historical Journal*, forthcoming.
22.   David Hayton, 'Anglo-Irish Attitudes: Changing Perceptions of National Identity among the Protestant Ascendancy in Ireland, *ca.* 1690–1750', *Studies in Eighteenth-Century Culture*, XVII (1987), 151.
23.   Colin Kidd, 'North Britishness'; also Rosalind Mitchison, 'Patriotism and National Identity in Eighteenth-Century Scotland', *Historical Studies*, XI (1978), 73–95; N. T. Phillipson, 'Nationalism and Ideology', in J. N. Wolfe (ed.), *Government and Nationalism in Scotland: An Enquiry by Members of the University of Edinburgh* (Edinburgh, 1969), pp. 167–88.
24.   Linda Colley, 'Whose Nation? Class and National Consciousness in Britain 1750–1830', *Past and Present*, 113 (Nov. 1986), 112; idem, *Britons*, p. 116.
25.   Letter to *The Times*, 21 March 1887.
26.   J. C. Beckett, 'Northern Ireland', *Journal of Contemporary History*, VI (1971), 123.
27.   Peter Gibbon, *The Origins of Ulster Unionism: The Formation of Popular Protestant Politics and Ideology in Nineteenth-Century Ireland* (Manchester, 1975), p. 136.
28.   Alvin Jackson, *The Ulster Party: Irish Unionists in the House of Commons, 1884–1911* (Oxford, 1989), p. 15.
29.   For some recent exceptions, see Thomas Hennessey, 'Ulster Unionist Territorial and National Identities 1886–1893: Province, Island, Kingdom and Empire', *Irish Political Studies*, VIII (1993), 21–36; Graham Walker, 'Empire, Religion and Nationality in Scotland and Ulster before the First World War', in I. S. Wood (ed.), *Scotland and Ulster* (Edinburgh, 1994), pp. 95–115.
30.   David Hempton and Myrtle Hill, *Evangelical Protestantism in Ulster Society 1740–1890* (London, 1992), esp. chs 8–9.
31.   For F. F. Moore, see Patrick Maume's contribution to this volume.
32.   Much of the pamphlet was in fact written by Edward Caulfield Houston: see Alvin Jackson, *Colonel Edward Saunderson: Land and Loyalty in Victorian Ireland* (Oxford, 1995), pp. 55–7.
33.   MacKnight, *Ulster as It Is*, II, 383.

34. *From Liberal Ulster to England* [London, 1886], p. 3.
35. An Ulster Presbyterian, *Ulster on its Own, or An Easy Way with Ireland* (Belfast, 1912).
36. This was usually a secondary line of defence: see, for example, Thomas Sinclair, 'The Position of Ulster', in S. Rosenbaum (ed.), *Against Home Rule: The Case for the Union* (London, 1912), pp. 173, 180–1.
37. George Hill, *An Historical Account of the Plantation of Ulster* (Belfast, 1877).
38. James Seaton Reid, *History of the Presbyterian Church in Ireland* (3 vols, Belfast, 1834–53). See also Robert Allen, *James Seaton Reid: A Centenary Biography* (Belfast, 1951).
39. *First Meeting of the Presbyterian Historical Society of Ireland* (Belfast, 1908). For Thomas Sinclair see Graham Walker's contribution to this volume.
40. See also Whitelaw Reid, *The Scot in America and the Ulster Scot* (London, 1912). Both Hanna and Reid were frequently cited by Unionist historians.
41. In addition to the sources already cited, see H. S. Morrison, *Modern Ulster: Its Character, Customs, Politics, and Industries* (London, 1920), ch. 1; Henry Maxwell, *Ulster was Right* (London, [1934]), pp. 37–9.
42. John Harrison, *The Scot in Ulster: Sketch of the History of the Scottish People of Ulster* (Edinburgh, 1888), preface; James Barkley Woodburn, *The Ulster Scot: His History and Religion* (London, 1914), p. 379.
43. A good example is James Heron, 'The Making of the Ulster Scot', in Henry Jones Ford, *The Scotch-Irish in America* (Princeton, 1915), pp. 555–75. Heron was a professor at the Assembly's College, Belfast.
44. T. M. Johnstone, *Ulstermen: Their Fight for Fortune, Faith and Freedom* (Belfast, 1914), p. 38.
45. Ibid., pp. 37, 48.
46. Woodburn, *Ulster Scot*, pp. 29–30. See also John Byers, *The Characteristics of the Ulsterman* [Belfast 1920?], p. 3.
47. Dennis Kennedy, *The Widening Gulf: Northern Attitudes to the Independent Irish State 1919–49* (Belfast, 1988), p. 62.
48. W. T. Latimer, *The Ulster Scot: His Faith and Fortune* (Dungannon, 1899), pp. 2, 7–8.
49. Robert Lynd, *The Present Crisis in Ireland* (Belfast, 1886), p. 14.
50. This contradiction has been investigated in Clare O'Halloran, *Partition and the Limits of Irish Nationalism: An Ideology under Stress* (Dublin, 1987).
51. See, for example, Maxwell, *Ulster was Right*, pp. 8, 49.
52. Lynd, *Present Crisis*, pp. 14–15.
53. Walker, 'Empire, Religion and Nationality', p. 112.
54. Woodburn, *Ulster Scot*, pp. 370–1.
55. *Tyrone Constitution*, 18 March 1892, quoted in Hennessey, 'Ulster Unionist Territorial and National Identities', 30; see also Sinclair, 'Position of Ulster', pp. 171–2.
56. For some suggestive parallels, see Colin Kidd, 'Teutonic Ethnology and Scottish Nationalist Inhibition', in *Scottish Historical Review*, forthcoming.
57. Johnstone, *Ulstermen*, p. 88; for a later affirmation of composite identity see William A. Carson, *Ulster and the Irish Republic* (Belfast, 1956), p. 56.

58.   Sarah Nelson, *Ulster's Uncertain Defenders: Protestant Political, Paramilitary and Community Groups and the Northern Ireland Conflict* (Belfast, 1984), p. 12.
59.   Beckett, 'Northern Ireland', 130–1; Kennedy, *Widening Gulf*, p. 232; Clem McCartney and Lucy Bryson, *Clashing Symbols? A Report on the Use of Flags, Anthems and Other National Symbols in Northern Ireland* (Belfast, 1994), p. 42.
60.   Lord Brookeborough *et al.*, *Why the Border Must Be: The Northern Ireland Case in Brief* (Belfast, 1956), p. 4.
61.   See, for example, Ronald McNeill, *Ulster's Stand for Union* (London, 1922), p. 2; Ulster Unionist Council, *Ulster is British* (Belfast, 1949), p. 24; W. Douglas, 'The Impossibility of an Irish Union', *The Bell*, XIV, no. 1 (April 1947), 33–40; Carson, *Ulster and the Irish Republic*, p. 55.
62.   John Hewitt, 'The Bitter Gourd: Some Problems of the Ulster Writer', reprinted in *Ancestral Voices: The Selected Prose of John Hewitt*, ed. Tom Clyde (Belfast, 1987), pp. 108–21; 'Regionalism: The Last Chance', reprinted ibid., pp. 122–5.
63.   Hewitt, 'No Rootless Colonist', reprinted ibid., p. 153.
64.   *Ulster, An Ethnic Nation? Papers Delivered to a Seminar held by the Ulster Society* (Lurgan, 1986).
65.   Steve Bruce, *The Red Hand: Protestant Paramilitaries in Northern Ireland* (Oxford, 1992), p. 227.
66.   Vanguard, *Ulster – A Nation* (Belfast, 1972), p. 11.
67.   Ibid., p. 10.
68.   Steve Bruce, *God Save Ulster: The Religion and Politics of Paisleyism* (Oxford, 1986), p. 145.
69.   Vanguard, *Ulster – A Nation*, p. 15. A similar appeal has been made by W. Martin Smyth in *A Federated People* [Belfast, 1985?], pp. 5, 8. Smyth's proposal for a federal union, to be entitled the Isles of the North Atlantic (IONA for short) reveals a streak of utopian speculation not normally associated with Protestant political culture.
70.   McCartney and Bryson, *Clashing Symbols*, pp. 55, 60.
71.   Jennifer Todd, 'Two Traditions in Unionist Political Culture', *Irish Political Studies*, II (1987), 1–26.
72.   *Festival of Britain 1951 in Northern Ireland: Official Souvenir Handbook* (Belfast, 1951). The Festival also stimulated interest in regional art and literature: see Sam Hanna Bell *et al.*, *The Arts in Ulster* (London, 1951).
73.   See, for example, Brookeborough, *Why the Border Must Be*, esp. pp. 7–12.
74.   Colley, *Britons*, p. 374.
75.   A. T. Q. Stewart, 'The Siege of Ulster', *Spectator*, 11 Jan. 1986, p. 15.

2 Thomas Sinclair: Presbyterian Liberal Unionist
Graham Walker

In the Ulster Unionist pantheon of heroes Thomas Sinclair occupies a very minor position. In a recent publication celebrating the Ulster Covenant of 1912 he is identified as the Covenant's author, yet omitted from the chapter on the leaders of the Unionist movement.[1] In Irish historiography he has also suffered comparative neglect; even in the monographs devoted to the development of Unionism as a mass movement he merits only a passing mention.[2] This chapter will attempt to show that a study of his career illuminates some very significant aspects of Unionist politics and culture, in particular the Presbyterian and Liberal contribution to the campaigns against Irish Home Rule.

I

Thomas Sinclair was born in 1838 into a family which had already made its mark on Ulster society. His father, Thomas Senior, was a devout Presbyterian and an elder and session clerk in the Fisherwick Place Church in Belfast. He and his brother John had set up in 1834 the firm of J. and T. Sinclair, provender merchants, and become prosperous. The Thomas Sinclair family home was the handsome mansion 'Hopefield' in the north of the city, a focus for much religious and political activity in the adult lifetime of Thomas Junior. Thomas Senior and his brother devoted much of their wealth to the Presbyterian Church as well as their activities and energies, and a church bearing the name 'Sinclair Seamen's' was built as a memorial to John after his death in 1856. This church was primarily constituted to serve the spiritual needs of the seamen of the dockland community in Belfast in which it was situated.[3]

The family name was also to become associated with another parish church. In 1859 Thomas Senior and his family took an active interest in the Revival activity which swept Ulster in that year. This outpouring of religious fervour and incidence of mass conversion has to be seen in the context of the upsurge of evangelicalism in Victorian society more generally, and of the impact of the social and economic forces occasioned by industrialisation and urbanisation.[4] However, the singular feature of the phenomenon in Ulster was that it affected Presbyterianism much more profoundly than any other denomination. In the short term, at least, it increased the numerical strength of the Church and extended its sphere of influence. Following a typically enthusiastic prayer meeting in the Revival year attended by Thomas Junior at a house in North Belfast, Thomas Sinclair Senior was persuaded to set about building a church for the district. This was perhaps an indication that eminent Presbyterians wished to exercise some control over the outbursts of religious fervour and direct them to the ends of strengthening the Church's presence.[5] In the event this led to the erection of Duncairn Church on the Antrim Road in 1862. In this Church Thomas Junior replicated his father's record of church service as elder, Sabbath school officer and session clerk, and fashioned his status as the leading Presbyterian layman of his generation.[6]

As a young man of Liberal politics – an enthusiastic admirer of Gladstone – Sinclair was a prominent contributor to debates within Presbyterianism concerning the disestablishment of the Church of Ireland and the question of the state's religious endowments. Sinclair's political activities will be considered in more detail below but it is important at this point to appreciate how representative he was of the strong strain in Ulster Presbyterianism which took a principled stance against the religious privileges conferred by the state upon the Anglican 'ascendancy' – and had its Liberal dissenting politics shaped accordingly. At the time of Church of Ireland disestablishment by Gladstone's Liberal government in 1869 Sinclair was an articulate critic of 'the State Church Party' and 'the Orange ascendancy': at this point the Orange Order was very much an Episcopalian organisation led by the landed gentry, and Presbyterian feelings about it ranged from the lukewarm to the irreconcilably hostile. Presbyterian resentments focused on the civil and religious disabilities and degradations which their church had to endure during the penal era of the eighteenth century. Along with Roman Catholics they had been compelled to pay tithes to the established Church of Ireland; moreover, marriages performed by Presbyterian ministers had been denied official recognition, an indignity with which the Catholic Church had not been burdened. The latter issue was resolved by legislation in 1844.

Sinclair's political motivation sprang directly from Anglican–Presbyterian tensions. Speaking in support of the Liberal candidate,

Thomas McClure, at the 1868 general election, he called for 'justice in religion' and argued that the act of forcing someone to support (in the form of the payment of tithes) a church of which he does not approve, was 'the antithesis of Protestant principles'. He went on to bracket Presbyterian religious grievances with those of Roman Catholics.[7] Sinclair, along with most Presbyterians, thus welcomed disestablishment, although there were by this time a number of Presbyterian Tories who took the view of the Reverend Henry Cooke, who died in 1868, that there were advantages to the establishment of Protestantism in some form. Sinclair's position was emphatically against any state endowments of any religion and in favour of strict equality of treatment. At a Presbyterian meeting to discuss Gladstone's Disestablishment Bill he proclaimed:

> There is one principle which has brought both Presbyterian and Catholic so far in this great struggle – the principle of full and impartial dis-endowment as alone suited to the present condition of Ireland – and the man who first departs from that principle, be he Presbyterian or be he Catholic, at his door lies the responsibility of inducing indiscriminate endowment; and be he Presbyterian or be he Catholic, all loyal Presbyterians should oppose and resist him.[8]

Disestablishment had clear financial consequences for the Presbyterian Church, regardless of debates about other effects. It meant an end to the endowment the Church had received from the Crown since the mid-seventeenth century: the so-called 'Regium Donum'. Ministers, many of whom were dependent on this income, were persuaded by laymen including Sinclair, to commute these payments (which they could have drawn until they retired) for a lump sum which was paid to the Church. The laymen in turn undertook to set up a Sustentation Fund to augment this sum, and promised that this would result in a rise in the ministerial income to £100 per year.[9] In the organisation and successful operation of the Sustentation Fund Sinclair was crucial, although the promised £100 figure was not reached until a long time after the Fund's establishment.[10]

The principle of 'full and impartial disendowment' was one of the guiding themes in Sinclair's politics for the rest of his life. From 1870, however, it was an issue with which he engaged in relation to the Roman Catholic Church. Very soon after his declaration of 1869, quoted above, Sinclair was resolutely opposing Catholic demands for denominational education funded by the state. In 1870 he was instrumental in forming the National Education League for the defence of a non-sectarian system; however, the willingness of this organisation to consort with the Orange Order on the issue riled Catholic Liberal supporters and underlined the extent to which education was a divisive question within Ulster Liberalism.[11] In 1871 Sinclair insisted that if the demand for denominational education had emanated from a Presbyterian quarter his emphatic adverse response would have been the same.[12] Later in his career, most notably in connection with the issue of a Catholic university, Sinclair consistently opposed the concept of state assistance. While aspects of his Gladstonian Liberal outlook, such as his attitude to land reform, were to undergo a certain amount of moderation, Sinclair never departed from the ideal of non-sectarian education and the principle of opposition to state privileges; his early convictions forged in the circumstances of the Anglican ascendancy never left him, and in his later career shaped much of his outlook in relation to the prospect of Irish Home Rule and enhanced Roman Catholic Church power and influence. This will be further explored.

There are other ways in which Sinclair's politics cannot be fully understood without an appreciation of the religious outlook which underpinned them. There was, for instance, his Church work among the poor. Sinclair's attitude here was that of a typically Victorian middle-class stress on self-help – on the part of the Church. He was strongly in favour of the Church taking responsibility for its own poor and repudiated the idea of leaving problems of poverty to the state and the Poor Law system. His aim, as expressed in a speech in 1872 to the Presbyterian Orphan Society, was that no Presbyterian child should be found in a workhouse or in receipt of parish relief.[13] Sinclair knew about poverty at first hand: he visited the homes of the poor in his district and when he spoke about the reverence of the poor for their Church it was not in a patronising spirit.[14]

His missionary work among the poor was first undertaken as a young man in the company of his mentor, James McCosh.[15] McCosh, a Scot, was a student of the Scottish Enlightenment philosophers, and a major intellectual figure in his own right. From 1856 to 1868 he was resident in Belfast and held the Chair in Logic and Metaphysics at Queen's College where Sinclair studied after finishing his schooling at the prestigious Royal Belfast Academical Institution. Sinclair was a student of McCosh and was clearly influenced by his broad-minded Presbyterian outlook and his quest to improve the educational and social conditions of the poor. McCosh in turn had been much influenced by the Scottish Churchman Thomas Chalmers, whose name was often invoked in Irish Presbyterian circles. The 'sister church' of the Irish Presbyterian Church from the time of 'the Great Disruption' in Scotland in 1843 was Chalmers's Free Church of Scotland.[16] McCosh considered Chalmers the greatest man he ever met[17] and it is likely that much of Chalmers's religious philosophy and sense of mission was filtered through McCosh to Sinclair. Certainly, both shared the evangelical paternalism which characterised Chalmers's efforts in Glasgow to strengthen the Church among the poor and to retain influence against the encroachments of the state.[18] Both Sinclair and McCosh identified a need for the Presbyterian Church in Belfast to address the challenges of the socio-economic factors which were breaking down old communal structures and shaping an increasingly individualistic and competitive society. Both followed Chalmers's example in focusing their energies on the un-churched; in Belfast this meant tackling drunkenness and anti-Catholic intolerance encouraged by Orangeism among the Protestant labouring poor. For McCosh and Sinclair, as for so many 'progressive-minded' Liberals and Radicals, the answer lay in better education: in the establishment in Ireland of a national, non-denominational primary and intermediate system.[19]

There is nothing to suggest that Sinclair, as a leading merchant capitalist, did not fully support a *laissez-faire* economic system, but he was 'enlightened' enough to be aware of the dangers of ignoring social problems and of exacerbating conflict between classes. In a speech in support of a 'Society for Providing Nurses for the Irish Poor' he said:

> If our men of capital go heartily into this matter, they may do more than merely relieve suffering. They may contribute no inconsiderable influence towards soothing the differences between capital and labour that are incident to a social state like ours. There are no surer solvents of jealousy and mistrust than beneficence and Christian charity. The one purifies a plutocracy of its luxury, the other purges a democracy of its socialism.[20]

For Sinclair the Church had to direct its energies to both philanthropic and educational work. It was imperative that it maintained its influence, in times of great social upheaval, in spheres such as poor relief, educational provision and social mores. Clearly, he saw the well-off as having a duty to tackle and alleviate the adverse social effects of the economic system, in the interests both of the system itself – which he saw as socially and economically progressive – and of the maintenance of the Church's position in a changing society. His religious impulse was of the contemporary evangelical kind with its stress on individual conversion, but it was accompanied by an awareness of the value of the communal spirit to the health of the Church. His ideal, like that of Chalmers, can be described as morally reformed, well-educated individuals forming 'godly' communities.

For a generation and more Thomas Sinclair was to articulate his thoughts on religious affairs and on political issues on which he was guided to a large extent by his religious convictions, through the medium of the Presbyterian General Assembly and other such forums and conventions. These thoughts invariably made a powerful impact well beyond the Presbyterian Church.

II

Ulster politics in the mid-Victorian era reflected the Conservative–Liberal polarisation of the rest of the UK.[21] Gladstone's democratic appeal to 'enlightened' members of the bourgeoisie, like Sinclair, and self-improving artisans, drew a significant response, particularly among Ulster Presbyterians. In the 1868 election the Liberals made advances, albeit ephemeral, in the Ulster borough constituencies, and in the 1870s they mounted an effective challenge in the rural areas on the question of the land system and tenant right. This culminated in the winning of eight county seats in 1880. Strong support for the Liberals built up among the predominantly Presbyterian and Roman Catholic tenant farmers.[22] Sinclair's views in this period were firmly anti-landlord, and he shared the Gladstonian presumption of the time that a just settlement of the land question would redirect Irish national feeling to the benefit of the British and Imperial connection. 'The strength of vast empires', he pronounced, 'lies in the skilful blending of various nationalities'.[23] Successive governments, he believed, had neglected Irish national feeling and were reaping the consequences. This, of course, was the period of the rise of Fenianism in Ireland, the movement for separation which adopted physical force methods.

Gladstonian Liberalism before the storm over Irish Home Rule mirrored much of Sinclair's personal creed. In its moral righteousness and crusading zeal it echoed Sinclair's brand of Presbyterian social evangelicalism. Gladstone pitched his message at independent-minded workers; likewise Sinclair urged Ulster workers in 1868 to vote for McClure since the latter, as he put it, 'respects their conscience'.[24] Sinclair believed that the 'right to private judgement' was the 'clearest privilege' that Protestantism conferred, but that it involved civil as well as spiritual responsibilities;[25] this was eminently of a piece with Gladstone's moral and civic programme. Moreover, the Gladstonian Liberal assault on privilege found a ready echo in Presbyterians like Sinclair who believed that Presbyterians did not receive a fair deal in terms of a share of public offices, and that the industrial bourgeoisie and mercantile class which was largely Presbyterian deserved fairer representation. Speaking for McClure in 1868 he said: 'Belfast is a mercantile town. It is the Glasgow of Ireland. It is monstrous that she should not have at least one of her merchants in Parliament.'[26] Sinclair's Gladstonian political faith remained resolute into the 1880s. He scorned Tory attempts to convince electors that they, the Tories, now supported tenant right. Blisteringly, he attempted to expose Tory blandishments to Presbyterians:

> Since disestablishment, the Presbyterian Church does not require to stand as a beggar at the door of the state; she is at liberty to manage her own affairs and prosecute her proper work, a noble example of a free Church in a free state.... Why, then, this Tory zeal for Presbyterianism? Gentlemen, it is a blind ... it is a cloak wherewith to cover ulterior objects. Strip it off, and you find the old ascendancy as naked as when born.[27]

However, Sinclair and other Ulster Liberals had even greater cause for concern in the leakage of Catholic support from the Liberals to Parnell and the Land League, and later the National League, in this period.[28] As Catholics went over increasingly to the cause of Irish Home Rule, led so astutely by Parnell, Liberal Protestants were forced to face the political implications of hardening sectarian positions around the issue of the Union. Protestant (mainly Presbyterian) and Catholic unity around land questions was to be subverted by the overarching sense of division over the constitutional question. For Protestant Liberals like Sinclair Parnell's identification of Home Rule with agrarian aspirations was a confidence trick to be exposed in the cause of Gladstone's reforming programme towards Ireland. In the event it proved to be the seeds of a major dilemma.

III

For all their awareness of the effectiveness of Parnell's parliamentary and extra-parliamentary campaigns for Home Rule, Sinclair and the Ulster Liberals were stunned by Gladstone's conversion to the measure in 1886. The fact that there were Liberals who had lost their seats in 1885 while fighting for Gladstone in opposition to Parnell, rendered them all the more incredulous. The majority of them saw it as a surrender and a betrayal.

At a special meeting of the General Assembly of the Presbyterian Church in March 1886 Sinclair seconded a resolution opposing Home Rule and predicted that such a measure would mean economic disaster for Ulster.[29] In the same month at a special Liberal convention in Belfast Sinclair moved a resolution (adopted by a majority) calling on Gladstone 'not to risk the fate of his remedial legislation on land by entangling it with the vexed question of Home Rule', and said that the establishment of a separate Irish parliament would be certain to result in 'disastrous collision between sections of people holding conflicting views upon social, economic and religious subjects'. His concluding words defined the outlook of the new Ulster Liberal Unionist Association (ULUA) which shortly emerged with Sinclair as its first president:

> We claim that it is to our distinctive honour that we have ever been in line with the great acts of remedial legislation that have marked the repentant relations of England to Ireland since Catholic emancipation. In that path we mean to continue. But we claim to be an integral part of the United Kingdom. There must be no Home Rule plank in the Ulster Liberal platform.[30]

Gladstone's Liberal Party split over Home Rule and his Bill was defeated in the House of Commons in 1886. It was mainly the Whiggish wing of the Liberal Party which defected. On the other hand, the Ulster Liberals were stoutly supported in their opposition to Home Rule by two of the great radical political figures of modern Britain: Joseph Chamberlain and John Bright. Chamberlain received a tumultuous reception at a gathering of Ulster Liberals, chaired inevitably by Sinclair in 1887,[31] while Bright wrote to Sinclair upholding the idea of Ulster's separateness from the rest of Ireland. 'Ulster', Bright contended, 'may be deemed a nationality differing from the rest of Ireland at least as much as Wales differs from England, but Wales is treated to a flattery which, if not insincere, seems to be childish, and Ulster is forgotten in the discussion of the Irish question.'[32] This is an interesting comment for the time (1887) since the opponents of Home Rule, including the Ulster Liberal Unionists, were taking care to argue that they opposed it in the interests of the whole of Ireland. Nevertheless, it might be indicative of the extent to which, even at the time of the first Home Rule crisis, Presbyterian Liberal Unionists were less than committed to the all-Ireland loyalism preached by the 'ascendancy' party leaders such as Colonel Saunderson.[33]

Indeed, there was always a significant tension between the overriding requirements of Unionist unity in the successive campaigns against Home Rule from 1886 to 1914, and the jostling for position of the different parties and class and group interests within the alliance.[34] From the perspective of the Ulster Liberal Presbyterians it was imperative that they make their presence felt and convey clearly the message that opposition to

Home Rule was not the monopoly of the Conservatives and the Orange Order. The latter groups certainly desired this too, at least from the point of view of influencing public opinion in Britain. However, this common desire did not preclude power struggles within Unionism, and the Liberal Presbyterians were always sensitive to the charge – issued often by fellow Presbyterians such as the Reverend J. B. Armour from around 1890[35] – that they were being turned into the mere tool of the Conservatives, the Orange Order and the Church of Ireland. Correspondingly, Sinclair strove in his keynote speeches of the period to play down, for example, the role of the Orange Order: in 1888 he claimed that there were only 40 000 'acting' Orangemen in Ireland.[36] He also introduced arguments which had a singular Presbyterian flavour: he was fond of referring to the illiteracy rates of the period in Ireland ostensibly to show that much of the nationalist support drew on people who could not be sufficiently informed of the issues surrounding Home Rule.[37] Literacy rates were higher among Protestants relative to Catholics, but they were also appreciably higher among Presbyterians relative to other Protestant denominations. In a way Sinclair might have been subtly signalling to his non-Presbyterian allies the importance of the Presbyterian community to the Unionist case from the point of view of propaganda, reasoned argument and general organisational skills.

It was also Sinclair who took the initiative in organising the spectacular anti-Home Rule Convention held in Belfast in June 1892.[38] The defeat of his Home Rule Bill in 1886 had removed Gladstone from office, but it was clear that he would make another attempt if the opportunity arose again. As it happened, one month after the Convention, the general election restored Gladstone as premier with Irish nationalist support.

The Convention remains an important landmark in the organisation of Unionist resistance to Home Rule. It was carefully stage-managed to answer Gladstonian Liberal and Irish nationalist accusations that Unionism was the creed of a narrow landed elite clinging on to privileges and manipulating Orange workers with sectarian rhetoric. Liberal representation was much in evidence and reflected Sinclair's hand in the proceedings. The speeches at the Convention were notably conciliatory towards Catholics and expressions of pride in Irishness were effusive; 'Erin go bragh' even adorned the Convention pavilion. Sinclair's speech was one of the highlights of the day and was primarily notable for its apparent threat of Unionist civil disobedience or passive resistance in the event of a Dublin parliament being established.[39] However, Sinclair was also concerned to give the lie to the claim that Unionists simply sought a sectarian ascendancy over the Catholic Irish.

With Scottish Presbyterian and English non-conformist opinion most clearly in mind he recounted the Liberal Presbyterian record of struggles fought alongside Catholics for equal rights and against privilege. He lambasted Gladstone's lieutenant, John Morley, for suggesting that the Unionists wanted to 'trample' on people whom they considered 'an inferior race'.[40]

As Gladstone duly prepared his second Home Rule Bill, a sense of profound crisis and emergency gripped Unionists. They possessed some doubt that the House of Lords would reject the Bill if, as was certain, it passed through the Commons. Out of the 1892 Convention there emerged an Ulster Convention League, the Watch Committee of which Sinclair chaired. He also featured in the ruling cabal of the Ulster Defence Union, another creation of the times. He and Thomas Andrews, another important Ulster business leader, headed the Liberal wing of these pan-Unionist organisations. The Liberal Unionists themselves sent a deputation, headed by Sinclair, to confront Gladstone in London; by their own account, their erstwhile political hero gave them short shrift and constantly interrupted Sinclair's exposition of the economic consequences for Ulster of Home Rule.[41] The deputation duly published their message to Gladstone on their return in the form of a pamphlet which appeared under the auspices of the Belfast Chamber of Commerce. The statement of aims read as follows:

> We are of opinion that the reasonable wants of Ireland would be fully met by any mode of dealing rapidly and simply with the land question, consistently with justice and honour; by some arrangement for local government, similar to that lately created in England and Scotland; by an adequate reform of private Bill procedure; and by such aid from imperial credit as would in a sensible and economic way assist the development of Irish industries, where and when such assistance might be required. The policy of legislative union which has succeeded as regards not the least important section of the people of Ireland, is the policy which, if patiently continued, will yet bring peace to our beloved and divided country.[42]

To the relief of the Unionists the House of Lords rejected the Home Rule Bill and the succession to office of Salisbury's Conservative government in 1895 ushered in a period of relative calm on the constitutional issue. It was, however, to be a period when the theory – held most strongly by the Liberal Unionists – that the remedy of Irish grievances and social and economic ills would of itself solve the Irish question, was to be put to a test.

Liberal Unionists like Sinclair simply could not accept that there were grounds for Irish nationalism as such; in his view it had to be about a struggle for power and privileges with Catholic Nationalists attempting to seize both from the old ascendancy. He saw Presbyterians as the major potential victims, a point he was especially at pains to stress to Scottish audiences in these years as he cultivated his covenanting roots and appealed as a former follower of Gladstone to the numerous Scottish Presbyterian Liberals.[43] However, he was also keen to play to the gallery of the business and commercial community of the West of Scotland, in so many ways a mirror of Belfast and its environs, and like the latter largely Liberal Unionist in their politics.

Thus, in 1895, to a Glasgow audience, Sinclair said that Ireland only needed fair treatment to become 'like Scotland', a 'bulwark to the Empire'; and at the same meeting he drew a Scottish parallel with the proposed Dublin rule as follows:

> It is just as if it were proposed to transfer the interests of shipbuilders and manufacturers of Glasgow from Imperial Parliament to the control of a legislature swamped by the crofters of the Highlands.[44]

Such statements are revealing of the outlook of Unionists like Sinclair. It was considered progressive to dissolve older national allegiances in a wider British and Imperial whole, and Sinclair seemed to be assuming that this was happening in Scotland to the extent that he could make an appeal to the sense of regional pride in the West of Scotland which had been fostered by the material benefits of Empire, in contradistinction to the rural and 'backward' Highlands. This may indeed have drawn applause from a business audience in Glasgow and there was certainly a strong regional identity in Clydeside and in other parts of Scotland. Nevertheless, this did not detract from a wider Scottish national consciousness which was arguably enhanced by Scotland's role in the Empire. Sinclair may have extrapolated unduly from the Irish situation, assuming too much about national identity on the basis of his reluctance to admit to the substance of Irish nationalist feeling. This may have handicapped him especially in his appeals to Presbyterian Liberals in rural and small-town Scotland.

Irish nationalism, in the course of the nineteenth century, became to a significant extent identified with ultra-montane Catholicism, and this decisively sharpened the Ulster Protestant sense of apartness. Sinclair and others were on surer ground in Scotland when they made their appeal for support with reference to the Catholic Church's growing strength in

Ireland and what was perceived to be its quest for power and privileges, especially in the educational sphere. In the Presbyterian mind, both in Ulster and in Scotland, there was little doubt that Catholicism meant intellectual 'enslavement'.

IV

In the era of 'constructive Unionism'[45] the Liberal Unionists in Ulster attempted to exert a positive reforming influence on such matters as the land question, local government reorganisation, agricultural development and technical education.[46] Shannon has credited them with much of the 'progressivism' of the government's Irish policy,[47] while Gailey has argued that the presence of Chamberlain in the government emboldened Sinclair, Andrews and other Liberal Unionists to press their views on their Conservative colleagues.[48] In 1896 Sinclair was made an Irish Privy Councillor.

Developments in the late 1890s and early 1900s certainly reminded Unionists of the precarious nature of their alliance in the context of political controversies over land reform and Presbyterian grievances. The former issue was marked by an upsurge in radical farmer politics, led by the Liberal Unionist T. W. Russell, a maverick figure who ultimately drifted to a position of electoral dependence on the Irish Nationalists, but who threatened seriously for a time to fragment the Unionist movement.[49] Liberal Unionist leaders like Sinclair were very much concerned to maintain unity and the powerful political influence of the landlords,[50] while progressing cautiously in the direction of reform. Sinclair's stance on the land question by the late 1890s was governed by a pragmatism derived from his relations with Conservative colleagues, and was largely devoid of the rhetoric he had employed in earlier days. He was acutely aware of the dilemma of reform in a context where reforms or the lack of them threatened to damage Unionist solidarity.

Presbyterian grievances over the matter of public appointments – they alleged Episcopalian discrimination against them – constituted another sensitive area. The issue prompted the establishment of the Presbyterian Unionist Voters' Association (PUVA) in 1898. Publication of statistics on public appointments by the PUVA caused Sinclair great concern,[51] both on account of the anti-Presbyterian bias they apparently revealed, and the dangers that such grievances, if unaddressed, might pose for the Unionist alliance. Only the appointment to the vice-royalty in 1906 of the

Presbyterian Lord Aberdeen, ironically also a Home Ruler, appears to have taken the sting out of the issue.[52]

On agricultural matters and the development of technical education, Sinclair, along with other leading Liberal Unionists, worked closely with Horace Plunkett, the champion of rural cooperatives and an outstanding 'progressive' figure in the late-nineteenth and early-twentieth-century period. The association with Plunkett is evidence of the Liberal Unionists' independent line; most of the Conservatives, particularly the landlords, distrusted Plunkett and saw in his schemes only their own ruin and a stimulus to Home Rule. Sinclair, quite emphatically, viewed Plunkett's work as the kind of desirable reforming programme designed to improve relations within Ireland and strengthen the Union. In this he faced down opposition from within the Unionist camp and did much to enhance the Liberal Unionist profile.[53] Plunkett himself paid tribute to the efforts of Sinclair and Andrews in championing his initiatives in hazardous political circumstances.[54]

Plunkett began a rural self-help movement centred on cooperative creameries in the late 1880s; by 1894 it had developed into the formation of a coordinating body called the Irish Agricultural Organisation Society (IAOS). Impressed by the Ulster Liberal Unionists' campaign for technical education he urged them to join forces with his movement in the cause of developing both agriculture and technical education. Sinclair and other Liberal Unionist leaders responded positively, and in 1895 Plunkett brought them together with Parnellite Nationalists in the Recess Committee (so called because it sat in the parliamentary recesses) to promote these objectives. An 'Ulster Consultative Committee' was set up along with it. Plunkett valued greatly the contribution of Sinclair and his followers and praised them for recognising – as urban businessmen – the importance of agriculture and of rural cooperative schemes.[55] The Recess Committee's lobbying resulted in the Unionist government at Westminster establishing in 1899 a new State Department of Agriculture and Technical Instruction (DATI) for Ireland. In effect this was 'agricultural devolution' for Ireland.

Notwithstanding the suspicions, and indeed hostility, of many Unionists Sinclair continued to support Plunkett in his work at the DATI. He braved an Orange outcry over his support for Plunkett's choice of T. P. Gill, a Catholic and a Nationalist, as secretary of the department.[56] The Liberal Unionists were instrumental in ensuring that the new system of technical or vocational education should be non-denominational. However, Sinclair did break with Plunkett over the latter's support for a Catholic university,[57] and in his final years Sinclair sorrowfully observed Plunkett's gradual movement towards a pro-Home Rule position.[58] Nonetheless, this cannot detract from the significance of Sinclair's influence on Plunkett's thinking – it may indeed be argued that Plunkett's major work, *Ireland in the New Century*, bore clear traces of the Liberal Unionist outlook epitomised by Sinclair regarding the Catholic Church's relationship to industry, business skills, technical education, and a culture of economic development in general. Plunkett's criticisms of the Catholic Church in these respects embroiled him in a controversy which led to his resignation from the DATI in 1907.[59]

For Sinclair it was one thing to participate in committees and organisations with Catholics and Nationalists within the Union and with safeguards against the exploitation of subjects like education for sectarian ends; it was quite another to pursue his objectives while at the mercy of a Dublin parliament which he believed would be unduly influenced by a power-hungry and, in terms of the demands of new technology and industrial development, backward Catholicism. Other observers offered a different interpretation. The Ulster playwright St John Ervine, then a Home Ruler, wrote of Sinclair in 1914:

> Thomas Sinclair, a man of singular integrity and judgement, had no difficulty whatever in working with Nationalists and Catholics on committees of the Irish Agricultural Organisation Society; but some perverse thing operating in his mind made him refuse to work with them in government. There were many men in Belfast such as he who had all the potentialities of great Irishmen, but, because of traditional prejudices and hatred, persisted in being only little Ulstermen.[60]

V

In the last ten years of his life Sinclair's Unionism increasingly focused on the perception of Home Rule as 'Rome Rule', thus blurring somewhat the lines of division between himself and Conservative Orangemen. Ironically, it was his belief that he was being steadfast in his Liberal principles which often occasioned his most strident warnings about Home Rule and Catholic power.

The 'devolution' schemes of 1904 and 1907 aroused much Unionist anxiety; they were viewed largely as a means to Home Rule. Unionists of all shades had come to the point where they could not be reassured that even a moderate administrative devolution plan would not be a stepping-stone to something else; they viewed the reunited Irish Nationalist Party as all-out for a generous measure of legislative Home Rule which, once in operation, could be massaged into something embodying greater independence and ultimately complete separation. By 1910, when the Liberals held power by virtue of the Nationalists and signalled their intention of abolishing the veto of the House of Lords and introducing a third Home Rule Bill, Unionists rejected any notion that safeguards supposedly protecting their rights and interests in any scheme could in practice prove dependable. They argued that 'paper guarantees' given by the Imperial Parliament could not be made effective in practice.[61] This was the line Sinclair took in several important interventions, and he made it clear that he saw the Catholic Church as the insatiable power behind the scenes ensuring that the new parliament do its bidding.

He drew on issues such as university education to support this view. In 1908 a Universities Bill had in effect provided for a state-endowed Roman Catholic university in Ireland, something Sinclair considered contrary to every principle of religious equality argued for by Liberals.[62] In 1910 Sinclair contended that safeguards intended to prevent sectarian abuses in university education had amounted to nothing and that three-fourths of Irish university education was now run in a sectarian fashion by the Catholic Church.[63] In the same year he was involved in a protest against the establishment of a lectureship at Queen's University in Scholastic Philosophy which he viewed as an endowment of Catholic teaching.[64]

There also occurred in 1910 the notorious 'McCann case' in Belfast which seemed to bear out Protestant fears about the practical effects of the Catholic Church's decree on mixed marriages, 'Ne Temere', issued in 1908.[65] Sinclair commented:

> Subject as they themselves are to Vatican control, no restriction of the powers of a Dublin parliament would be permitted which would limit the Church in its use of the Ne Temere decree. Rather would she insist that the substance of that decree be enacted in an Irish Parliamentary statute.[66]

In 1911 the Catholic Church issued another decree, 'Motu Proprio', which seemed to Protestants to be an attempt to secure the immunity of the Catholic clergy from the process of civil or criminal law. For Sinclair this further demonstrated the Church's determination to assert its domination over individual judgement – a sacred Liberal and Protestant principle – and its authority in matters of legislation when it decided that its interests were at stake. In an Irish parliament, he argued, a legislature dominated by Catholic members would give paramount weight to the claims of the Church and the minority would be powerless to prevent it. Any 'safe-guards' built in to prevent such a development would, he believed, be ignored and in such circumstances it would be impossible to make them effective short of using force.[67]

Such arguments as these were constructed by Sinclair on the basis of his perception of the Catholic church accumulating special privileges and infringing Protestant liberties, and they derived fundamentally from Sinclair's Liberal political heritage. They were also essentially Presbyterian arguments reflecting the Presbyterian fear of an Anglican ascendancy in Ireland being replaced by a Roman Catholic ascendancy.[68] They were the kind of arguments which led to the popularising of the 'Home Rule is Rome Rule' slogan but in many ways their painstaking rea-soning and their Liberal underpinnings got lost in their adoption as a rally-ing cry, and the identification of opposition to Home Rule with the sectarianism of Orangeism was not, in the fevered circumstances of 1910–14, significantly modified by Liberal Presbyterian polemicists such as Sinclair.[69]

Nevertheless, the Liberal Unionist Presbyterians could still be said to have made their mark out of proportion to their numbers. During the third Home Rule Bill crisis they continued to make strenuous efforts to distin-guish themselves and their part in the Unionist opposition movement. Sinclair was instrumental in organising another convention, this time of Presbyterian Unionists in February 1912.[70] The purpose was again to high-light the non-Conservative and Orange section of the movement, and to appeal to the non-conformists of England and the Presbyterians of Scotland. The appeal to the latter in particular was embodied explicitly in the convention's resolutions, and Sinclair, in his address as Chairman, recalled Scottish assistance for Ulster Presbyterians during the persecu-tions of 1641 and expressed confidence that aid would again come from this source. He also identified the Ancient Order of Hibernians (AOH) – '(composed of men) utterly inexperienced in financial and industrial affairs' – as the vehicle through which the Catholic Church would exercise domination in a Home Rule Ireland.

The convention was notable first for the stress on fears of a future Catholic ascendancy: an ethnic homogeneity was promoted, based on reli-gious identity and cultural assumptions about Catholicism, rather than racist notions.[71] Secondly, an element in this ethnic identity was the cele-bration of the myth of the 'Ulster Scots' as a people with exceptional resolve, and resourcefulness and genius.[72] This can be interpreted as an expression of the Presbyterian pride in their own cultural distinctiveness and of the sense of moral righteousness which had long characterised the

Presbyterian community in Ulster and had found political expression in causes as various as the United Irishmen of the late eighteenth century, Gladstonian Liberalism, and Presbyterian opposition to – and support for – Home Rule.

By 1912, at the height of its resistance to Home Rule, Unionism was bound up above all with ideas of Ulster particularity. This was the culmination of a process of 'Ulsterisation' which Jackson sees as developing rapidly, and out of political necessity, after 1905, although there are other historians who would date it earlier.[73] The iconography of Unionist resistance in the 1912–14 period was built around apocalyptic concepts of Ulster standing firm – and alone if necessary. To this process of image-fabrication Sinclair contributed much; indeed, it might be claimed that the Liberal Presbyterian Unionists were the most enthusiastic proponents of an Ulster identity which, in terms of imagery and propaganda, drew so much on such distinctively Presbyterian themes as the Scottish cultural heritage. It is Sinclair who is widely credited with composing the text of the Solemn League and Covenant of 1912, by which Unionists pledged to resist Home Rule.[74] This seems likely, given that it was based on the Scottish example of the 1640s. In view of its impact as a statement of solemn and binding intent, and as the subject of a massive show of strength and resolve, the Covenant amounted to something of a hi-jack of the Unionist identity by one tradition. Even allowing for intermarriage and a general blurring of denominational boundaries among Protestants, it might be said that the Presbyterians of Scottish descent were able to stamp their cultural imprint on the Unionist cause more definitively by virtue of their relatively greater social coherence and intellectual and religious purposefulness. Those Unionists of English settler descent were divided more sharply by social class and by denomination, and were overshadowed in the employment of mobilising myths and imagery.

The promotion of 'Ulsterness' owed much to the way in which Irish nationalist imagery and ideology forced Unionists to cultivate an alternative ethnic identity, but it arguably stopped short of being a fully-fledged nationalism.[75] Unionists in general, including the Liberal Unionists, insisted they were British and wanted simply to remain within the Union and the Empire. This loyalty co-existed with Ulster and Irish forms of identity. Unionists generally did not, at least before 1914, disparage or disavow expressions of Irishness. They did claim, at least in theory, a right as Ulstermen to self-determination, although as Sinclair made clear in his contribution to the publication *Against Home Rule*, this was regarded as a last line of defence.[76] Sinclair contended that Ireland consisted of two nations but his references to the 'Unionist unit' concentrated in the

Province of Ulster, and the 'Ulster Scot' as no 'ordinary immigrant' are better understood as arguments for Unionists to be regarded as a distinctive ethnic people whose right to British citizenship was paramount, and could not be denied to them.[77] It is likely that Sinclair still viewed a wider British and Imperial identity as a progressively capacious structure encompassing diversity, a 'higher' and more worthy focus of loyalty and allegiance. However, there was a discernible tension in Unionism between the 'progressivist' and secular language of claims made for the benefits of the Union and British citizenship, and the sense of Ulster particularism shaped by religious and cultural factors which were decidedly exclusivist, and heavily orientated to the Presbyterian self-image.[78] Sinclair, tireless in the service of Presbyterian virtue, embodied the tensions and ambiguities.

Sinclair died in February 1914, at the height of the Home Rule controversy. He had become one of Carson's most trusted lieutenants – and has been celebrated as such.[79] He was a central figure in the Ulster provisional government which had been constructed during the crisis, and he had been responsible for drawing up its constitution.[80] Obituarists, however, stressed his restraining influence on some of his more extreme colleagues.[81] The tributes flowed from political allies and opponents alike[82] and, if anything, the Presbyterian Church's sense of loss was even greater than that of the Unionist movement. He had been, above all, a dedicated custodian of his Church's heritage and, according to his own perception of them, his Church's beliefs and principles.

VI

A study of Thomas Sinclair is in many ways a study of the Presbyterian community and its centrality to Ulster Protestant culture. He epitomised a sense of cultural as well as religious mission and a supreme confidence in the soundness of Presbyterian principles and values. He blended compassion and a drive for social justice with an unbending moralism. He assumed the superiority of the Presbyterian conception of what was best for the country, and held a Whiggish view of Ulster's progress to which the Presbyterian contribution regarding social, economic and cultural achievements was crucial. He embodied a sense of cultural elitism which characterised much Presbyterian argument.

To study Sinclair is also to appreciate the importance of the Liberal Unionists to the Unionist anti-Home Rule cause, notwithstanding their numbers relative to the Conservatives.[83] Without the Liberal Unionists, there would have been no significant representation of the crucial busi-

ness, industrial and financial interests (largely Presbyterian) who strengthened the case against Home Rule from an economic point of view. Sinclair
and his fellow Liberal Unionists were necessary to give credence to the
Unionist argument that they valued the Union and the Empire as a socially
progressive political structure. The perception of Unionism as essentially
sectarian was perhaps inevitable given the role of the Orange Order as a
mobiliser of popular Protestant resistance. However, the arguments put by
Sinclair on the subject of Catholic sectarianism and the threat to Protestant
liberties deserved as much attention as the Orange demonstrations.
Cogently built into them was the crux of Unionist concerns: only in the
context of the UK parliament did they feel that their social and economic
welfare, cultural vitality and religious liberties would be secure. Sinclair
deserves greater recognition as one of Ulster Unionism's most practised
advocates.

NOTES

1.   G. Lucy (ed.), *The Ulster Covenant* (Ulster Society, 1989).
2.   A. T. Q. Stewart, *The Ulster Crisis* (London, 1967); P. Buckland, *Ulster
     Unionism* (Dublin, 1973).
3.   Information derived from the *Presbyterian Quarterly Visitor*, November
     1988; also Rev. T. Hamilton, *History of the Irish Presbyterian Church*
     (Belfast, 1992, reprint), chapter XX.
4.   See D. Hempton and M. Hill, *Evangelical Protestantism in Ulster Society*
     (London, 1992), chapter 8; P. Gibbon, *The Origins of Ulster Unionism*
     (Manchester, 1975), chapter 3.
5.   See Thomas Sinclair's foreword to W. Gibson, *The Year of Grace*
     (Edinburgh and London, 1909).
6.   Information derived from centenary booklet of Duncairn Parish Church
     (1962).
7.   Report of meeting in Thomas Sinclair Papers, PRONI D3002/1.
8.   Ibid. Date of meeting 8 April 1869.
9.   See F. Holmes, *Our Irish Presbyterian Heritage* (Presbyterian Church in
     Ireland, 1985), p. 132.
10. See cuttings regarding Sustentation Fund in Sinclair Papers D3002/1.
11. P. Bew and F. Wright, 'The Agrarian Opposition in Ulster Politics,
     1848–87', in S. Clark and J. S. Donnelly Jnr (eds), *Irish Peasants*
     (Manchester, 1983).
12. D3002/1, date of meeting 8 December 1871.
13. D3002/1, 22 February 1872.
14. Ibid.
15. W. M. Sloane (ed.), *The Life of James McCosh* (Edinburgh, 1896).

16. F. Holmes, *Thomas Chalmers and Ireland* (Presbyterian Historical Society, 1980).
17. Sloane, op. cit., p. 140.
18. See S. J. Brown, 'Reform, Reconstruction, Reaction: The Social Vision of Scottish Presbyterianism c. 1830–1930', *Scottish Journal of Theology*, vol. 44 (1991), pp. 489–517.
19. Sloane, op. cit., chapter IX passim.
20. D3002/1, n. d.
21. See B. M. Walker, *Ulster Politics: The Formative Years* (Belfast, 1989).
22. See R. McMinn, 'Presbyterianism and Politics in Ulster, 1871–1906', *Studia Hibernica*, vol. 21 (1981), pp. 127–46.
23. D3002/1, 18 November 1868.
24. Ibid.
25. D3002/1, 8 April 1869.
26. D3002/1, 18 November 1868.
27. D3002/1, cuttings on election meetings 1880–81.
28. Bew and Wright, op. cit.
29. Speech quoted in F. Holmes, 'The General Assembly and Politics', in R. F. G. Holmes and R. Buick Knox (eds), *The General Assembly of the Presbyterian Church in Ireland 1840–1990* (Presbyterian Church in Ireland, 1990).
30. Resolution quoted in J. R. Fisher, *The Ulster Liberal Unionist Association: A Sketch of its History 1885–1914* (Belfast, 1914), pp. 15–17.
31. See T. McKnight, *Ulster as It Is*, vol. II (Belfast, 1896), pp. 196 ff.
32. D3002/1, Bright to Sinclair, 6 June 1887.
33. See McKnight, op. cit.; and chapter by Ian McBride in this volume.
34. See A. Jackson, *The Ulster Party* (Oxford, 1989), passim; also Gibbon, op. cit. and Buckland, op. cit..
35. See R. McMinn (ed.), *Against the Tide* (PRONI, 1985), especially p. xxxviii.
36. D3002/1, 22 March 1888.
37   Ibid.
38. Fisher, op. cit., pp. 33–5; McKnight, op. cit., pp. 288–90.
39. Speech cited in Holmes, *Our Irish Presbyterian Heritage*, p. 136; also Buckland, op. cit., p. 16.
40. See report in *The Times*, 18 June 1892.
41. See document reproduced in P. Buckland, *Irish Unionism 1885–1923: A Documentary History* (Belfast, 1973), p. 273.
42. Pamphlet in D3002/1.
43. See, for example, speech to General Assembly of Church of Scotland in 1893, D3002/1.
44. *Northern Whig*, 9 March 1895.
45. The best account is A. Gailey, *Ireland and the Death of Kindness* (Cork, 1987).
46. Fisher, op. cit , p. 39.
47. C. Shannon, 'The Ulster Liberal Unionists and Local Government Reform 1885–1898', in A. O'Day (ed.), *Reactions to Irish Nationalism* (Dublin, 1987).
48. Gailey, op. cit., p. 146.

49. See A Jackson, 'Irish Unionism and the Russellite Threat 1894–1906', *Irish Historical Studies*, vol. XXV, no. 100 (November 1987).
50. See chapter by David Burnett in this volume.
51. Gailey, op. cit. , p. 155.
52. McMinn, 'Presbyterianism and Politics'.
53. See Gailey, op. cit., p. 156 regarding Sinclair's letter to Arthur Balfour saying that attacks on Plunkett were attacks on his brother Gerald's policies.
54. See letter from Plunkett to Andrews, quoted in S. Bullock, *Thomas Andrews* (Dublin, 1912), Appendix.
55. See T. West, *Horace Plunkett, Co-operation and Politics* (Gerrards Cross, 1986), pp. 45–6; H. Plunkett, *Ireland in the New Century* (Dublin, 1982), p. 218.
56. West, op. cit., pp. 54–5.
57. Ibid., p. 64.
58. Ibid., pp. 121–5.
59. See epilogue of 1905 edition of *Ireland in the New Century* for Plunkett's account of the controversy.
60. St John Ervine, *Sir Edward Carson and the Ulster Movement* (Dublin and London, 1915), pp. 70–1. See also chapter by Patrick Maume in this volume.
61. See ULUA Pamphlet 'The Home Rule Crisis' (1911) in D3002/1.
62. *Belfast Newsletter*, 10 April 1908.
63. D3002/1, letter to *The Scotsman*, 26 April 1910.
64. See McMinn, *Against the Tide*, pp. 194–5.
65. See P. Bew, *Ideology and the Irish Question* (Oxford, 1994), pp. 31–4.
66. D3002/1, letter to *The Scotsman*, 24 April 1910.
67. See *Northern Whig*, 6 January 1912.
68. See Holmes, 'The General Assembly and Politics'.
69. T. G. Houston was another such polemicist – see, for example, his pamphlet 'Ulster's Appeal' (1913).
70. See report in *Belfast Weekly News*, 8 February 1912. This is the source for what follows regarding the Convention.
71. See Hempton and Hill, op. cit. , p. 183.
72. The 'Home Rule era' saw the publication of a number of books extolling the virtues of the 'Ulster Scots' and presenting the Home Rule issue as a struggle essentially between them and the Catholic Irish. See, for example, J. Harrison, *The Scot in Ulster* (Edinburgh, 1888); C. Hanna, *The Scotch-Irish* (London, 1902); J. B. Woodburn, *The Ulster Scot* (London, 1914).
73. Jackson, *Ulster Party*; but see also Gibbon, op. cit., who sees the 1892 Convention as marking its emergence.
74. Lucy, op. cit., p. 43; Holmes, *Our Irish Presbyterian Heritage*, pp. 136–7.
75. For a guide to the scholarly debate on this very complex question, see A. Jackson, *Ulster Party*, chapter 1; also G. Walker, 'Empire, Religion and Nationality in Scotland and Ulster before the First World War', in I. S. Wood (ed.), *Scotland and Ulster* (Edinburgh, 1994).
76. T. Sinclair, 'The Position of Ulster', in S. Rosenbaum (ed.), *Against Home Rule* (London, 1912); see also chapter by Ian McBride. By 'Ulster' Sinclair

meant the six counties plus 'the important adjacent Unionist sections of Monaghan, Cavan and Donegal'.

77. Sinclair, op. cit. For a discussion of Unionism and ideas of citizenship rights and obligations, see D. Miller, *Queen's Rebels* (Dublin, 1978).
78. Certain publications of the time were geared to this end: see Woodburn, op. cit., a key Presbyterian text.
79. Lucy, op. cit., p. 43.
80. Bew, op. cit., p. 36.
81. Sinclair Papers, PRONI D3002/5.
82. See McMinn, *Against the Tide*, pp. 142–3.
83. See Bew, op. cit., chapters 1–2.

3 The Modernisation of Unionism, 1892–1914?
David Burnett

INTRODUCTION

The roots of Irish Unionism are long. Countering O'Connell in 1834, C. D. O. Jephson declared, 'we are all divided now into Repealers and unionists'.[1] Parliament agreed, and for the next fifty years approved of the Union as both an essential imperial defence and as an umpire between the Irish parties. However, the organisation of various Unionist bodies between 1884 and 1886 represented a new situation. A Liberal government at Westminster threatened to pass a bill granting self-government to Ireland. Unionists believed this threatened a Catholic Nationalist hegemony in all aspects of Irish society. Thus, a myriad of anti-Nationalist factions were brought together. Protestant class and denominational differences were subsumed by a simple desire to preserve the Union with Great Britain and, as a result, Protestant security.

The Home Rule bill of 1886 was defeated in the House of Commons by a combination of Conservatives and Liberal Unionists.[2] The same alliance emerged in Ireland and was augmented by long-standing, cross-denominational bodies such as the Orange Order. Unionism was a broad church, ranging from landed elements, who moved in British socio-political circles, to a variety of plebeian and bourgeois groups generally more localist in outlook.

Irish Unionism was numerically weak in both Ireland and the House of Commons (outnumbered four to one by Nationalists). But Irish Unionists had important political weapons. The landed and titled had close personal and economic ties with British aristocratic cousins who dominated Westminster; and they controlled a significant geographic area, north-east Ulster, in terms of votes and MPs returned.[3] The former allowed Irish Unionists to influence Unionist Party policy on Ireland out of all proportion to their numbers, important when the Unionists were in office, while the latter provided a tangible counter to Nationalist claims that Home Rule was the will of the Irish people. Ulster, unlike any other part of Ireland, contained a vertically integrated Unionist community.[4]

Late Victorian politics remained the preserve of landed and titled elites and, with direct access to the leadership of a party of government, Irish Unionism was well placed to withstand Nationalist pressure for Home Rule. Moreover, with the Unionist-dominated House of Lords in reserve, the Home Rule legislation of a Liberal government was not assured to become law. Unionists relied upon the *quality* of their argument, and a favourable response from the State as embodied in Parliament, to maintain the constitutional *status quo* for the whole of Ireland; the question of Ulster, and the *quantity* of anti-Home Rulers there, remained in reserve.

However, this was also a time of challenge to the established political leadership of the landed peers and gentry.[5] Democracy was the political watchword of the day and the will of the majority was gradually usurping the patronage of the wealthy and titled. The growth of organised working-class politics and new collectivist ideas demanding greater revenue from taxation to tackle a range of issues were two important consequences. Liberals and Labour reacted quickly to this scenario, promising wealth-creation by government intervention and wealth-redistribution by government planning respectively. Unionists produced no agreed policy response and embarked upon a quest for such over the next thirty years, usually embracing some form of social imperialism.[6] Irish Unionists were sympathetic to this idea but disliked any other issue taking priority over the Irish Question. As Ireland became less important as an issue in British politics, the influence of the Irish Unionist elite within the party began to wane.

Moreover, Irish Unionist leaders encountered similar pressures from below, with many in the Unionist stronghold of Ulster keen to support progressive legislation and greater democracy in party decision-making[7] (the two were connected). Thus, some form of modernisation in these areas, to prevent the disintegration of the class consensus so vital to the party's electoral success, was always a prime concern. The subsequent decline of Irish landlordism and the emergence of a confident and determined bourgeois leadership, between 1892 and 1914, resulted in the dominance of Ulster Unionism.

HOBSON'S CHOICE – REFORM AND SECURITY, 1892–1900

In the 1890s the Ulster Liberal Unionist Association (ULUA) provided a counter-weight to the dominant, landed Conservatism of Irish Unionism, doing much to convince the Unionist masses, centred in Ulster, that reform remained a party priority. Peter Gibbon concluded that these two wings of Irish Unionism were engaged in a 'conflict for [the] leadership of

Unionism' and that the Belfast Convention of June 1892 marked a watershed, with the 'urban entrepreneurs' emerging victorious; there was a 'common recognition of a distinct northern cause'.[8] This has been decisively countered[9] but the importance of the ULUA and its leaders remains neglected; why were these talented men unable to transform this 'distinct northern cause' into a distinctly northern organisation and perpetuate this? The answer lies in the relationship between the landed conservatives and the urban liberals and in the unresolvable nature of the problems facing Irish Unionism in the 1890s.

Liberal Unionists were not trying to usurp the leadership of the landed conservatives; rather they valued the latter's influence and desired a compromise to resolve the conservative–reformist dilemma. Both agreed, for example, that Unionism was best served by a British power base and the ULUA sent deputations to Hartington and Chamberlain, mimicking Irish Conservatives' relations with the Salisbury leadership.[10] These were taken seriously by British commanders; after all, the Irish Question was the entire basis of the Unionist alliance. Moreover, with the landed elite also the paymasters of the various Unionist organisations in Ireland, and the Unionist voter contributing little or nothing to expenses, the loss of the former would seriously disrupt Unionist efficiency.

Land and local government were the key areas the ULUA wanted to see reformed so as to maintain the Unionist consensus. By the election of 1892, some Unionist candidates in rural Ulster constituencies felt they had to denounce landlord obstinacy over land reform. Thus, three positions were to emerge within the Liberal Unionist wing of the party: conservative (pro-landlord), reformist (anti-landlord) and a middle group seeking compromise.

Converted whigs, such as Hugh de Fellenberg Montgomery, a County Tyrone landlord, represented the first group. He feared that Protestant farmers, by prioritising land reforms above the Union, were establishing a dangerous precedent. Replying to R. M. Dane, newly elected MP for North Fermanagh in 1892, Montgomery explained that his support had been for Dane as a Unionist, not as a farmers' candidate; having asked farmers to support landlords as Unionists, the latter 'were bound to practice [*sic*] what we preached'. Montgomery's fear was that the farmers, by advocating compulsion, were admitting a dangerous principle because Nationalists would twist it into a

conspiracy for undermining British rule, by ruining and expelling the gentry and that protestant [*sic*] tenants in adopting the demand are cutting a rod for their own backs, as – the principle once admitted –

there is nothing to prevent a Radical government from applying it to any body of Protestant occupiers that a Popish or Fenian majority wish removed out of any part of Ireland to make room for 'men of their own'.[11]

The legal framework of society would be undermined by Nationalist numbers and British betrayal; reform meant Nationalist empowerment and a renewed, intensified thrust for hegemony. Landlordism and its boons for Unionism (wealth and influence) would be sacrificed, only for the Protestant beneficiaries of reform to suffer the same fate later. Rather than risk this, Unionism should defend the *status quo* by advocating land reform which gradually helped the farmers and compensated the land-lords.[12] Dane actually agreed with much of this. His platform advocacy of compulsion was tempered by a fear of its consequences and he hoped the party would find a way to target this for the exclusive benefit of Ulster's Protestant farmers, avoiding Montgomery's doomsday scenario.[13]

The compromisers were mainly ULUA leaders, such as Thomas Sinclair,[14] Robert MacGeagh, Thomas Andrews and Adam Duffin. These were Gibbon's 'urban entrepreneurs' who defeated landlordism, captured Unionism for Ulster and created a bold, sectarian monolith. Reality was different. Sinclair and MacGeagh, for example, were sympathetic to the landlord case, preferring to extend the Ashbourne Act (1885) and continue inducement.[15] Duffin believed compulsion could work with adequate compensation to landlords but realised that the enormous sum this would necessitate was not available from Treasury coffers.[16] Therefore, compulsion would degenerate into a Nationalist crusade to break the land system without compensating the landlords, to be justified as a payback for ancient 'robbery'. This mirrored Montgomery's fear about empowering Nationalists.

These men did organise popular resistance in Ulster against the second Home Rule bill, using the Ulster Convention League (UCL) and Ulster Clubs Council (UCC).[17] Both bodies were keen to reassure southern Unionist leaders about their aims, and deputations from north and south visited each other and agreed to cooperate.[18] This unity was reliant upon a common analysis of the crisis, that their best defence lay in Parliament with the party leadership. The UCL and UCC were contingency plans to confront Gladstone in the unlikely event he squeezed the bill through both Commons and Lords. As such, the Belfast Convention was nothing more than an organisational version of Chamberlain's Ulster rhetoric in the Home Rule debates of 1886 – 'a terrible nut for the G.O.M. to crack'.[19] The ongoing relationship between north and south was best illustrated at the election of 1895 when the southern, landlord-led Irish Unionist Alliance and the three main northern groups operated a joint committee to control and target funding.[20]

Sinclair had initiated organisational reform in 1892 to contain popular unrest over land reform at a time of crisis. However, efforts to perpetuate the UCL's momentum, after the defeat of Home Rule in the Lords in 1893, by reorganising it as the Ulster Defence Union (UDU), proved more difficult. This was to be a permanent organisation in Ulster of 600 representatives, elected by local colleges of every registered Unionist voter, to ensure Unionist discipline and readiness against any crisis.[21] Within a year this body had experienced major difficulties and after five years had completely disappeared. The enthusiasm of the Convention had ebbed away. Why?

The immediate difficulty was that of convincing conservatives of the value of a populist, provincial organisation. Montgomery's South Tyrone Unionist Association had refused to affiliate to the UCL, preferring the philosophical and financial comfort of the IUA; several other associations retained similar doubts.[22] The UDU was too much a slippery slope to caucus politics[23] and irresistible pressure for compulsion as party policy. For reformists, the UDU was a permanent response to a temporary crisis now past;[24] with Nationalism split and impotent and Gladstone defeated, party commitment to deliver reform was now wanted.

The reformists, led by T. W. Russell and Thomas Lea, advocated radical land reform as the only way to prevent Protestant farmers from succumbing to Nationalism's promise that compulsion would follow Home Rule.[25] Landlord influence in Westminster was deemed inadequate defence against this, indeed to be counterproductive, pushing frustrated Protestants towards the Nationalist panacea. The only real safety lay in a contented Protestant 'democracy'[26] as an alternative to that of Nationalism. This meant comprehensive land reform, even at the risk of empowering Nationalists – exactly what Montgomery feared. Unionists such as Dane actually fitted better with the compromisers than with the reformist group and the compromisers were inclined towards the conservatives.

However, many Protestant farmers in Ulster remained unconvinced that reforms had to be gradual and small to keep Nationalism at bay; and many middle-class social climbers, thwarted by the party's influence with Dublin Castle in determining appointments by patronage, shared this view. After the comprehensive defeat of Home Rule in 1893, these groups saw little to fear from making good the party's claim that the Union was the basis of progress.[27]

Since the mid-1880s, successive Unionist Chief Secretaries had pioneered a strategy dubbed constructive unionism.[28] Its creator, Arthur Balfour, summed this up as being 'as relentless as Cromwell in enforcing obedience to the law, but, at the same time...as radical as any reformer in redressing grievances'. The aim was to help contain Irish Unionist factionalism (conservatives were to be consulted on legislation, reformists appeased by the ultimate enactment of reforms) and maintain good Irish–British Unionist relations.

In 1896, Russell persuaded the Unionist government to introduce a land bill, similar to the defunct Morley bill which landlords had opposed as too radical, to placate disaffected farmers. Russell's efforts to build on this made him the hate-figure of landlords who feared Montgomery's scenario would follow.[29] By 1900 they had taken revenge by using their powerful contacts with party command to force Russell from his junior ministry, whereupon he took his case to Ulster's rural constituencies.[30] The Unionist alliance was unravelling. Constructive unionism was castigated by all as either too conservative or too radical. Russell's departure publicised the failure of the ULUA to effect a compromise and they were now branded part of a landlord conspiracy to deny reforms; the accusation that the Unionist Party was a self-serving clique became common.[31]

Similar problems had surrounded local government reform. In 1888 Sinclair confided to Montgomery that he favoured local government reform because it was the best alternative to Home Rule (and also a lesser evil than Chamberlain's provincial councils scheme) but he was worried that the left wing of the ULUA was moving too quickly and could hand local control to Nationalists.[32] ULUA policy therefore included safeguards for the gentry who dominated the Grand Jury system threatened by reform; democratic local government should not be allowed to bludgeon landlordism from Irish administration.[33]

Irish Unionism, therefore, looked like its British counterpart – an uncomfortable coalition of defensive landlords and bourgeois aspirants, controlling the scope and pace of reform for their own ends. To a large extent this was true but there were unique Irish conditions which complicated matters.

Chief among these was the perception of the Irish Nationalist threat. While British parties began to develop socio-economic policies capable of recruiting opponents' supporters, Irish parties remained static; neither Unionists nor Nationalists could win votes from the other. Irish Unionism therefore found it difficult to isolate socio-economic reforms (generally supported by Irish Unionist voters) from the constitutional question because empowering the masses also meant empowering Nationalists. The latter were seen as unconvertibles,[34] refusing the opportunities proffered by membership of the United Kingdom and intent only on abusing reforms to achieve ascendancy, not equality or progress.[35]

Thus, the blanket nature of reforms under constructive unionism threatened Unionist influence in Irish society while to ignore such reform threatened grassroots revolt. Irish Unionism faced a philosophical Hobson's choice; to maintain the authority of the constitution *in toto*, opposing blanket reforms to keep Nationalism at bay, at the risk of alienating popular support; or to champion reforms as the ideal of British constitutional liberty but, in so doing, risk empowering Nationalists who would undermine the constitution and Unionist security. Liberal Unionist leaders perceived the constitution as the guarantor of wider liberties and material progress. Thus, blanket reforms of the moment had to be diluted to prevent Nationalist empowerment and ensure the continuity of the only state structure capable of delivering greater reforms in the long term. Tensions within Unionism remained. Neither constructive unionist legislation nor Irish Unionist alternatives offered a coherent strategy to resolve the fundamental problem of the 1890s – how to satisfy Unionist demands for reform so as to deny the empowerment of Nationalists as a consequence.

Those proposals which had been implemented (broadly those advocated by the ULUA) were seen as inadequate by independent unionists and the land question was still unresolved. The emergence in Ulster of a pro-union but anti-landlord farmers' movement, decrying Home Rule as a bogey and accompanied by those hostile to 'the clique', was one result. Such grassroots disaffection threatened the Unionist class consensus and, consequently, the party's ability to retain seats in Ulster; parliamentary clout, and the argument that many Irishmen rejected Home Rule, would be seriously weakened if Nationalists could exploit these divisions. By 1900 Irish Unionism was still struggling to come to terms with democracy and collectivism but they could not ignore the modernising agenda.

MODERNISATION, 1900–5?

As we have seen, legislation was by definition all-embracing. Unionist needs could not be segregated from Nationalist and the latter's empowerment was assured to some degree. Constructive unionism was thus misconstrued by contemporaries as a plot to convince Nationalists of the benefits of Union, to be 'killing home rule with kindness'. But the government's interest was in keeping Ireland quiet, and 'kindness' had been a consequence of this, not a policy in itself.[36] Nevertheless, Irish Unionist leaders became angry and demanded partisanship from the Unionist administration in Dublin Castle; constructive unionism was perceived as moving British commanders towards neutrality between Nationalist and Unionist.[37] Moreover, as there was no sign of Nationalists accepting the constitutional position in return, kindness was condemned for empowering Nationalists without adequate compensation. Faced with reduced influence in Dublin Castle and a constituency threat from Russell and other dissidents, Irish Unionist leaders panicked. Home Rule was declared a real threat, supporters were asked to defend the Union; the grassroots were expected to rally but they did not. Russell pointed to kindness as tacit admission by British Unionists that the Union was safe and Home Rule a bogey, and portrayed the Irish Unionist efforts to re-establish influence with Dublin Castle as the clique seeking to secure the means by which they prospered at the expense of the wider unionist family.[38]

Colonel Edward Saunderson, the Irish Unionist leader, was a prime target for the emerging independent unionist groups and personified the weaknesses of the old elite.[39] Russell had continually blasted him as the only Unionist MP yet to accept the principle of compulsion; a local linen boss standing as an independent unionist, James Orr, had given him a bruising battle at the 1900 election; and from 1901 he suffered the wrath of extreme Protestants, led by Tom Sloan, who accused him of endorsing ritualism in the Episcopalian church.[40] Together, their critique was simple; Irish Unionism was too close to London and British and party concerns and too removed from its constituency.[41] Hindered by ill-health, Saunderson had no answer save an appeal to his record against Home Rule. A breaking-point was nearly reached after a highly public verbal assault by Sloan at a Twelfth of July demonstration in 1902. Saunderson's Protestantism was questioned following a parliamentary debate over the inspection of convent laundries. He was so shaken that he resigned as Grand Master of Belfast Grand Lodge and by January 1903 there was speculation he would also retire from Parliament.[42] Unionism looked ripe for defeat at the hands of the re-unifying Nationalist party, revitalised with the patronage of kindness and victory at the first local government elections in 1899.

Unionist reformists had argued that democratisation of local government would show British voters that efficient government in Ireland was possible without Home Rule; Liberal Party commitment to Home Rule could be dropped as Nationalists would have a stake in Irish society and there would be no need to dismantle the Union.[43] Furthermore, Unionists in Ulster could take control of their own affairs and initiate reforms; empowering Nationalists would be fine when no party of government supported Home Rule. This was a desire for a return to the pre-1886 consensus on the Union. Against such theorising, however, there was the immediate threat of Nationalists controlling the socio-political life of areas Unionists deemed their own.[44] Southern Unionism, the heart of Irish landlordism, did not have the numbers to compete at elections and many areas in Ulster itself had local Nationalist majorities. Southern Unionists, already familiar with Nationalist control of local administration such as Poor Law and battered by the experience of boycotting, resigned themselves to defeat.[45] In Ulster, the intensity of local government contests revived party bitterness. Thus far, kindness had provided *causes celébrès* for the party to rally around more than hurting the Unionist masses directly;[46] loyalist anger came from the psychological blow of a Unionist administration rewarding Catholic Nationalism with patronage and appointments, creating fears about the future. Local government brought this fear into Unionist homes.

Returns for the first elections in 1899 showed the partition of Ireland more starkly than ever before. Not only was the north–south divide apparent but also a more detailed Nationalist–Unionist split within Ulster localities. The comprehensive nature of the reform, covering County, rural and urban councils, split Ulster into Orange and Green segments.[47]

Initially though, the new system had seemed to operate in a non-party atmosphere, even in Orange strongholds such as County Armagh. Here, the new County Council, dominated by Unionists, accepted the idea of affiliating to a national board of County Councils in Dublin, over-ruling the objection of William Allen, an Orange leader from Lurgan, that it was a Nationalist plot.[48] This solidarity was a false dawn, and in the next six years Allen and his like were to become the mainstays of Ulster Unionism and helped reinvigorate the party throughout the province, mixing innovation with a return to basics. With their leaders unable to counter Unionist dissidents, the task of realigning the Unionist class consensus had fallen to others. The modernisation challenge would be accepted by local Unionists and local government would provide a vehicle.

Local Unionist leaders (a combination of wealthy grandees, elder politicians, barrister apparatchiks and aspiring young mandarins) became increasingly important political players. Since 1885–86 constituency organisation had depended on the enthusiasm of this small band of party activists; subscriptions, revision contests, election work, social events and propaganda were their sphere and they enjoyed a large degree of autonomy.[49] This group now supplied many candidates for local government elections, even when the contest was billed as non-party.[50] Uncontaminated by kindness, thanks to their non-parliamentary status, fervently Protestant (often Orangemen), concerned with their locality and especially the Unionists of the area, and non-landed, these men, such as Allen, initiated a distinct 'Ulster' Unionism. The reason for this was not a change in identity or anything so amorphous; the crisis of political necessity provided little option. Ulster was simply the area where most Protestants lived and, by virtue of numbers, Unionism there could do what all-Ireland Unionism could not. The defence of hearth and home and empire espoused by the old elite[51] remained the central philosophy, the home had just become a little less grand.

The most important aspect of the local contests was that whoever won would be able to decide the nature of reforms for the locality, as Council powers were considerable. They could build roads, schools, markets and general infrastructural improvements, administer gas, water and later electricity schemes, and decide the rates-level to pay for these. The Local Government Board, which had ultimate responsibility for the system, was distrusted by Unionists as a proponent of kindness but as the source of capital, providing loans to augment local coffers, could not be ignored. Local Unionists and Castle kindness had come head-to-head. The former's response was to ensure that, when in control, crucial issues were targeted to Unionist needs so as to deny empowerment of Nationalists. In the towns at least, this helped resolve the dilemma which had bedevilled reformists in the 1890s.

Unionist-controlled councils initiated improvements similar to those in other localities throughout Britain and Ireland. Where there was the opportunity to provide a service, such as a new road or water scheme, which devolved no political clout to anyone, Unionists prided themselves on their inclusive attitude; but when local schemes involved a distribution of influence as a consequence, Unionists operated an exclusive system. This was achieved by either blatant jobbery or careful targeting of resources so as to ensure Unionist districts benefited most; moreover, it was a mirror image of Nationalist strategy throughout the whole island.[52]

The North Armagh towns of Lurgan and Portadown, both with Unionist controlled Councils, demonstrated this strategy in action. The first election in Lurgan had been characterised as non-party and free from sectarian feeling, echoing the atmosphere at the County Council, but this was misleading. At meetings held by Nationalists to support Dr Magennis for the County Council and two other locals for the Rural District Council, Father O'Hare C. C. urged Catholics, 'to keep the reins of the chariot [in] their own hands' and not to vote for any Protestant or Unionist.[53] This was echoed by Father O'Connor of Portadown who urged Catholics to vote for their co-religionists at the impending County Council election so as to hold their own 'green spots' as retaliation against Portadown Unionist Club.[54] This body had endorsed 15 candidates to ensure Protestants won all the seats on the urban council, even opposing a popular and experienced Catholic, James Grew.[55] In Armagh city, where the political divide was nearly equal, local elections were fought on open party lines and deeply embittered relations; and S. C. Clarke in Enniskillen was convinced that, '[a]s the County Council has such farreaching [*sic*] powers now the election is almost more important to us than a parliamentary one'.[56]

Lurgan and Portadown had provided the bulwark of Saunderson's support when defeating Orr in 1900.[57] Local leaders had been crucial in securing that solidarity[58] and none more so than Allen who was being tipped as Saunderson's successor. Indeed, some Orangemen had been keen to see Allen usurp Saunderson before the 1900 election, presumably to preclude just such a challenge as Orr's. Allen had rebuffed such notions but was widely believed to be nursing the constituency for the future.[59] Between 1901 and 1904, Allen and other local leaders helped the beleaguered Saunderson to combat the independents by outbidding them on key issues such as socio-economic improvement, Protestantism and democracy. Local leaders provided alternative party responses to national questions which Saunderson and his MPs could not answer. While the Ulster Party's first rank could not walk away from kindness without straining relations with British Unionism to breaking-point, the party's second rank had no such scruple.

One example of this was in education. Arthur Balfour had rekindled the passions of the University question in 1899 by suggesting the endowment of denominational colleges. Non-conformists were opposed, believing their taxes would be funding Anglican and Catholic establishments, and feared this would set a precedent for primary and secondary structures. British insensitivity had opened the traditional split between the Protestant denominations which seemed irreconcilable. However, local government reform gave councils a major say in their district's schools; the Department of Agricultural and Technical Instruction (DATI) liaised with the education sub-committee of a council to agree the transfer of funds from the former to the latter. In Lurgan, this translated into Unionists holding the purse strings.

When, in 1901, DATI agreed to transfer the reserve funds of Lurgan council into the hands of a local priest and Nationalist leaders, a microcosm of the national scene emerged. The Catholic case to DATI was that a new school being built by the Council was in a predominantly Protestant area and unsafe for Catholics to commute to and from; therefore money should be given to local Catholics to build their own. DATI agreed to requisition the Council's reserve fund to allow a convent school for girls to be built. This was seen by DATI as a compromise, protecting young girls without initiating denominational education in full. For Protestants in Lurgan it was no such thing. Dublin Castle had been castigated for ignoring Ulster's concerns for the benefit of the South and West and now Horace Plunkett's scheme had arrived in Lurgan to effect a similar injustice.[60] Protestants paid the vast majority of rates yet the Catholic church was to be the beneficiary; the redistribution of wealth was no longer an issue affecting the landlord class alone. Denominational education had thus been reduced by kindness to a simple choice, Protestant or Catholic. Lurgan councillors chose the former and took DATI to court. In January 1902 Saunderson's meeting in Lurgan gave H. G. MacGeagh, the chair of the Council's education committee, the chance to politicise the affair. Plunkett's interference was derided as selfish and political, an effort to gain Catholic support for his election campaign in Galway, having been ousted from South County Dublin by diehard Unionists.[61] MacGeagh was returned to the Council a year later with the biggest vote yet recorded[62] and kindness was soon condemned for moving beyond neutrality to straightforward Nationalist bias.[63]

Unfortunately for Saunderson the simplicity of choosing sides in such local fracas did not translate to high politics. In 1902 the Unionist government introduced an Education Act for England and Wales which Saunderson supported, despite the protests of non-conformists about its denominational character. The Ulster Party leaders still believed that if Dublin Castle's methods were to be changed this could only happen with support from party command in Parliament, thus relations there had to be maintained,[64] even at the expense of constituency displeasure; but as no change occurred Saunderson was left to look like a supporter of kindness.

At the end of 1903, Portadown Council took the Valuations Commissioner to court to contest his decision that the local convent was exempt from paying rates.[65] The council won the case in January 1904 to a fanfare of local Unionist praise.[66] This was an important step in the fight against Sloan's Belfast Protestant Association, which tried to establish branches in the urban centres of Lurgan, Portadown and Lisburn[67] by holding monthly meetings. Their appeal was to the Protestant working classes' fears that they were being sold to Nationalist slavery by the inaction of their representatives. Even Allen and James Malcolm (Jr), both Orange stalwarts and personal acquaintances of Saunderson, had not felt able to fully support the colonel's line on the Education bill or convent laundries.[68]

But the fact that local Unionists offered counter-measures had done much to remove Saunderson and his dithering from the picture and the BPA's campaign deflated, then died.[69] The crucial issue for the pro-union electorate was not Saunderson's class but his loyalty to the locality and Belfast Sloanites compared poorly to the colonel's local cadre.

Therefore, this had not become a question of representation but one of representativeness (echoing Tory Democracy – a policy line which satisfied the masses rather than a means to have working men selected as parliamentary candidates). If the Ulster Party defended the interests of *all* unionists, and not just the party's elite, disaffection would fade; working men knew they had neither the time nor money to run for office.[70] Popular dissent, organised into an electoral threat by Russell, Sloan and others, was tantamount to asking the Ulster Party to choose between its constituency base and British colleagues tainted by kindness. As such, there always remained an opportunity for the Ulster Party to outbid its rivals for popularity. The key was to establish the issues which mattered to the electorate and to represent those interests against British treachery and Nationalist aggression. Despite the party leadership's inability to distance itself from London command and kindness, local leaders were holding the breach by offering Unionist 'purity' as an alternative – progressive socioeconomic policies which did not deprive Unionists of power. By offering local variants of national questions, which placed the needs and wants of the electorate before the intrigues of party command, local Unionism at least was responding to the demands of its electorate.

Saunderson was thus encouraged by his supporters to be more active locally. Having failed to satisfy local opinion on every major issue since 1900, he was asked to help organise a major campaign to win government funds for a drainage scheme around Lough Neagh and the River Bann to prevent perennial flooding. This would show his constituents that the Ulster Party's priorities lay with its supporters, undoing the damage of the past. The initial campaign had been organised in Portadown but the affair quickly took on wider significance, covering several Ulster constituencies and even winning some support from Russellites and Nationalists. Saunderson's role was to liase with the Chief Secretary, Wyndham, and bring the government on board.[71] His failure to achieve anything, after months of negotiations, sat uncomfortably against the success of infrastructural improvement campaigns for Nationalist areas which had received government assistance.

Again, kindness was derided and again the Ulster Party were perceived as remaining faithful to party command even when nothing of substance had been done to offset a genuine grievance.[72] The 'Ulster Revolt' which

resulted in 1904, was a response to grassroots criticism that the party was
at best impotent and negligent, and at worst corrupt and self-serving;
hostile votes against Balfour's government, in debates where the result
would not be affected, were as far as the parliamentary party could go in
embracing the language of purity cultivated by local elders since 1900,
without becoming wholly independent of the Unionist Party.[73]

However, local leaders had no new powers to help the party resolve the
land issue, now polarised around compulsion and inducement. Debate
among landlords, with their cause disowned by Ulster Party MPs, had
moved from whether or not they would accept reform to how this could
best be achieved.[74] Influence with Dublin Castle was thus paramount to
ensure that inducement was the strategy chosen. In 1903, Wyndham's
Land Act provided just such a generous package, not only satisfying the
landlords but also many farmers. Even Russell approved, despite the fact
that this was far short of compulsion and invoked the wrath of hardline
farmer opinion.[75] However, this split did not work to the direct credit of
the Ulster Party because the scheme was correctly heralded as the outcome
of Lord Dunraven's Land Conference. Saunderson had not participated in
this, preferring to remain wed to the Landowners' Convention and British
backbenchers who had taken on his cause.[76] Wyndham's success was that
the bill was regarded by all parties as a fair settlement; Castle neutrality
had had its finest hour. The reward for the Ulster Party was that the economic arguments of Russell had been largely negated and if the issue of
representativeness (the clique) could now be resolved, the dissidents'
critique could crumble.

In 1904–5, Unionist MPs who desired party modernisation to meet such
lingering criticisms constructed the Ulster Unionist Council (UUC). This
body formalised the political pattern of the preceding five years without
abandoning the old leadership. Local Unionist leaders, who had shared the
burden of countering the dissidents, were now admitted to a wider leadership structure on an electoral college system similar to that advocated for
the UDU in 1893.[77] Allen, for example, became one of the UUC's three
honorary secretaries. These bourgeois leadership partners were different to
those of 1892 described by Gibbon. While ULUA representatives had
remained active Unionists they were not central to the UUC initially.
Instead, the new men were predominantly Orange and Conservative
Unionists scarred from local government battles with Nationalists. They
brought expertise to Unionist constituency organisation, providing models
for ill-organised divisions to follow, and they acted as messengers to the
leadership, voicing local concerns. With land reform now a reality,
Unionism was embarked on a reorganisation concerned with outbidding

its critics on the key issues of democratic organisation and Protestantism. Allen's definition of Unionism meant doing 'all in their power to prevent the Papacy from ruling Ireland'. He realised others would prefer to see Unionism merely as maintaining the legislative link with Britain but the perpetuation of crisis imposed by kindness and Nationalist aggression had rendered reductionist theory inappropriate.[78] By 1905, modernisation of policy and organisation had been accepted by Ulster Unionists; the price to be paid was the copperfastening of an insular provincialism and sectarianism.

The creators of the UUC were William Moore and C. C. Craig. Both had quickly risen to prominence as the Ulster Party MPs whose priority was their locality. C. C. Craig had been elected as an independent-minded Unionist of Tory/Orange complexion who would put Ulster's interests before those of party or personal advantage; and Moore warned British Unionists that if forced to choose between kindness and having to leave the party to stand as an independent, he would choose the latter.[79] The Ulster Revolt was being taken to new lengths by young turks whose solidarity lay in their attitudes to policy. British command would have to choose between kindness and their populist Ulster wing.

The devolution affair brought the crisis surrounding kindness to a head.[80] The revelation that Wyndham's staff were preparing plans to devolve self-government to Ireland ensured that kindness was seen by Ulster Unionists as a coherent policy reaching a conclusion. Moore and C. C. Craig led the assault, which resulted in Wyndham's removal and the appointment of Walter Long. Kindness seemed to have been defeated and the Ulster Party's old influence restored but the reality was that the fraternal relationship between the latter and British command had all but broken down.[81]

AN 'ULSTER' UNIONISM, 1906–14

At the election of 1906 the Ulster Party regained the bulk of Protestant support against the independent unionists. Russellites, Sloanites and the Independent Orange Order were bundled together as Nationalist dupes, reliant on Catholic votes to achieve nothing but the destruction of the best defence against Home Rule legislation – the Ulster Party. Having accepted reforms and reasserted its independence and Protestantism, the Ulster Party turned the tables on its critics. Had locals chosen the independents' candidates? Were they all in favour of the Magheramorne Manifesto advocating Home Rule? What would be the price for their reliance on Catholic votes?[82] The Liberal Party had won the election, resurrecting fears of Home Rule;

although this did not materialise, Liberal policy continued (then intensified) the patterns of Unionist kindness. The crisis facing Ulster Unionists was British treachery in the contest with their Nationalist opponents.

Between 1907 and 1909, the Ulster Party used the UUC to try to bolster weak constituencies, setting up local associations and securing parliamentary candidates vital for financial assistance.[83] The object was not only to test Nationalist defences and boost Unionist morale but to revitalise relations with British party leaders – to tackle that part of the crisis they could actually do something about. One important step had been Long's acceptance of the leadership of the Ulster Party after Saunderson's death in October 1906; now, Lonsdale and Moore were securing funds from party coffers to help the revitalisation campaign. However, the Ulster Party's ideal – local purity – was not the reason behind British benevolence. The defeat of 1906 and the intensifying intra-party feud over tariff reform had left party leaders with little choice but to keep the Ulster Party's 23 MPs on board.[84] Although by 1908 Long had effectively withdrawn from Ireland with the acceptance of a safe London seat, party command continued to utilise loyalism as part of their critique of the Liberals and for the unifying effect of anti-Home Rule politics on the party. This perfunctory relationship showed that loyalism had been relegated from the vanguard of the party to a supporting role.

By 1910, the bitterness of local politics and two quick general election defeats coloured Unionism in general. While there were still periods of political calm, and subsequent Unionist apathy and disunity, the duration of these had become shorter. Significant figures in the Ulster Unionist leadership now perceived a 'permanent crisis' ahead which would have to be faced without full British support.[85]

Colonel R. H. Wallace, an Orange leader who had suffered defeat and Nationalist abuse at the local government elections in 1899, exemplified the Ulsterisation of Unionism. He organised an Orange Emergency Committee in Ulster, which from 1908 was sending aid to persecuted southern loyalists, and helped construct a Provincial Grand Lodge for Ulster in 1912; he informed Long of failing loyalist morale, a result of British Unionist neglect; he was organising drilling in the winter of 1910–11; and he emerged as a 'hawk' during the 1912–14 Home Rule crisis, favouring the arming of the Unionist masses.[86] Long acknowledged in 1911 that he 'quite understood' that Wallace was 'with the party of No Surrender'.[87] In 1912, Thomas Sinclair, the veteran ULUA leader, contributed an essay to the Unionist publication, *Against Home Rule*, where he expounded the virtues of the Ulster-Scot; later, he would write the words of the Ulster Covenant.[88] These were unlikely partners, but with no one else to turn to, every faction within Ulster Unionism looked to the other. The formation of the Ulster Volunteer Force embodied this spirit of self-reliance. British Unionists sought to utilise the Ulster cause for their own electoral ends[89] and were ready to accept Home Rule, even for Ulster, if an election returned a Liberal–Nationalist majority. Ulster Unionists were not prepared to accept Home Rule for Ulster (or a significant part of it) under any circumstances; local government had provided adequate demonstration of life under Nationalist rule. The reality behind the thousands of UVF men and women prepared to offer themselves as a blood sacrifice for 'Ulster' in 1914 was much the same; to defend the home and family from Nationalist tyranny by preserving the Union and its 'imperial citizenship'.

CONCLUSION

Modernisation was always a key Unionist concern; too much *or* too little could bring party disintegration. Juggling factional interests and keeping the party together remained paramount and, by 1914, had been significantly achieved by reducing Unionism from its all-Ireland roots to a populist, Ulster base. The reasons for this lay in the severity of the crises facing Unionism (British treachery, popular disaffection, Nationalist challenge in the localities) and the inability of the old leadership to resolve these. The emergence of a more open party structure and the approval of many major reforms came about with pressure from below. Thus, Ulster Unionism had responded to the demands of its democracy. Yet, populist pressure for reform had not meant pressure for a new form of politics. Ulster's Unionists still feared Catholic nationalist ascendancy and still believed self-government would result in the realisation of Montgomery's scenario; *all* Protestant property and status would be at the mercy of a perpetual and vengeful Nationalist majority. As such, grassroots requests for the modern politics of reform had never involved asking the Ulster Party leadership to do so for the benefit of all.

NOTES

1.   Mirror of Parliament, 4, WIV, 1834. 1363.

2.	Joseph Chamberlain and Lord Hartington led Radical and Whig groups from Gladstone's party to become Liberal Unionists; with the Conservatives they were known as the Unionists.

3.	P. Buckland, *Irish Unionism I: The Anglo-Irish and the New Ireland 1885–1922* (Dublin & New York, 1972), pp. xiv–xv; *Irish Unionism II: Ulster Unionism and the Origins of Northern Ireland* (Dublin & New York, 1973), ch. 1. A. Jackson, *The Ulster Party; Irish Unionists in the House of Commons, 1885–1911* (Oxford, 1989), ch. 2.

4.	Jackson, *Ulster Party*, pp. 11–12.

5.	D. Cannadine, *The Decline and Fall of the British Aristocracy* (London, 1990), pp. 8–15, 25; and Ireland, pp. 168–9, ch. 5.

6.	A. Sykes, *Tariff Reform in British Politics, 1903–13* (Oxford, 1979).

7.	Jackson, *Ulster Party*; policy, ch. 4; organisation, ch. 5.

8.	P. Gibbon, *The Origins of Ulster Unionism: The foundations of popular Protestant politics and ideology in nineteenth-century Ireland* (Manchester, 1975), pp. 127–35.

9.	H. Patterson, 'Redefining the Debate on Unionism', *Political Studies*, xxiv, 1976, pp. 205–8. Jackson, *Ulster Party*, pp. 5–21.

10.	PRONI, Adam Duffin papers, MIC 127/3,4,5,6,11 as examples for 1886 and 1893. J. R. Fisher, *The Ulster Liberal Unionist Association: A sketch of its history, 1885–1914* (Belfast, 1914), p. 88. A. Jackson, 'Irish Unionism and the Russellite Threat, 1894–1906', *Irish Historical Studies*, xxv, 100, Nov. 1987, pp. 376–404, p. 384, and *Ulster Party*, pp. 45–6, 50–1, 81–2.

11.	PRONI, Hugh de Fellenberg Montgomery papers, D627/428/189, Montgomery to Dane, 12/7/92. Printed in P. Buckland, *Irish Unionism, 1885–1923; a Documentary History* (Belfast, 1973), p. 197.

12.	This was known as inducement: state-aided land reform which compensated landlords who voluntarily sold to tenants.

13.	HFMP, D627/428/182, Dane to Montgomery, 11/6/92; printed in Buckland, *Documentary History*, pp. 196–7.

14.	See chapter by Graham Walker in this volume.

15.	HFMP, D627/428/44, Sinclair to Montgomery, 1/5/88, and D627/428/79, MacGeagh to Montgomery, 23/1/89; D627/428/99, Montgomery to G. de L. Willis (draft), 26/4/89, 'my Belfast friends agreed with me'.

16.	ADP, D1631/3/2, debate with T. W. Russell in *Northern Whig*, 17/12/89, also letter 22/4/92.

17.	PRONI, South Antrim Constitutional Association minutes, D2165/1, 31/1/90, first reference to the idea of an Ulster Unionist consultative body. UCC minutes, D1327/1/1.

18.	PRONI, ADP, D1631/3/2, report of the Dublin Convention, 23/7/92. UCC minutes, D1327/1/1, 22/5/93. Thomas Sinclair papers, D3002/3, UCL programme, report of Belfast Convention, from *Ulster Echo*, 17/6/92.

19.	J. Loughlin, 'Joseph Chamberlain, English Nationalism and the Ulster Question', *History*, 77, no. 250, June 1992, pp. 202–19, esp. pp. 213–19. Chamberlain to Hartington, 27/10/87, quoted in Jackson, *Ulster Party*, p. 193.

20.	PRONI, UCC executive minutes, D1327/1/2, 9/7/95, 6/8/95, 23/9/95; minutes of the Joint Committee held in London, D1327/1/8, 11/3/95. Jackson, *Ulster Party*, pp. 208–9.

21. TSP, D3002/1, UDU manifesto from *Ulster Echo*, 17/3/93, inaugural meeting report, *Northern Whig*, 25/10/93. The terms UCL and UDU were synonymous.

22. HFMP, D627/428/193, Duffin to Montgomery, 27/8/92; Jackson, *Ulster Party*, pp. 207–8.

23. PRONI, R. H. Wallace papers, D1889/3/2, series of letters; by spring 1895 a haphazard effort to secure canvassers and speakers for *British* constituency work at the coming election had taken priority over any plans for an Ulster caucus; only *surplus* cash from this campaign would go to local organisation.

24. UCC executive, D1327/1/2, 13/8/95, after the 1895 election, the UCC and UDU were organising victory meetings while the Joint Committee with the IUA was disbanded. RHWP, D1889/3/4/E, J. A. McConnell to Wallace, 9/8/99, complained that Finnegan's involvement in Revision work had put them 'at sixes and sevens', showing that even Orange/Conservative Unionists, who valued the UDU's idea of constant vigilance, ran out of patience.

25. HFM, D627/428/36, A. C. Sellar to Montgomery, 13/3/88. J. Loughlin, 'T. W. Russell, the Tenant Farmer interest, and Progressive Unionism in Ulster, 1886–1900', *Eire-Ireland*, xxv, I, 1990, pp. 44–64, pp. 47–8. Jackson, 'Russellite Threat', p. 384.

26. This meant a large numbers of supporters, usually from the working classes, e.g. 'the Orange democracy'.

27. See note 17; Abercorn, Sinclair, Ewart and Doloughan (a farmers' representative) all preached this at the Convention.

28. A. Gailey, *Ireland and the Death of Kindness: The experience of Constructive Unionism, 1890–1905* (Cork, 1987). Jackson, *Ulster Party*, pp. 115–16, 168.

29. HFMP, D627/428/273, Montgomery to J. Chamberlain, 31/7/95, complained of Russell's 'antics'.

30. Jackson, 'Russellite Threat', *IHS*, pp. 390–4.

31. Jackson, *Ulster Party*, p. 224.

32. HFM, D627/428/44, Sinclair to Montgomery, 1/5/88.

33. J. R. Fisher, *Liberal Unionist*, pp. 85–6, 89–91.

34. PRONI, Joshua Peel papers, D889/3/1c/52, Peel to J. B. Lonsdale, 26/1/04; British Unionists were 'blind to history and the fact they [Nationalists] never can be placated'.

35. TSP, D3002/1, Sinclair's pamphlet, *Thirteen Reasons Why Unionists Object to the Home Rule Bill of 1893*.

36. A. Gailey, 'Unionist Rhetoric and Irish Local Government Reform, 1895–9', *IHS*, xxiv, 93, May 1984, pp. 52–68, also *Kindness*. Jackson, *Ulster Party*, p. 168.

37. JPP, D889/3/1b/297, Peel to J. G. Shera, 23/1/00, complained that this Unionist government 'insists on political etiquette as regards patronage and nomination'.

38. Jackson, 'Russellite Threat', pp. 392–3.

39. R. Lucas, *Colonel Saunderson, MP: A memoir* (London, 1908); A. Jackson, *Colonel Edward Saunderson; Land and Loyalty in Victorian Ireland* (Oxford, 1995). Saunderson was MP for North Armagh, 1885–1906.

40. Jackson, *Ulster Party*, p. 234. J. Boyle, 'The Belfast Protestant Association and the Independent Orange Order 1901–10', *IHS*, xiii, 50, Sept. 1962, pp. 117–54. To balance this article, see H. Patterson, 'Independent Orangeism in Edwardian Belfast; a Reinterpretation', *Proceedings of the Royal Irish Academy*, vol. 80, sect. c (1980), pp. 1–27.

41. Orr's election leaflet, 24/9/00, 'I am a North Armagh man myself, living in the heart of the Constituency, and accessible at all times to the Voters.'

42. Boyle, 'Belfast Protestant Association', p. 31. An important revision of the episode is Patterson, 'Independent Orangeism', pp. 9–10. *Lurgan Mail*, 10/1/03 and JPP, D889/3/1c/258, Peel to Lonsdale, 10/3/05.

43. Fisher, *Liberal Unionist*, p. 85.

44. JPP, D889/3/1a/434, Peel to D. P. Barton, 2/3/97, warned it would be an 'unjust ... placing of the property owners at the mercy of their political foes'; P. Bew, *Ideology and the Irish Question* (Oxford, 1994), pp. 74–5.

45. Cannadine, *British Aristocracy*, pp. 171–2.

46. Jackson, *Ulster Party*, pp. 246–53.

47. C. Shannon, 'The Ulster Liberal Unionists and Local Government Reform, 1885–98', *IHS*, xviii, 1972–73, pp. 403–23, p. 423.

48. PRONI, Armagh County Council minutes, LA2/2GA/1, 1/7/99, 28/8/99.

49. Jackson, *Ulster Party*, ch. 5.

50. RHWP, D1889/3/4/A, McConnell to Wallace, 13/2/99. Lurgan had 13 Unionists and a Protestant working man from 15 councillors, despite a 'non-party' election.

51. HFMP, D627/428/111, Montgomery to Earl of Erne, 28/10/[89] (copy), dis-cussing a county defence association of all classes against lawlessness and treason. This was a common theme from Ulster Party MPs during the 1886 and 1893 Home Rule debates. JPP, D889/3/1d/323, Peel to Lonsdale, 22/8/11, saw a women's organisation as useful in showing the British public that Home Rule imperilled 'hearths and homes and young families'. B. Barton, *Brookeborough, the making of a Prime Minister* (Belfast, 1987), pp. 29–58, notes defence of home and locality as the motivation behind the Special Constabulary, 1919–20.

52. Bew, *Ideology*, pp. 74–5.

53. *LM*, 25/2/99.

54. *LM*, 4/3/99.

55. *Portadown News*, 21/1/99.

56. JPP, D889/3/1c, Oct. 1903–April 1909. PRONI, Clarke and Gordon (solici-tors) papers, D1096/1c/2/34, Clarke to Rev. O. W. Clarke, 2/9/02.

57. *LM*, 22/9/00, 29/9/00.

58. *PN*, Nov.–Dec. 1902. SACA, D2165/1, 14/9/00. Officers of this Association likewise defended W. G. Ellison-Macartney when he was Parliamentary Secretary to the Admiralty and the department overlooked Belfast.

59. *LM*, 15/9/00. JPP, D889/3/1c/121,599, Peel to Lonsdale, 24/6/04, 22/10/06.

60. *LM*, 30/11/01.

61. *LM*, 18/1/02.

62. *LM*, 17/1/03.

63. JPP, D889/3/1c/52, Peel to Lonsdale, 26/1/04, 'There is deep discontent amongst protestants and loyalists ... [that] the present Government would do more for the enemy than a Liberal Government.'

64. Jackson, *Ulster Party*, pp. 244–53.
65. *PN*, 24/10/03.
66. *PN*, 16/1/04.
67. *LM*, 4/1/02, 23/8/02; *PN*, 23/8/02, 27/9/02, 25/10/02, 22/11/02. RHWP, D1889/3/16, *Belfast News Letter*, cutting, 13/1/06, BPA monthly meetings in Lisburn had stopped before the by-election of February 1903.
68. *PN*, 11/10/02, 27/12/02.
69. *LM*, 6/9/02; *PN*, 22/12/02, 27/12/02. Jackson, *Ulster Party*, pp. 103, 113. Sloan was thus integrated into the Ulster Party, 1903–5.
70. *LM*, 4/3/05, 18/3/05, describing the formation of the North Armagh Unionist Association and the deference of urban and rural working-classes' representatives to party elders. The Lurgan Orange and Working Men's Association reported an increased membership of 25 per cent since 1904.
71. *LM*, 4/5/01, 9/11/01.
72. *LM*, 21/2/03, Allen, frustrated by Ulster Party–Dublin Castle dithering, proposed that locals should devise their own scheme and present it to the government as a *fait accompli*.
73. *LM*, 24/10/03 (Saunderson first threatened the government), 5/3/04, 2/4/04, 16/4/04 (A. T. Farrell, Orr's election agent in 1900, was at this meeting).
74. Jackson, *Ulster Party,* pp. 160–1.
75. Jackson, 'Russellite Threat', p. 396; *Ulster Party*, pp. 160, 163. Russell had realised compulsion was financially impossible; now he publicly admitted such.
76. Jackson, *Ulster Party*, p. 162.
77. Buckland, *Documentary History*, pp. 201–5. F. S. L. Lyons, 'The Irish Unionist Party and the Devolution Crisis of 1904–5', *IHS*, vi, 21, Mar. 1948, pp. 1–22. Jackson, *Ulster Party*, pp. 235–40.
78. *LM*, 2/9/05.
79. SACA, D2165/1, 12/1/03, AGM selection of C. C. Craig; Hansard, ser. 4, 1904, cxxxix. 779.
80. See note 76; the crisis was seen as the rationale behind the formation of the UUC until Jackson's revision.
81. Jackson, *Ulster Party*, pp. 276–81, Long's appointment did not satisfy Moore that Castle kindness had been overturned. Buckland, *Documentary History*, p. 202, shows A. J. Balfour's subsequent 'contamination'.
82. RHWP, D1889/3/16, J. Craig to Wallace, 16/1/06, castigated James Woods MP (his Russellite opponent) as dependent on Nationalist votes and therefore obliged to support Home Rule. *LM*, 10/11/06, Moore challenged the 'Russellite-Sloanite-Nationalist combination' at the North Armagh by-election.
83. PRONI, UUC papers, R. D. Bates correspondence with constituency organisers, D1327/23/1a, May 1907–Sept. 1911. Jackson, *Ulster Party*, pp. 292–3, on Austen Chamberlain's flirtation with the Ulster Party, 1906–8.
84. Jackson, *Ulster Party*, p. 55.
85. PRONI, Frank Hall papers, D1496/8. Jackson, *Ulster Party*, pp. 313–19.
86. Buckland, *Documentary History*, p. 185; PRONI, UUC Year Books, D972, 1909, Report of Grand Lodge meeting, 9/12/08; RHWP, D1889/1/2/3, 127,

Wallace to Sproule, 22/12/10 (copy). A. Jackson, *Sir Edward Carson* (Dundalk, 1993), p. 37.

87.   RHWP, D1889/3/20/a-b. Long to Wallace, 7/8/11.
88.   S. Rosenbaum (ed.), *Against Home Rule; the Case for the Union* (London, 1912), pp. 170–81.
89.   J. Smyth, 'Bluff, Bluster and Brinkmanship; Andrew Bonar Law and the Third Home Rule Bill', *Historical Journal*, 36, 1, 1993, pp. 161–78.

4 Ulstermen of Letters: The Unionism of Frank Frankfort Moore, Shan Bullock, and St John Ervine

Patrick Maume

Cultural Unionism is often called a contradiction in terms. The Victorian Irish Protestant intelligentsia who claimed the intellect of Ireland was against Home Rule[1] have been eclipsed by political defeat and by artists of the Irish Revival from Protestant/Unionist backgrounds who adopted nationalism as part of their rebellion into artistic self-definition. Belfast Unionism, the product of a provincial commercial city, took less interest in the arts than the Dublin variety. Its literary self-expression was left to local antiquarians, minor regional writers (often linked to Protestant churches, the Orange Order, or various branches of the Unionist establishment) or Ulster-born writers in London who still identified with their origins.* Only in recent years has Belfast supported a significant literary intelligentsia, and few of its members have Unionist affiliations. Because of the strength of regionalism among twentieth-century Ulster writers, the intellectual atrophy of Ulster Unionism after the demise of its Dublin counterpart and the marginalisation of the Irish Question in British politics after 1922, critics underestimate the Unionist commitment of earlier writers and forget the role of the London-based Ulsterman of letters.

This chapter discusses the role of Ulster Unionism in the life and writings of three such London-based writers, and relates it to their grapplings with the wider problems of modernity: the changing roles of men and women, the crisis of Protestant faith, the growth of nationalism to challenge Empires, and the uneasy position of artists balanced between provincial narrowness and the hopes and terrors of the global marketplace.

I

Frank Frankfort Moore (1855–1931) was the son of a successful Belfast clockmaker and jeweller. Moore was educated at Belfast Royal Academical Institute and knew several modern languages. He wanted to be a poet, and at 20 published a book of poems which brought a friendly letter from Longfellow; but he had to live, so he joined *The Belfast NewsLetter*.[2] His linguistic knowledge and love of travel made him a foreign correspondent. Moore went to the Congress of Berlin and covered the Zulu War. (He saw South Africa as a second Eden and despised its black inhabitants.) He became arts reviewer, leader-writer and eventually assistant editor.[3] He was a compulsive writer – never revising – with an uncannily acute and retentive memory.[4]

Moore wrote adventure stories for the Society for the Promotion of Christian Knowledge.[5] This was a business transaction; he simultaneously composed 'ungodly' light comedies for the London stage. (His marriage to Grace Balcombe, whose sister Lucinda married Bram Stoker, gave access to the theatrical world.) Moore rebelled against his father's strict Protestantism. He admired Tyndall's declaration of scientific materialism at the 1874 Belfast conference of the Belfast Association, and laughed at the outrage of local Presbyterian ministers.[6] Moore later jeered at Evangelicals as hypocrites, denounced old-fashioned Ulster notions of parental authority, and compared the Ulster Revival to outbreaks among West Indian negroes.[7]

Moore despised newspaper work and resented confinement in a philistine province when his talents qualified him for the metropolis. He expressed his resentment in libellous theatre reviews;[8] he imitated the polished brutality of 'tough-minded' London Tory journalists; he developed a cult of the eighteenth century. He explored Smithfield for antique furniture, seeing the Catholic ghetto more closely than most Belfast Protestants of his class and time.[9] He found the inhabitants of the West of Ireland friendlier and more picturesque than Northerners.[10] He joined a Gaelic society (perhaps inspired by the scholar John Knott, another brother-in-law) and tried to interest Belfast businessmen in *The Voyage of Maelduin*;[11] he wrote historical novels describing the Cromwellian conquest as seen by the defeated, with a brave and resourceful Jesuit among the characters.[12]

Moore's loyalties were never in doubt. He denounces Cromwell's crimes, but the Protector appears as a Carlylean Great Man. Moore felt the same respect for the terrible disciplined zeal of the Ironsides and the vigorous philistine entrepreneurship transforming Belfast around him; he was a modern commercial writer selling into the wider British market. His Gaels are inefficient fantasists; the Jesuit, though benevolent, is a ruthless shapeshifter resembling the evil Jesuits of Evangelical fiction. Moore occasionally portrays upper-class Catholics as representatives of a sophisticated though outworn civilisation teaching social graces to its raw, virile successor;[13] but he hated and feared the mass Catholicism of the Western peasantry and the Belfast slums as the enemy of individual freedom and economic progress. He saw the Land League as disreputable adventurers, petty gombeenmen and assassins ostracising and destroying anyone with the slightest tendency towards individuality.[14] This view was reinforced by witnessing League activities and the squalid bickerings of the Parnell Split.[15]

These views reflect snobbery and cultural chauvinism (though not biological racism; Moore emphasises Irish success outside Ireland).[16] This is conspicuous in three anti-Home Rule satires published anonymously in 1892–93. In *The Diary of an Irish Cabinet Minister* the Tories grant Home Rule to discredit it; the 'patriots' squander their budget, fail to plunder Ulster's wealth, split into six factions, and flee to their shebeens amidst the sardonic laughter of Parnell's ghost.[17] *The Viceroy Muldoon* adds satire on the provisions of the Second Home Rule Bill.[18] *Larry O'Lannigan, J.P.: His Rise and Fall* depicts nationalist magistrates appointed by the Liberals as drunken, illiterate, faction-fighting, priest-ridden, chicken-stealing, poteen-making buffoons; an eviction is thoroughly well-deserved.[19]

In 1893 Moore left Belfast for London; he promptly published a book depicting former colleagues and employers as ignorant opportunists.[20] He was enormously successful as a commercial novelist; after eleven years in London he moved to Lewes, cultivated a formal eighteenth-century garden[21] and still collected antique furniture.

Moore's interest in Ulster revived with the Ulster Crisis. In 1914 he published two major pro-Unionist books: a novel, *The Ulsterman*, and *The Truth About Ulster,* a collection of reminiscences. These were not universally welcomed by Unionists, for some of his comments resembled nationalist criticisms.[22] *The Ulsterman* opens on Eleventh Night in a mid-Antrim village; the Orangemen are ludicrously ignorant. The most prominent character, James Alexander, is a mill-owner self-made with the help of an early fraud (nationalists claimed northern prosperity derived from commercial dishonesty). He makes vulgar displays of wealth; he gets tipsy; his bullying manner and aggressive use of Ulster dialect gall his better-educated children;[23] he is so provincial he distrusts Carson for his Southern accent. Willie Kinghan, an ambitious lawyer-politician (placehunting Unionist lawyers were denounced by nationalists and distrusted by many Unionists) courts two wealthy girls simultaneously while avoiding breach of promise.

Moore is unquestionably Unionist. Neither Kinghan nor Alexander does any real harm. In the South impoverished gentlemen like Kinghan become self-pitying spongers; in the North he must develop his talents.[24] Alexander is a genuine wealth-creating entepreneur; his crudities reflect a society invigoratingly open to social mobility, his children have acquired education and culture. All the characters, including the cultivated Thorntons and the wealthy Catholic Powers, despise Home Rulers and denounce the Liberals as corrupt.

While Moore's image of nationalists derives from the 1880s, he presents a 'new' Unionism based on economic modernisation. He claims disingenuously that religious divisions were disappearing before the Home Rule Bill revived them. Both Alexander's sons marry Catholics. Technology breaks paternal tyranny. His younger son uses his motor-bike to visit his Catholic ladylove when his father thinks he is at the Scarva sham-fight; he finally defeats his father by threatening to sell to a rival firm a device which he invented and patented.[25] His motor-bike also carries UVF dispatches. An UVF review contrasts with the Twelfth; all classes are represented, many participants are not Orangemen, everyone knows why they would rather die than surrender. Moore defended the UVF as a restraining force, without whom civil war would already have begun. If the Government persisted, uncontrollable riots would bury Home Rule in bloodshed.[26]

Moore's suggestion that modernisation would make Unionists of Catholics underestimated the depth of sectarianism and the ability of nationalists to sustain a state. *The Truth About Ulster* inclines towards partition and a two-nation theory.[27] Moore responded to the activities of Sinn Fein after 1916 by recycling old polemics against the Land League.[28] In 1923 he wrote a long, fascinating newspaper series on his memories of late-Victorian Belfast.[29] Moore told his readers:

It is better to be separated from the rest of Ireland than from Great Britain. That great Irishman, Oliver Goldsmith, wrote the allegory of the mad dog, and it may be applied to the situation.... Sir James Craig will, I am sure, prove the Pasteur of the Province.[30]

Moore then returned to Sussex, where he died in 1931.[31]

II

Moore once wrote that Gissing's novel *New Grub Street* gave every journeyman writer an uneasy conscience. A cynic might compare Moore and Shan Bullock to Gissing's flashy journalist Jasper Milvain and doomed, overworked artist Edwin Reardon.[32] Moore and St John Ervine saw themselves as entrepreneurs whose achievements mirrored the creativity of commercial Belfast. Bullock, who spent years drafting and rewriting naturalistic novels about rural Fermanagh for a relatively small audience, is the artist as traditional craftsman or even peasant farmer. He worked as a civil servant, supplementing his salary by journalism; he recorded the domestic joys and constraints of a married London clerk in his novel *Robert Thorne*.[33]

One source of fellow-feeling between Moore and Ervine was experience of despotic evangelical fathers. Moore despised his father's world, but Bullock was haunted by fear and admiration for Thomas Bullock JP, a Victorian patriarch who sired eleven children and blamed his town-bred wife for their 'softness'.[34] Born in poverty, Thomas Bullock gave up secure employment as Lord Erne's steward for the precarious independence of a tenant farmer. He was a Freemason but not an Orangeman, seeing as troublemaking the Orangeism Lord Erne shared with labourers and smallholders.[35] He struggled with the flood-meadows of Lough Erne, cursing Free Trade for ruining agriculture; his children emigrated, geologists undermined his Evangelical faith, and his later life was marked by black fits of despair: yet his boast that he lived a man's life and never sold himself into slavery like his degenerate son echoes through the son's novels.[36] The old man had Puritan contempt for fiction as lies. The austere naturalist aesthetic of his son's novels distrusts art as falsification; writers appear as fantasists, seducers and incompetents.[37]

Shan Bullock saw the integrity and intolerable narrowness of Puritan Ulster, the glamour and danger the city showed the provincial. In his early days as a London clerk he slid towards nihilism and squalid dissipation, but was rescued by marriage and Matthew Arnold's version of Christianity.[38] Bullock was deeply attached to his wife,[39] but dissatisfied with the scrupulous domesticity of *Robert Thorne*. While male vanity and egotism and female strength and resourcefulness appear in his stories of rural life, Bullock implies that urban white-collar life precludes a particular inarticulate masculine integrity and makes women (whose traditional roles are less affected) stronger than men. He dreams of escape to Canada or New Zealand, to 'a man's life'.[40]

This discontent drives Bullock's artistic commitment. He wrote interlocking novels set in the countryside of his youth, and is often seen as a naive chronicler of rural life, limited by indecision about his characters.[41] He is in fact a highly self-reflexive writer describing irresolvable conflicts of values in all their complexity, knowing any form of representation involves falsification. He made self-doubt an art-form.

Critics often note Bullock's strong emotional attraction to the strange, ragged Catholics who looked down from the barren hills of South Fermanagh to the fertile Protestant loughside.[42] His intellectual commitment to Unionism is usually overlooked.

Bullock's Unionism is clearest in *The Awkward Squads* (1893) and *The Red Leaguers* (1904). *The Awkward Squads* consists of four short stories; the title story depicts rival groups of Catholic and Protestant Volunteers drilling in anticipation of the Second Home Rule Bill. The Catholics live across the Cavan boundary; when a leader proposes a drill-site his followers protest 'That's in Fermanagh...the inemy's country'.[43] Long before Partition, Bullock knew he inhabited a border zone.

The Orange Volunteers are ignorant, bigoted and undisciplined but the Catholics are crueller, verbose, superstitious and intolerant. The most powerful story, 'A State Official', dramatises the Unionist view of boycotting. An eccentric rural postmaster, inarticulately asserting individuality, refuses to boycott a grabber. The old man is ostracised, attacked and driven mad. The title highlights the inability of the state to protect the individual against communal tyranny. Bullock knew the old man.[44]

The Red Leaguers is set in the near future, in a time of apparent peace with few soldiers in Ireland. It combines memories of Land League terror and Boer War doubts about British power with older fears. In 1641 Protestants were massacred at Belturbet (the Bullocks' market town); Enniskillen held out but isolated Protestant garrisons were butchered after surrender.[45] Growing up around Crom Castle, Bullock heard traditions of the 1689 siege by ruthless Lord Galmoy, and the slaughter of Jacobites after the battle of Newtownbutler.[46] In Bullock's childhood men slept with guns for fear of Papists; he played a practical joke on one such individual.[47] In *The Red Leaguers* these fears come true.

The narrator, Red Shaw, is a Protestant soldier of fortune returned to his native countryside after fighting in Cuba and South Africa. He loves Leah Hynes, a local Protestant girl; she prefers Jan Farmer[48] (son of Thomas Farmer, a large tenant-farmer). Shaw spitefully joins local Catholics in a conspiracy and discovers a secret society is organising Boer-style 'commandos' (flying columns) for a nationwide uprising.

On the chosen night Shaw leads his commando down from mountainous Armoy into the rich Protestant lowlands of Gorteen. The first few Protestant farmhouses are captured before shots are fired and drums beaten. In hours of confused fighting, Protestants are shot defending their farms; an isolated Catholic village is massacred, and rebels slaughter the perpetrators. The landscape of Gorteen, and named individuals, are familiar from earlier Bullock novels; this creates a terrible vivid sense of neighbours killing one another. Eventually Red Shaw asserts control. The Protestants are dead or captured except for Thomas and Jan Farmer, who realised something was brewing and retreated with a few neighbours into an old Planter castle prepared for siege. Protestant men are sent as prisoners to Belturbet; their womenfolk (including Leah) look after the farms. Dublin has fallen after fierce fighting; a Republic has been proclaimed. Everywhere outside Ulster British rule has collapsed, but Protestant forces hold large areas of the seven north-eastern counties. The Republic proclaims universal tolerance. Protestant prisoners will be safe until the fighting is over, then must swear allegiance or leave Ireland.

It soon becomes clear there is no effective central leadership, though some Protestant strongpoints (including Derry and Crom Castle) fall in uncoordinated attacks by local commanders. Shaw's attempts to storm the Farmers' stronghold fail ignominiously; his commando returns to its farms or drifts off to bigger battles. Shaw takes Leah to Dublin, where the provisional Irish Parliament is hopelessly factionalised while its peasant soldiers lose interest and resume their everyday lives. The British navy blockades Ireland; having secured her international position by alliances with Germany and America, Britain lands an army and the reconquest begins. Shaw realises he cannot force Leah to love him, frees her to return to Jan Farmer, and escapes to France. (The echo of King James's flight is probably deliberate: there are several such historical allusions.)

The view of nationalist rhetoric as ultimately irrelevant to the peasantry is a standard Unionist theme, like the image of nationalist political incapacity; but where Moore insinuates that nationalist factionalism reflects age-old barbarism, Bullock calls it the legacy of misrule. The nationalists include a coward and a psychopath, but also honest and intelligent patriots. They generally behave well; the worst atrocity is committed by Orangemen. Even the squabbling leaders are sincere, though incapable of implementing their noble sentiments. (This should not obscure the shortcomings of Bullock's picture. Would leaders capable of organising such a widespread and effective conspiracy prove so immediately and utterly incapable of administering the country? How could an old regime which – outside Ulster – collapsed so suddenly and completely, be reinstated even by a victorious army? Shaw's flight conveniently excuses Bullock from describing the relations between Catholics and Protestants after the reconquest.)

Bullock's description of the fall of Crom Castle attributes the land-lords' fate to their self-indulgent isolation; they should have given their tenants access to a wider civilisation.[49] The fate of the Ulster colony rests neither with landlords nor Orangemen, but with the strong-farmer virtues of Thomas and Jan Farmer. Thomas Farmer is Thomas Bullock. Who is Jan?

In *The Cubs*, Bullock's fictionalised account of his schooldays, Jan is the first-person narrator. In *By Thrasna River* Jan is again the first-person narrator identifiable with the young Bullock; he dislikes a sentimental visiting writer from London. In *Irish Pastorals* the narrator is a cousin of Jan, revisiting Fermanagh; Jan mocks his clumsy attempts at haymaking.[50] In *The Red Leaguers* the shadowy Jan is Bullock as he might have been; the well-meaning, indecisive, foolish Red Shaw is a hostile self-portrait of the artist as Lundy.

This underlies the book's ultimate failure. Shaw is an interesting study in self-doubt, but not a convincing soldier of fortune. Bullock sees far greater potential for savagery, but shrinks from the full horror of a future where hillmen would shoot Protestant farmers in the fields of south-eastern Fermanagh.

Bullock's hope of averting that future rested on Horace Plunkett. He worked with the great cooperative pioneer, and some later novels (notably *Master John* and *Hetty* (1911) – dedicated to Plunkett) reflect Plunkett's hope that through economic reform and an enlightened Arnoldian Anglicanism the gentry might yet create a prosperous rural civilisation within the Union. The alternatives are the hillmen and the nihilistic specu-lator Dan the Dollar.[51]

From 1910 Bullock, like Plunkett, reluctantly accepted Home Rule as inevitable. He distrusted Home Rulers, but saw no future for an 'Ulstershire' cut off from Ireland and attached to an uninterested England; he thought the Ulster leaders should make the best terms they could. He enthused over Redmond's speech at the outbreak of war, and worked for the Irish Convention in 1917–18.[52]

Unlike Plunkett, Bullock eventually supported Partition. His son served in the war; his relatives were scattered across the Empire. He could not blame the Ulster Protestants for refusing to live under murderers. His last published novel, *The Loughsiders*, describes a capable though unattractive farmer depriving the heirs to a neighbouring farm of the heritage they would have squandered anyway.[53] It can be read as a parable of the Plantation, or a meditation on the legacy of Thomas Bullock (d. 1917). Bullock called it 'The Story of a Man'.[54]

Despite a last visit to Fermanagh Shan Bullock remained in Surrey until his death in 1935, still writing novels which publishers turned down as old-fashioned.[55]

III

Moore was the product of mid-Victorian confidence and the great expansion of Belfast. Bullock, son of a declining rural society, has a stronger sense of personal economic and cultural insecurity. His only literary venture into Belfast was the official biography of Thomas Andrews, undertaken at Plunkett's suggestion. For Bullock, Andrews is an urban replica of his father; a Man, working with things not words.[56] Andrews had a darker significance for St John Ervine (1883–1971), whose generation came to manhood under the shadow of the Boer War and was crushed on the Western Front. The older men saw these wars as temporary setbacks. The death of Andrews in the *Titanic* recurs in Ervine's work as a symbol of the decline of the British Empire and the nineteenth-century liberalism and economic dynamism which created his native Ballymacarrett.[57]

Ervine's father died soon after the birth of his son in 1883; his mother was a deaf-mute. The boy was brought up by his maternal grandmother, who kept a little shop on the Albertbridge Road until she died in 1893.[58] She was a strong Evangelical, full of Christian love though not entirely suited to bringing up a boy on her own. (Ervine knew nothing of the facts of life until an unusually late stage of childhood, and had severe disciplinary problems at school.)[59] She took him on frequent visits to relatives in North Down, providing memories of rural and small-town society which inspired some of his best work.[60]

The child thought East Belfast with its shipyards and Orange parades the most romantic place in the world. Only as he grew up, realised why working-class girls lost their looks after marriage, and became a low-paid clerk at the age of 14, did he see the trap.[61] A talented schoolteacher had interested him in the theatre, widely seen in Belfast as a gateway to the Pit (of Hell).[62]

For 300 years his ancestors lived and died in Down, with one exception – his maternal grandfather went to America and died there.[63] This desertion of his grandmother gave Ervine one of his recurring plots. Sometimes it is the story of a strong woman betrayed by a feckless man, sometimes a brave adventurer fleeing the stifling love of an uncomprehending woman.[64] In 1901 Ervine went to London; he abandoned the religious faith of his grandmother.

In London Ervine became a City clerk. He saw the grandeur of London, and realised the provincialism of Belfast and his own naivety and aesthetic starvation.[65] He also saw the poverty of the slums and the indifference of the city; he burst into tears outside the Mansion House at the sudden thought that of so many millions not one knew or loved him. He became a socialist, joined the Fabian Society, and supported Home Rule. He sent his first play to George Bernard Shaw, never thinking a busy writer might resent it.[66] Shaw replied with helpful advice, beginning a friendship which survived even Shaw's gibe that Ervine's lengthy biographies could be summarised in ten pages[67] and Ervine's accusation that Shaw was a potential dictator, his philosophy crueller than Calvinism.[68]

Ervine became a freelance journalist, contributed to the avant-garde socialist magazine *The New Age*, and worked in repertory theatre. From 1910 he acquired a literary reputation, publishing two novels and several plays. Ervine mostly dealt with Irish themes, but also used British settings and was attacked as insufficiently national by the critic Ernest Boyd because he wrote primarily for British audiences.[69]

Ervine's early work presents Ulster Protestant society as hardworking, resourceful and commonsensical but corrupted and exploited by Evangelical Protestantism and Orange bigotry. His first mature play, *The Magnanimous Lover*, depicts an Ulsterman who has 'found religion' returning from Liverpool to offer marriage to the woman he impregnated and abandoned ten years previously. She rejects his loveless legalism.[70] Critics accused Ervine of immorality; he replied with vituperation.[71]

Ervine's most considerable play, *John Ferguson*, is a subtler and more respectful critique of evangelicalism. The noble old farmer John Ferguson, facing death and reduced to poverty after a lifetime's toil, trusts God's justice even when a malevolent landlord threatens his family with eviction and rapes his daughter. Ferguson's son, incited by a feeble-minded tramp incapable by Act of God of realising the moral significance of his action, kills the rapist. Ferguson discovers his son's guilt, forgets his lifelong belief in expiation and begs the murderer to escape; but the young man gives himself up to save an innocent suspect. Ferguson looks for consolation in the Bible and finds David's lament for Absalom; Ervine endorses the old man's ethics but sees his faith as childish.[72]

Ervine is far less sympathetic to Orangeism and Unionism in general. He met Carson once and disliked him;[73] he ridicules him as a placehunting Tory lawyer supported by illiterate Orange stonethrowers and senile idiots whose catchcries disgust the intelligent younger generation.[74] In *The Mixed Marriage* (the prototypical 'Troubles Play')[75] employers use

Orangeism to divide striking workers; one bigot, told *Maria Monk* is a fake, protests 'He'll be disbelievin' the Bible next.'[76] Ervine's support for Home Rule derived from technocratic confidence rather than cultural revivalism. The craftmanship of the shipyard worker and the labour of the housewife showed the rationality of Ulster Protestants; they would shake off bigotry and join a new generation of Catholics to organise trade unions, deal with the slums, secularise education and banish the clergy from politics. He said Horace Plunkett and AE represented the new Ireland.[77] He ignored the influence of Catholicism and the Gaelic revivalist and physical force elements of the Irish revival. He expected a continuing link with Britain; socialists of his generation often saw the Empire as a great developmental force. His wife and many friends were English, he wrote for English audiences; when he was briefly manager of the Abbey he tried to forge closer links with British provincial theatres.

Ervine saw the First World War as a 'Great European Disaster' inflicted on the young by the old, and considered avoiding conscription; but he felt it his duty to go, and soon after the Easter Rising he went.[78] (He joined an Irish rather than a British regiment, due to an impulse of hatred for a London crowd cheering Casement's execution. Ervine often admitted an emotional admiration for the rebels while hating their worldview, just as he responded to Catholicism aesthetically while denouncing it as a tyranny.) In later life he contrasted the idealism of Dominion volunteers who travelled thousands of miles to fight for a commonwealth of free nations with the selfish peasants idealised by Sinn Feiners and Catholic apologists.[79] He admired the soldiers' good humour; even their bawdy songs had Shakespearean vigour.[80] He saw crowds pulped by artillery and realised that his belief in organisation, efficiency and progress led to the crushing of countless individuals.[81] In May 1918 he lost a leg and spent the rest of his life in pain.[82]

He found Ireland in turmoil, denounced the atrocities of both sides, and hoped the all-Ireland Dominion settlement advocated by Plunkett might emerge from the chaos.[83] Ervine attended a press conference given by de Valera in New York and was horrified to hear that Ulster Protestants who would not accept the Republic should go 'back' to Britain. Thus began a lifelong hatred of de Valera, eclipsing his dislike of Carson.[84] The Civil War completed Ervine's disillusion. When Collins was shot and Plunkett burnt out, Ervine cursed the Irish[85] and transferred his allegiance to Northern Ireland, which seemed a haven of peace in comparison.

London was almost equally detestable. The Georgian literary ideals of his generation, which found expression so late and was cut down so early, were replaced by new forms of mass entertainment which he loathed as mechanical and dehumanised, and by Modernism, which he called juvenile pretentiousness.[86] He became a literary curmudgeon, trading abuse with modernist polemicists in his *Observer* column. He achieved financial success with well-crafted West End plays (such as *The First Mrs Fraser*); potboilers financing his attempts to make sense of his life.

Ervine was torn by conflicting emotions, unable to discipline his nonfictional work. His play *The Ship* dramatises the conflict between his knowledge of the achievements of modernity and the horrors of modern war in a story loosely based on Thomas Andrews and the *Titanic*. He cannot resolve the conflict and imposes a resolution. He meant to debunk Irish nationalism in an iconoclastic life of Parnell, but felt possessed by Parnell and eulogised him.[87] He spent the profits of *The First Mrs Fraser* on six years' research about General Booth; he had heard Booth in Belfast, and his grandmother admired the Salvation Army when the world mocked them.[88]

Ervine 'found God' in the trenches.[89] Just as many nineteenth-century Protestants embraced revivalism in reaction against Calvinist harshness, Ervine declared Pelagius was an Ulsterman and upheld Pelagianism against the determinists Paul, Augustine, Calvin, Marx and Shaw. He combined theological liberalism with a mystical strain reminiscent of AE.[90] Ervine believed everyone contained a spark of the divine and could become divine through their own efforts; only in this sense did he think Jesus divine. He rewrote the stories of Moses and Jesus (the latter as a self-portrait) considering himself as much 'inspired' as the writers of Scripture.[91] He mounts the Great White Throne, ushering Annie Horniman into Heaven and gloating as he consigns some particularly nasty Sinn Feiners to Hell.[92]

His desire to assert individuality against the machine transmuted his socialism into extreme individualism. He had always admired small entrepreneurs such as his grandmother; he still advocated social reform; he was haunted by the seemingly inexorable decline of liberalism before communism and fascism, and concerned at bureaucratic and undemocratic tendencies in the Labour Party;[93] in a period of reviving *laissez-faire* his ideas no longer appear so wildly eccentric as in the eras of Attlee and Butskell. Nevertheless his individualism has strains of cruelty and egotism; his Pelagianism implies that those who fail have only themselves to blame.

Ervine's attempt to reconcile the human affections and the demands of modernity lies behind his support for rural revival (the war veteran hero of *The Ship* escapes from the family shipyard to a farm, though Ervine does not fully endorse this: Ervine's later years were spent in Devon), Zionism (he believed the Jews should have their own state so they could civilise the Arabs and become a normal nation)[94] and feminism. (He advocated contraception and economic independence for women because he believed these led to efficient motherhood, without husbands if necessary. Pregnancy, motherhood and concubinage recur in his later writings, perhaps in reaction to the Ervines' childlessness. He detested homosexuality as desertion of the duties of husband and father.)[95] It also inspires his version of Ulster Unionism.

Ervine claimed that Northern Ireland combined localism and cosmopolitanism, enjoying a vigorous local culture within a wider association of self-governing nations. He contrasted it with 'Eire', which 'freed' itself from the Saxon only to impose new restrictions on its citizens and sink into reactionary peasant selfishness exemplified by wartime neutrality.[96] Ervine visited the Province frequently, kept contact with local artistic circles, and wrote plays such as *Boyd's Shop* giving a sentimental picture of small-town Northern life.[97] He stated his version of Unionism in a biography of Lord Craigavon which took six years to write.[98] His play *Friends and Relations* (London, 1942) expressed his hopes for the future, depicting the revitalisation of an Ulster business dynasty by the exclusion of decadent parasites and pseudo-intellectuals in favour of an illegitimate female heir with the family entrepreneurial drive, and a diffident but talented male artist.[99]

Ervine's hopes for a marriage of business and art in a rejuvenated Ulster were over-sanguine. The traditional business elite was commercially moribund, while Ervine's artistic friends respected him but disliked his praise for a reactionary and intolerant Establishment.[100] The serious points in *Craigavon: Ulsterman* were lost in sprawling diatribes against 'Eireans': he evaded Craigavon's darker qualities, and the book was so angry even Lady Craigavon and the Stormont Cabinet were upset.

Ervine's last major work was a biography of Shaw.[101] Ervine died senile in 1971, unaware of the violence engulfing Ulster.[102]

A nationalist interpretation of these writers might attribute their artistic and personal limitations to Unionism and expatriation. This would present them as wilfully forsaking their Irish heritage, and trace a proto-fascist rake's progress from Moore's arrogant imperialism through Bullock's urban anomie to Ervine's solipsistic self-deification and transformation from Edwardian Socialist to Victorian Radical.

This contains some truth, but not enough. London brought financial and emotional insecurity, but also new opportunities, freedoms and perspectives. Staying in Ulster meant aesthetic starvation, white-collar drudgery, puritan conventicles, and silence. Their expatriate Unionism was no less (or more) authentic than the nationalism of many whose identity was formed by exile. Nationalism is no guarantee of literary achievement: Gaelic chauvinism and Irish parochialism have ruined minds. These writers voiced serious criticism of nationalist shortcomings, and their standpoint gave distinctive insights. The abyss which confronted them reflected the impact of Darwinism as much as the conflicts of Ireland. The world market, Evangelical Protestantism, and the modern crisis of religious faith have shaped Irish life; it is not discreditable that these writers rarely resolved such themes, and could not avert the horrors they foresaw. These London-based Ulstermen of letters were products of the Home Rule debates, when the problems of Ireland were the centre of British political controversy; but the issues they raised lie at the heart of the modern world.

NOTES

1. John Tyndall, quoted in Jonathan Parry, *Democracy and Religion: Gladstone and the Liberal Party 1867–75* (Cambridge, 1986), p. 43.
*. Such writers were not always Unionist, nor men. My title alludes to Frankfort Moore's novel.
2. 'In Belfast By The Sea', Part 10, *Belfast Telegraph*, 12 November 1923.
3. 'In Belfast ...', Part 13, 3 December 1923; Part 49, 19 May 1924; *A Journalist's Notebook* (London, 1895).
4. 'In Belfast...':, Part 38, 10 April 1924 :'Old Fogey' 'Frankfort Moore as Journalist... Some Personal Reminiscences', *Northern Whig*, 15 May 1931 .
5. 'In Belfast...', Part 27, 3 March 1924.
6. 'In Belfast...', Part 33, 24 March 1924; Part 35, 31 March 1924; *The Truth About Ulster* (London, 1914), pp. 221–6.
7. *Truth About Ulster*; *The Ulsterman* (London, 1914). See also jokes in 'F. Littlemore', *A Garden of Peace: A medley in quietude* (London, 1919). Publisher's letter in National Library of Ireland copy confirms authorship.
8. 'Old Fogey', 'Moore as Journalist'.
9. 'In Belfast...', Part 16, 24 December 1923; Part 31, 17 March 1924.
10. *Truth About Ulster*, pp. 251–6.
11. Ibid., pp. 94–6. Knott; J. B. Lyons, *What Did I Die Of?* (Dublin, 1991).
12. *Castle Omeragh* (London, 1903).
13. E.g. Lydia Montgomery, *The Ulsterman*, ch. XIX.
14. *Truth About Ulster*, pp. 181–3; Moore, *A Friend Indeed* (London, 1916), chs XIII–XXI.

15. *Journalist's Notebook.*
16. *A Friend Indeed.*
17. *The Diary of an Irish Cabinet Minister* (Belfast, 1892).
18. *The Viceroy Muldoon* (Belfast, 1893).
19. *The Rise and Fall of Larry O'Lannigan, J.P.* (Belfast, 1893). National Library of Ireland and (Belfast) Linenhall Library catalogues attribute these to Moore, confirmed by *Journalist's Notebook* pp. 112–13.
20. *Journalist's Notebook* ; 'Old Fogey' 'Frankfort Moore as Journalist'.
21. Described in *A Garden of Peace.*
22. 'H. C. L.', *Belfast Telegraph*, 10, 20 June 1924; for a defence, 'Plain James', *Northern Whig*, 21 May 1931.
23. Re-reading *The Ulsterman* in old age, C. S. Lewis's brother found it painfully reminiscent of his own relationship with his father: Clyde S. Kilby and Marjorie Lamp Mead (eds), *Brothers and Friends: The Diaries of Major Warren Hamilton Lewis* (Harper & Row, San Francisco, 1982), pp. 278–9.
24. *Ulsterman*, pp. 54–5.
25. Ibid., chs I, XIV and ch.XXVIII, p. 297.
26. Ibid., pp. 128–31; *Truth About Ulster*, ch. I.
27. *Truth About Ulster*, pp. 70–2.
28. *A Friend Indeed.*
29. 'In Belfast by the Sea', 61 parts, *Belfast Telegraph*, 8 September 1923–30 June 1924 (twice weekly).
30. 'In Belfast...', Part 22, 4 February 1924.
31. Obituary, *Belfast Telegraph*, 12 May 1931.
32. *Journalist's Notebook.* Their friendship: *Truth About Ulster*, p. 71.
33. Bullock to P. S. O'Hegarty quoted John Boyd 'Ulster Prose' in Sam Hanna Bell (ed.), *The Arts in Ulster* (London, 1951), pp. 105–9. *Robert Thorne* (London,1907). His other London novels are *The Barrys* (London, 1898), *A Laughing Matter* (London, 1908), *Mr. Ruby Jumps the Traces* (London, 1917).
34. See Bullock's account of his youth, *After Sixty Years* (London, 1931) and Peadar Livingstone, *The Fermanagh Story* (Enniskillen,1969), pp. 252–3.
35. *After Sixty Years*, pp. 31–2.
36. Ibid., pp. 61, 90–6, 164. For Lough Erne floods in Bullock, John Wilson Foster, *Forces and Themes in Ulster Fiction* (Dublin, 1974), pp. 31, 34–5.
37. Fantasist: Harry Thomson, *By Thrasna River* (London, 1895). Seducer: Frank Barry, *The Barrys*. Incompetent: the narrator of *A Laughing Matter*. (Bullock was also influenced by resentment at the English reading public for preferring stage-Irish novels to his own careful works. He is self-consciously Irish and complains about English ignorance of Ireland, like many Unionists.)
38. 'My Sin' in *Mors et Vita* (London, 1923), verses composed spontaneously after his wife's death. Arnold: *Robert Thorne*, pp. 255–7.
39. *Mors et Vita*. Note affectionate but overbearing wives in *Robert Thorne, A Laughing Matter* and *Mr. Ruby Jumps the Traces.*
40. Robert Thorne and his family emigrate to New Zealand. Mr. Ruby's brief rebellion is ephemeral but his son goes to Canada. (Bullock's son emigrated to America but was not successful: Plunkett–Bullock

Correspondence, Plunkett Papers, Plunkett Foundation, Long Hanborough Business Park, Oxfordshire.)

41. E.g. Wilson Foster, *Forces and Themes*; Boyd, 'Ulster Prose'. Bullock *is* a valuable recorder of rural life and attitudes; cf. Henry Glassie, *Passing the Time: Folklore and History of an Ulster Community* (Dublin, 1982), pp. 773–4.

42. E.g. Benedict Kiely, 'Orange Lily', *Irish Bookman*, June 1947, quoting *After Sixty Years*, pp. 32–3.

43. *The Awkward Squads*, p. 15.

44. *The Cubs* (London, 1906) ; *By Thrasna River*, pp. 2–4. See Boyd, 'Ulster Prose'.

45. Lord Ernest Hamilton, *The Irish Rebellion of 1641* (London, 1920).

46. *After Sixty Years*, pp. 191–3.

47. *By Thrasna River*, pp. 85–8, ch. IX; *Master John* (London, 1909), pp. 109–19.

48. Farmer (Mac Scoloige) is a Fermanagh name; Livingstone, p. 427.

49. *Red Leaguers*, pp. 228–38; *After Sixty Years*.

50. 'The Haymakers', *Irish Pastorals* (London, 1901).

51. See Plunkett's pamphlet *Noblesse Oblige* (Dublin, 1907) and introduction to *After Sixty Years*. Cf. the enlightened Plunkettite Hugh Jarman in *Hetty*. Master John is explicitly contrasted (pp. 129–30) with Dan, who appears in *Dan the Dollar* (Dublin, 1906).

52. This account of Bullock's political attitudes is based on the Plunkett–Bullock correspondence (about 55 letters, c. 1905–23) held by the Plunkett Foundation.

53. *The Loughsiders* (London, 1924). For critical comment, see John Wilson Foster, *Forces and Themes*.

54. Harrap (publisher's) publicity material in my copy of *The Loughsiders*.

55. Unpublished MSS. in Queen's University, Belfast.

56. *Thomas Andrews* (Dublin, 1912), especially Plunkett's introduction and pp. 21, 28.

57. Especially *Changing Winds* (London, 1917), *The Ship* (London, 1922), *Craigavon: Ulsterman* (London, 1949).

58. *Dictionary of National Biography*; John Boyd, 'St. John Ervine – A Biographical Note', *Threshold*, Summer 1974. There are discrepancies between these accounts. Boyd seems more reliable.

59. Unpublished autobiography quoted in Boyd, 'Ervine – A Biographical Note'.

60. *Craigavon: Ulsterman* pp. 6–7.

61. *If I Were Dictator* (London, 1934), pp. 53–4.

62. *The Theatre in My Time* (London, 1933) pp. 15–16; Boyd, 'Biographical Note' .

63. *Some Impressions of My Elders* (London, 1923), p. 205. Boyd, 'Biographical Note'.

64. The woman: *Mrs. Martin's Man* (Dublin, 1914). The man: *The Wayward Man* (London, 1927).

65. Ervine autobiography in Boyd, 'Biographical Note'.

66. *The Mountain and Other Stories* (London, 1928), p. 205.

67. Shaw to Ervine, 29 October 1932, Dan H. Laurence (ed.), *Collected Letters of Bernard Shaw, Volume 4: 1926–50* (London, 1988), p. 313.

68. *Some Impressions of My Elders*, pp. 209–11, 234–41; *If I Were Dictator*, pp. 115–18.
69. Ernest A. Boyd, *The Contemporary Drama of Ireland* (Boston, 1917), pp. 179–92.
70. *Four Irish Plays* (Dublin, 1914).
71. Robert Hogan, Richard Burnham and Daniel Poteet, *The Modern Irish Drama IV: The Rise of the Realists 1910–15* (Dublin, 1979), pp. 200–3; *The Critics* in *Four Irish Plays*.
72. *John Ferguson* (Dublin, 1915). See also John Cronin (ed.), *Selected Plays* (Washington, DC, 1988), containing *The Mixed Marriage, John Ferguson, Boyd's Shop, Friends and Relations*.
73. *Craigavon: Ulsterman*, p. 190.
74. *Sir Edward Carson and the Ulster Movement* (Dublin, 1916); *The Orangeman* in *Four Irish Plays; Mrs. Martin's Man*, pp. 174–6.
75. Niall Cusack, 'A Most Undesirable Person' – St. John Ervine, Ulster playwright', *New Ulster 4* (Summer 1987).
76. *The Mixed Marriage* (Dublin, 1911), p. 5.
77. *Sir Edward Carson*, pp. 32–42.
78. *Changing Winds* (Dublin, 1917) fictionalises his hesitations; while awaiting military service he wrote this novel, whose hero writes a novel while awaiting military service.
79. *Some Impressions of My Elders*, pp. 46–54.
80. *The Organised Theatre* (London, 1924), pp. 63–4.
81. 'A Testament of Middle Age' in F. J. Harvey Darton (ed.), *Essays of the Year, 1930–1* (London, 1931).
82. Boyd, 'Biographical Note'.
83. *Some Impressions of My Elders*, chapter on AE.
84. Ibid., pp. 57–9.
85. Ervine to Dudley Digges, 28 August 1922, in Robert Hogan and Richard Burnham, *The Modern Irish Drama: Volume 6; The Years of O'Casey 1920-6* (Gerrards Cross, 1992), p. 65.
86. *The Organised Theatre*, passim.
87. Preface to first edition of *Parnell* (London, 1925).
88. Preface to *God's Soldier: General Booth* (2 vols, London, 1924).
89. *A Testament of Middle Age*.
90. Most movingly in his last novel, *Sophia* (London, 1942) about a recently-dead woman coming to terms with her past.
91. *If I Were Dictator*, pp. 8–39 ; *A Journey to Jerusalem* (London, 1936), passim.
92. Ervine, preface to Rex Pogson, *Miss Horniman and the Gaiety Theatre, Manchester* (Rockliff, 1952); *Craigavon: Ulsterman*, pp. 39, 318. (They deserved it.)
93. *If I Were Dictator; The State and the Soul* (London, 1939); *Is Liberty Lost?* (London, 1944). Postwar anti-socialist writings are more strident: *Private Enterprise* (London, 1948); Preface to Florence Wilson, *The Cookin' Woman: Irish Country Recipes* (Edinburgh, 1949; first edn Belfast).
94. *A Journey To Jerusalem*, pp. 300–9; see also the assimilationism of Shylock in Ervine's philo-semitic sequel to *The Merchant of Venice, The Lady of Belmont* (London, 1923).

95. E.g. *Oscar Wilde: A Present Time Appraisal* (London, 1923), especially pp. 44–5.
96. *The State and the Soul; Craigavon: Ulsterman*, passim.
97. *Boyd's Shop* (London, 1936).
98. John Boyd, *The Middle of My Journey* (Belfast, 1990), p. 112 describes its reception.
99. See the hostile comments of David Kennedy, 'The Drama in Ulster', in Bell (ed.), *The Arts in Ulster*, p. 62.
100. Boyd, *The Middle of My Journey*, pp. 107–14.
101. *George Bernard Shaw: His life, work and friends* (London, 1956).
102. Boyd, *The Middle of My Journey*, pp. 113–14.

5 The Protestant Experience of Revolution in Southern Ireland

Peter Hart

Between 1911 and 1926, the 26 counties that became the Irish Free State lost 34 per cent of their Protestant population.[1] To put this number into context, over the same period the Catholic populations in both the north and south fell by 2 per cent and the Protestant population in Northern Ireland rose by 2 per cent. Over the previous 30 years, the two groups within the 26 counties had declined at almost exactly the same – gradually decreasing – rate (Protestants by 20 per cent, Catholics by 19 per cent).[2] So this catastrophic loss was unique to the southern minority and unprecedented: it represents easily the single greatest measurable social change of the revolutionary era. It is also unique in modern British history, being the only example of the mass displacement of a native ethnic group within the British Isles since the seventeenth century. Did the political and demographic crises coincide? How voluntary was this migration, and what were its causes? How sectarian was the Irish nationalist revolution?

Protestant experiences of the revolution in southern Ireland ranged from massacre and flight to occasional inconvenience and indifference, from outraged opposition to enthusiastic engagement. Even within the small, troubled district of Kilbrittain in West Cork – a hot zone of republicanism and violence – the conflict could mean radically different things to different people.

Dorothy Stopford had a good revolution. A recent graduate of Trinity College, she spent part of 1921 and 1922 as the dispensary doctor in Kilbrittain. As a pipe-smoking woman wearing riding breeches and an eye-glass, she caused a minor sensation, but neither her politics (republican) nor her religion (Church of Ireland) prevented her from getting along with her neighbours.[3] To the local republican activists, her Protestantism was merely a curiosity: 'I sternly refuse all efforts to be converted and say I prefer to go to Hell. Then they all exclaim that they know it's wrong but they can't believe I will go to Hell – we have great sport.'[4] At the same time, 'I am on excellent terms with all the gentry and Protestants, they are very nice and broadminded.'[5] Her life did not lack variety: 'I went to a work party at the Rectory the other day and sewed an apron and we had prayers and sang hymns. I was much amused....I met all the ladies of the parish. Next minute I am out fishing or ferreting with the I.R.A. You can guess which I prefer.'[6]

For Dorothy Stopford, the guerrilla war raging in West Cork added the spice of adventure to a pleasant life ('it is always fun here, something happening every minute'). For John Bolster Barrett, also living in Kilbrittain, the same period was one of unrelenting fear:

> I had to sleep or try to sleep many nights in the open sometimes unable to protect myself from rain and cold....I was unable to get provisions for my house except by long, secretive journeys to loyal shops in Bandon. Many of my friends and neighbours of the same political adherence were murdered in West Cork, some in their beds, a few more shot on the way to and from Bandon whither they had gone for food. I am a member of the Church of Ireland and I was told on two occasions by Sinn Feiners that all the Protestants in West Cork were going to be shot. During this time my house was raided several times at night....I had therefore to sleep in the fields, my wife bringing me food secretly. These are only a few of the experiences I have gone through....I have never been restored to the health I enjoyed previous to 1920. Sometimes I suffer from long fits of depression, also from loss of memory.[7]

How representative were Stopford, Barrett and Kilbrittain? What follows is an exploration in outline of the Protestant experience of revolution in the three southern provinces of Munster, Leinster and Connaught. I am stopping at the border of Ulster rather than Northern Ireland because, although the minority communities of Cavan, Monaghan and Donegal shared the general demographic fate of their fellow Free State counties, their political history had far more in common with the rest of Ulster than with their southern neighbours.[8] For the purposes of this essay, therefore, 'southern' means what it meant before Ireland was partitioned.

WHEN DID THE PROTESTANTS LEAVE?

To understand why, we must first ask when. Clearly, if much of the population decline took place before 1919 – before or during the Great War – or if it was spread evenly over the whole 16 years between 1911 and 1926, this fact would call for a very different interpretation than otherwise. Fortunately, the change can be dated using church records. Unfortunately, neither national nor diocesan membership or attendance records exist for the Church of Ireland – by far the largest Protestant denomination in the south – but observers within the church do consistently indicate late 1920 as the turning point. 'It is the bare truth to say that we have lost more of our people during the last three years than in the fifty-three years since disestablishment', wrote one in 1923.[9] This impression is supported by the annual reports of Board of Education of the united dioceses of Cork, Cloyne and Ross. These reveal a 30 per cent drop in the number of pupils between 1911 and 1926, nearly three-quarters of which took place in 1920–22.[10]

My analysis of 19 complete parish Preachers' Books in West Cork – including the Kilbrittain area – confirms this pattern.[11] Attendance at Sunday service, averaged year by year, was higher in 1918 and 1919 than in 1911 or 1914. After 1919, attendance fell by 22 per cent, with more than two-thirds of the decline taking place in a single year – 1922.

Methodist congregations in Cork district followed an almost identical path, as did congregations throughout the three southern provinces. Methodist membership was higher in 1918, 1919 and 1920 than in 1914, but fell precipitously thereafter. Once again, 1921–23 were the crucial years, accounting for 74 per cent of the lost population.[12]

The salience of the year 1922 suggests at least a partial explanation for this timing, and for the decline as a whole: the withdrawal of the British Army and disbandment of the Royal Irish Constabulary early that year. And indeed, departing soldiers, sailors, policemen and their families (assuming all of the latter did leave) do account for about one-quarter of the emigrants, a significant contributing factor although ultimately a minor one.[13] They played no part in the West Cork figures discussed above, for example. Indeed, this transfer accounts for a much greater proportion of the Catholic population loss recorded in this period. Moreover, Irish-born Protestants left at almost exactly the same rate as those born outside the country.[14] Since almost all members of the armed forces in Ireland were British, it is clear that the movement was far more than that of an alien 'garrison'; these were overwhelmingly Irish men, women and families that were leaving.

These figures also eliminate another common explanation for the decline: the impact of the Great War. As staunch imperial patriots, Irish Protestants were widely believed to have served and died in disproportionately large numbers, thus crippling their home communities.[15] Many families were shattered by the loss of their sons ('Hardly a week passed without news of a casualty, a brother, a cousin, an older sister's fiancé, or a friend').[16] The rural gentry, true to their martial traditions, suffered heavily as a class ('The world we had known had vanished. We hunted again, but ghosts rode with us').[17] This mattered little in demographic terms. At most, the war induced a slight, temporary, decrease in overall numbers in 1915 and 1916, apparently soon compensated for by the stoppage of emigration.

In any case, southern Protestants were no more willing to sacrifice themselves for Britain than their Catholic neighbours. Ulster's enlistment rate far outstripped that of the rest of Ireland, where there was little overall difference in enthusiasm between Catholics and non-Catholics. In many southern counties, Protestants were actually less likely to enlist in either the Army or Navy than their Catholic neighbours, and made up a much smaller proportion of reservists. Occupation, not religion, determined the pattern of recruitment. Farmers and their sons made particularly reluctant soldiers, no matter what their denomination.[18] Thus, while southern Protestants did go to war in considerable numbers, they were in fact one of the least affected communities in the British Isles. It was not the world war that blighted southern Protestantism, but what came after.

HOW LOYAL WERE THE LOYALISTS?

Between 1912 and 1922, Irish politics was transformed by a host of new and renewed organisations: Ulster, National and Irish Volunteers (later the Irish Republican Army), Sinn Fein and Cumann na mBan, the Ulster Special Constabulary and the National Army, the Irish Transport and General Workers' Union and the Labour Party. Vast, unprecedented, numbers of men and women gave their names, money, time, votes, freedom or lives for the causes these groups represented. Not so the Protestant men and women of Connaught, Leinster and Munster. In this great era of mass mobilisation, they produced neither party nor private army, nor did they contribute more than a scattering of members to anyone else's. This set them apart from their co-religionists not only in the six counties of Northern Ireland but also in Cavan, Monaghan and Donegal, thousands of whom joined the Ulster Volunteer Force in 1913–14 and self-defence associations and the Ulster Special Constabulary in 1920–21.[19]

As John Henry Bernard, the Church of Ireland Archbishop of Dublin, wrote to Lloyd George after the Easter Rising, 'the one class in Ireland which has *not* had resort to arms in support of its political opinions in 1913–16 is the Unionist class in the South and West'.[20] The cause of southern unionism was represented by the Irish Unionist Association (and after 1919 by the breakaway Unionist Anti-Partition League) and a few Unionist clubs, but their membership was drawn from a tiny elite. The former had only 683 members in 1913, and the latter were small in number and size at best, at the height of the Home Rule crisis in 1914.[21] Even these largely disappeared after 1914 and failed to reappear in subsequent crises.[22] There was no need for an electoral machine, as unionist candidates only ran in and around the cities of Dublin and Cork in the General Election of 1918 (and only in the University of Dublin in the 1921 election for a southern parliament) and were almost as scarce in the local council elections of 1914 and 1920.

What of Protestant nationalism? Protestant home-rulers were a rare but identifiable breed, largely irrelevant after 1918. Protestant republicans such as Dorothy Stopford or Albinia Brodrick were far more exotic creatures, although not confined to any class or area.[23] When a pumpkin bearing the words 'Up Sinn Fein' appeared amidst the Kanturk church harvest festival decorations in 1921, the outrage was traced to the sexton who, it turned out, was 'well in with the rebels'.[24] Rarer still were Protestants in the IRA, who could be counted on one hand. Thus, while it would be fair to say that the vast majority of Protestants would have preferred that southern Ireland remain part of the Union, this was for the most part a passive, unexpressed preference. As a group, they were politically inert.

Most importantly, what Protestants – the vast majority of them – did not do during the guerrilla wars was resist the IRA or assist government forces. What the Royal Irish Constabulary and the British Army needed above all was information: who the local volunteers were, where their arms were hidden, when an ambush was being prepared. With the exception of a very few isolated individuals, Protestants did nothing to provide such intelligence, and generally avoided contact with soldiers and policemen. Official reports and memoirs are unanimous in this regard. John Regan, the County Inspector of the Limerick RIC, wrote of 'southern loyalists' that 'for many I had the most profound contempt. Certainly there were some who deserved great praise, but on the whole they were a poor lot....The Government could expect little help from them.'[25] One constable stationed in the west recalled that 'we wouldn't be a bit better in with Protestants than Republicans. We'd be less better in with them...because they were afraid to be accused of giving us news...they kept away from us altogether.'[26] In Dublin, the Irish command's official history noted that 'a considerable minority were professedly loyal but were so intimidated that they refused to give information even when they themselves had been the sufferers by I.R.A. action'.[27] A military situation report on the midlands and Connaught in December 1921 described 'active loyalists' as 'an inconsiderable class'.[28] A survey of army commanders in Munster in the spring of 1921 produced the same conclusions: 'Personally I have no very high opinion of the politic value of the loyalist'; 'Few in these counties are reliable'; 'I can see no sign of any effort to actively help the government'; 'I would say that their action is very passive....Whether they know things or not, I cannot say, but I do not think any try to be of any assistance in the way of intelligence.'[29]

The West Cork Protestants I have interviewed confirm these impressions. 'Even if you knew something, you wouldn't say it.'[30] Several told of their fathers asking British officers not to talk to them or visit them, to 'go away or you'll get me shot'.[31] 'There might be the odd one' who informed on the guerrillas but for the most part, 'people were too afraid to do it'.[32] 'They kept their tongues in their cheeks.'[33] This was felt to be true of any expression of anti-nationalist or anti-IRA dissent. To rural and small-town Protestants, 'talk' meant trouble even under normal circumstances.[34] During the revolution it could be terrifyingly dangerous. 'You could get into trouble from anything – without thinking.'[35] As one man told me: 'they kept quiet because they were afraid; I mean if I said something to you tonight you would say something to somebody else and somebody else and it would have got worse every time.'[36] 'You'd get into trouble very quickly and when you got into trouble it was hard to get out of it. We couldn't say a word anyway.'[37] W. B. Sanford wrote of the southern Church of Ireland as a whole that 'the general policy adopted was "Lie low and say nothing", "Wait and see".'[38]

Despite this strong communal consensus that 'you didn't speak out if you had any sense', there were those who were 'outspoken' or 'stern' or who 'passed remarks'.[39] Such people were considered 'stupid' and 'foolish' troublemakers, dangerous not only to themselves but to the whole Protestant community. Those who did proclaim or act on their loyalty in this way did so knowing they were on their own. James McDougall, a businessman who had to flee Cork, stated bitterly that he 'wasn't like the spineless so-called "loyalists" I knew there'.[40] Tom Bradfield, another devout unionist (shot by the IRA), declared that he was 'not like the rest of them round here'.[41] Even among Irish Grants Committee claimants, who had to demonstrate their loyalty to the Crown to receive compensation from the British government, only fifteen out of approximately 700 Cork applicants (or 2 per cent) said that they had provided information to the authorities.[42]

This withholding of support was not prompted by self-preservation alone, but also by alienation from British forces and methods themselves. Southern Protestants of all classes were repelled by British counter-insurgency tactics and by the new police recruits, the notoriously undisciplined Black and Tans and Auxiliaries. 'Those awful men! Everyone hated them, Roman Catholics and Protestants alike.'[43] Nor did this indignation stop at the Ulster border.[44] Protestants were probably less likely to be mistreated or to be singled out as the objects of retaliation, but they were far from immune. The only known Protestant volunteers in Munster were two young Tipperary men who joined after being beaten by the police.[45]

Active resistance to IRA raids and demands was as unusual as collaboration with the authorities and even more dangerous. When it did occur it was spontaneous, unorganised and almost always punished with the utmost severity. Tom Sweetnam of Ballineen became one of the first Protestants to be driven out of Ireland by the IRA after he fired on a group of Volunteers trying to break into his house in 1918.[46] Most Protestants, however, had neither the arms nor the inclination to engage in self-defence. Even non-violent resistance – the simple refusal of demands – often met with a harsh response. Survival depended upon submission. 'Loyalism', like unionism, was a matter of preference rather than practice, and most southern Protestants were loyalists in name only: a name usually applied by others in any case.

HOW SECTARIAN WAS THE REVOLUTION?

It was the Home Rule crisis that first raised the spectre of sectarian violence in the south, just as it did in Ulster. A survey of resident magistrates in early 1914 gathered predictions and fears from all three provinces. The Sligo RM warned that 'it is idle to suppose, if trouble comes, good fellowship can be upheld or that it is really now more than superficial'.[47] In Ballinrobe there was 'some apprehension of attacks on houses of Protestants who are taking such steps as are possible to protect themselves'. In Ballinasloe it was feared that 'the minority might be in danger of suffering if the Volunteers were not properly controlled'. In Kerry, 'the spirit of religious intolerance is stronger than for the past three years'. In West Cork, 'old sores have been re-opened during recent years and religious bigotry has been revived. On the part of the minority there is a widespread fear of possible outrages against their lives and property.' Many

RMs believed that fighting in the north would precipitate reprisals against Protestants in the south. When publicly expressed, such apprehensions or accusations of Catholic intolerance (the stock in trade of Unionist propagandists) produced, not reassurance, but an angry backlash. Members of the Limerick County Council condemned Munster Protestants for not contradicting such reports and warned: 'the worm may turn...and those people who may remain silent now may have reason to regret it'.[48]

These fears vanished practically overnight with the outbreak of war and were not revisited until the conscription crisis of 1918 (the Easter Rising having had no great impact on communal relations).[49] Thus we move from one might-have-been to another. What might have occurred if the British government had attempted to enforce conscription in Ireland? Sinn Fein and the Irish Volunteers would undoubtedly have resisted, with massive popular support – including from some Protestants. In this eventuality, Volunteer plans called for 'persons known or suspected to be in sympathy with the enemy to be confined to their houses, under penalty of being shot at sight'.[50] Heading this list were those who refused to sign the anti-conscription pledge or subscribe to the campaign fund.[51] Many Protestants both signed and gave when asked, out of conviction or prudence. Many did not and were threatened and harassed. 'They are making the Protestants join in now, or if not, they will be boycotted, or have to go to England's war', wrote one correspondent from Drinagh, Co. Cork in May 1918.[52] The County Inspector of the Longford RIC reported in June that the breach between the communities was 'wider than it ever has been in my experience'.[53] One Church of Ireland clergyman wrote from King's County that

> the Protestant people are being terrified into signing the pledge against conscription under threats of fire and sword....A higher up Sinn Feiner came here with the list and threatened me that I would be treated just like the British soldiers they would be fighting against if I did not sign it, murder for me and my family and my place would be burned down.[54]

Protestant homes were also frequent targets for nocturnal raids, as much to intimidate as to acquire arms.

This crisis, too, passed without the augured confrontation but the conscription *débâcle* did launch the IRA's insurrection. By the end of 1920 the guerrillas were engaged in an escalating struggle for mastery throughout southern Ireland, with their survival depending on the silence and acquiescence of the civilian population. As British forces came to grips with the new threat, fast-rising republican casualties bred suspicion and fear, and a mounting desire for revenge. Each British success would produce a frantic search for informers and a desperate need to hit back at their enemies.

As revolutionary violence spiralled upwards, more and more of its victims were civilians, and more and more of them were Protestant. Scores of Protestant men and women were shot in the winter and spring of 1920–21, throughout the south. Perhaps hundreds of others barely escaped the same fate and were driven from their homes. Not all of those shot were Protestant but they numbered far in excess of their share of the population. In County Cork, for example, the IRA deliberately shot over 200 civilians between 1920 and 1923, of whom over 70 (or 36 per cent) were Protestant: five times the percentage of Protestants in the civilian population.[55]

An even greater bias can be seen in the IRA's arson campaign over the same months, their response to British reprisals against property. The guerrillas struck back against private homes, hundreds in all, the great majority of which were owned by Protestants. This also reflected a class bias, as many were country houses of the gentry or aristocracy. By no means all, or even most, fell into this category: the common factor was religion. Of 113 houses burned by the guerrillas in Cork, seventeen (or 15 per cent) belonged to Catholics. Similarly, none of the more than two dozen farms seized from 'spies' in that county were owned by Catholics.

These attacks had little or nothing to do with the victims' actual behaviour. Although almost all of those shot were accused of being 'spies' or 'informers', this label covered a wide range of 'anti-National' or 'anti-Irish' offences. Simple dissent or non-cooperation with IRA demands condemned many. Many were condemned by nothing more than 'talk'. As suggested above, very few were actually guilty of aiding the enemy. A large number seem to have been killed simply as a warning to others. Moreover, despite the near-complete absence of political organisation, IRA units commonly believed themselves to be opposed by a loyalist underground, and these conspiracy theories multiplied as the war progressed. The Freemasons, perennial nationalist and Catholic bogeymen, were felt to be particularly menacing, followed at a distance by the YMCA.[56]

Most Protestants were thus faced with an acute dilemma for which there was no solution. 'The Protestants were caught, you see, in the middle of the road.'[57] With the escalation of the war came political polarisation, a harsh division (at least in republican eyes) between 'us' and 'them' – Protestants and Catholics, British and Irish, nationalist and unionist. 'They became not only different from us', recalled Lionel Fleming, 'they were against us.'[58] Neutrality and passivity could not overcome past divisions and abiding ethnic and political stereotypes. In the Irish revolution, an unobtrusive unionist was still a unionist, as Richard Williams found out when the IRA burned his house outside Macroom in June 1921. As described by the local reporter for the *Southern Star* (with considerable candour) his situation could stand for that of thousands of others. 'Whether Mr. Williams gave offence to Sinn Fein or endangered any of its adherents in the military sense, one would be very slow to believe.' Nevertheless,

> Mr. R. C. Williams has been a consistent Unionist in his politics, though he never openly identified himself with politics. He has always held his opinions quietly but firmly, and though at times, when the cry of intolerance was raised by Southern Protestants, to damage the National cause, he might have done a little more to 'nail the lie to the mast'; still he always enjoyed a large amount of popularity, esteem and respect.... The nation was engaged in a life and death struggle and there was little possibility of success adopting a neutral attitude.

Or, as a friend of Williams told me: 'They could have left him alone, I suppose, but they didn't leave anyone alone, that's the point.'[59]

The war continued to escalate right up to the July 1921 truce, and anti-Protestant violence rose along with it. Indeed, just before the fighting stopped, the Munster IRA had begun to seize Protestants to use as hostages. The County Inspector for South Tipperary commented that 'it looks as if a religious war was about to develop'.[60] The truce brought comparative peace, along with the prospect of far worse if it failed. 'One of them', a correspondent to the *Irish Times* from Limerick, lamented 'the state of paralysis into which they ["the southern Protestants"] have allowed themselves to fall....All of them have not yet experienced such pogroms as that of West Cork; but few have been without distinct intimation in some shape or form that they stand selected for special attention.'[61]

If hostilities had resumed, British commanders planned to pursue a far more ruthless course of action, and expected the IRA to follow suit. Willing Protestants (and any other 'loyalists') would have been evacuated into concentration centres – towns and villages emptied of 'rebel sympathizers' – and organised and armed as a 'civil guard'. In other words, they would be expected to participate in the reconquest of the country.[62] IRA intentions may be gauged by Sean Moylan's declaration that 'if there is a war of extermination on us...by God, no loyalist in North Cork will see its finish'.[63] It is hard to imagine anything other than the most terrible – and terminal – consequences for the southern minority under these circumstances.

What did happen after the Anglo-Irish treaty in many areas still exceeded all but the worst expectations. In effect, the guerrillas (most of whom opposed the treaty) picked up where they had left off six months earlier, pursuing the same imagined enemies, ex-soldiers and policemen as well as Protestants. Anyone suspected of collaborating with the enemy was in danger. This drive for revenge was fuelled by anger at anti-Catholic violence in the North, heavily publicised in southern newspapers. The Belfast boycott was reapplied, mainly against Protestant traders, and Protestant houses were seized throughout the south, ostensibly to provide shelter for northern refugees. The following letter, sent to scores – possibly hundreds – of homes in the spring of 1922 by western IRA units, illustrates the logic of reprisal:[64]

I am authorised to take over your house and all property contained therein, and you are hereby given notice to hand over to me within one hour from the receipt of this notice the above land and property. The following are reasons for this action:

(1) The campaign of murder in Belfast is financed by the British Government.

(2) As a reprisal for the murder of innocent men, women and children in Belfast.

(3) You, by supporting the union between England and Ireland, are in sympathy with their murder.

(4) In order to support and maintain the Belfast refugees.

It was not just individual households that were to be 'deported', but whole communities.[65] The Church of Ireland Bishop of Killaloe wrote in June of north Tipperary:

There is scarcely a Protestant family in the district which has escaped molestation. One of my Clergy has had his motor car and a portion of his house burned. Some other houses have been burned. Cattle have been driven off farms. Protestant families have been warned to leave the neighbourhood. Altogether a state of terrorism exists.[66]

In Ballinasloe:

If the campaign against Protestants which has been carried on there since the end of last month is continued in similar intensity for a few weeks more, there will not be a Protestant left in the place. Presbyterians and members of the Church of Ireland, poor and well-to-do, old and young, widows and children, all alike have suffered in intimidation, persecution and expulsion.

The campaign is carried out in the nightime, by unnamed persons, who give no reason for their action. The system which usually is followed is, first, the despatch of an anonymous letter giving the recipient so many days, or hours, to clear out. If this notice is disregarded, bullets are fired at night through his windows, bombs are thrown at his house, or his house is burned down (as in the case of Mr. Woods). In one case, an old man who had not left when ordered to do so was visited by a gang, who smashed everything in his cottage – every cup and every saucer, and then compelled him to leave the town, with his crippled son, the two of them destitute....The list of those proscribed is added to constantly, and every Protestant is simply waiting for his turn to come.[67]

Similar campaigns of what might be termed 'ethnic cleansing' were waged in parts of King's and Queen's Counties, South Tipperary, Leitrim, Mayo, Limerick, Westmeath, Louth and Cork.[68] Worst of all was the massacre of 14 men in West Cork in April, after an IRA officer had been killed breaking into a house.[69] Such events were often prompted by an unwavering belief in loyalist intrigue. The West Cork massacre was partly animated by the conviction that the victims had been plotting against the republic. Protestant houses in Mullingar were attacked by gunmen and arsonists and their inhabitants ordered to leave after a rumour was spread that 'the Protestant young men of the town have been drilling in fields in the neighbourhood'.[70] In each case, and in hundreds of lesser incidents, the language and intent was explicit: 'It is time they and their sort were out of the country!'[71] The simultaneous onset of civil war in the south and comparative peace in the north removed much of the pressure from Protestant communities in the south, but they continued to be favourite targets for anti-Free State reprisals up until the 1923 ceasefire.

Several points need to be made about the 1920–23 period as a whole. First, murder, arson and death-threats were a very small part of a much wider pattern of harassment and persecution. For every such case, there were a hundred raids, robberies or other attacks. Most rural and small-town Protestants spent these years in a constant state of anxiety, waiting for the next knock at the door. Would they want food, shelter, money, a horse or car – or something worse? Thousands of Protestant families had guerrillas billeted upon them for days or weeks at a time, even between the truce and the civil war. Some families maintained squatters on and off for years – a kind of IRA *dragonnade*.

This everyday violence went far beyond the IRA. Not all the members of that organisation – 'the three letter word' as it was cautiously known – were involved in robbery and extortion, but by no means everyone involved was a member. The revolution made Protestants 'fair game' to any of their neighbours, whether angry or covetous. While survivors of this period stress the number of Catholics who remained good neighbours, and it is clear that many disapproved of these attacks, it was Protestants and not their neighbours who were singled out for attention.

Attacks on churches, cemeteries, rectories and public buildings provide a further index of the growing sectarianism of nationalist violence. Almost beneath notice amidst the whirl of rebellion were the frequent acts of minor vandalism and harassment, as when 'young toughs' in Dublin stoned a Methodist church on the first anniversary of the Rising.[72] Beginning in the conscription crisis, however, churches were marked for destruction in order to intimidate or punish their congregations. Such was the case in Kilbonane, Co. Cork, when two Church of Ireland families refused to sign the anti-conscription pledge, and in nearby Mallow after a recruiting meeting.[73] Many later attacks appear to have no motive other than religious or ethnic animosity. At least three churches in Clare, and at least two in Sligo were burned before the truce, for example.[74] These were not 'official' acts of the IRA, but it is very likely that its members were involved. Other denominational targets included schools, orphanages and Freemasons' and Orange halls. At least nine Masonic lodges were burned, and a greater number were seized, looted and wrecked in the course of the 'troubles'.[75]

THE PROTESTANT EXODUS

The timing and context of population loss turn the census figures into a political and social event, and turn Protestant decline into a Protestant exodus. Almost all of the people who left did so between 1921 and 1924, in a sudden, massive upheaval. Police and other observers first noticed unusual levels of emigration and property sales in the spring and summer of 1921, in Leitrim, Sligo, Tipperary, Cork and King's County.[76] These continued through the year and rose dramatically in 1922, causing a minor refugee crisis in Britain.[77] The rate of departures apparently began to slow again in 1924 but by early 1926 nearly 40 per cent had gone for good.

This statistic captures only a fraction of the displacement caused by the revolution, however. From the winter of 1920 onwards, thousands of men spent many nights away from home, sleeping in barns or fields. While IRA volunteers were going on the run from their enemies, these people were on the run from the IRA. 'I know people – they never used to sleep inside their houses at all anytime, they just slept outside, and they were people minding their own business I'd say, they had no politics, no nothing.'[78] Hundreds of men and families left home altogether, for days, weeks or even years, returning when it seemed safe. Many did so more than once. One such was George Applebe Bryan, a Dunmanway merchant. He barely escaped being murdered in the West Cork massacre of April 1922 when his assassin's gun jammed. He hid and attempted to leave town next day by train (along with hundreds of other men throughout the region), but was prevented by an IRA picket. 'He took refuge in various friend's houses, changing every night, and eventually crossed to England.'[79] Bryan suffered a nervous breakdown but recovered enough to start a guest house in Bristol with his wife, supported by several relief agencies. His main concern throughout was to return home, which he attempted to do in June 1922 and finally did after the end of the civil war in 1923. Bryan's case can stand for many. These people did not leave quickly, easily or 'voluntarily'; they clung to their land or business for as long as possible. As remarkable as the number who left, therefore, is the number who stayed or returned.

All of the nightmare images of ethnic conflict in the twentieth century are here: the massacres and anonymous death squads, the burning homes and churches, the mass expulsions and trains filled with refugees, the transformation of lifelong neighbours into enemies, the conspiracy theories and the terminology of hatred. Munster, Leinster and Connaught can take their place with fellow imperial provinces Silesia, Galicia and Bosnia as part of the postwar 'unmixing of peoples' in Europe. We must not exaggerate. The Free State government had no part in persecution. Cork was not Smyrna, nor Belfast. Nevertheless, sectarianism was embedded in the Irish revolution, north and south. Any accounting of its violence and consequences must encompass the dreary steeples of Bandon and Ballinasloe as well as those of Fermanagh and Tyrone.[80]

NOTES

1. By 'Protestants' I refer to Protestant episcopalians, Presbyterians and Methodists, not including those described as 'others' in the census. For a discussion of the statistics of Protestant population loss, see R. E. Kennedy, *The Irish: Emigration, Marriage and Fertility* (Berkeley, 1973), pp. 110–38.
2. *Census of Ireland, 1926*, Vol. III, Part 1, Table 1.

3. Dorothy (Stopford) Price, 'Kilbrittain' (NLI, Dorothy Price Papers, Ms. 15,343[2]). See also L. O Broin, *Protestant Nationalists in Revolutionary Ireland: the Stopford Connection* (Dublin, 1985).
4. Dorothy Stopford letter, 9 Nov. 1921 (NLI, Dorothy Price Papers, Ms. 15,341[8]).
5. Stopford letter, 8 July 1921.
6. Stopford letter, 9 Nov. 1921.
7. John Bolster Barrett statement (PRONI, Southern Irish Loyalist Relief Association Papers, D989B/3/8). See also his file in the Irish Grants Committee Papers (PRO, CO/762/165).
8. The population loss for Leinster, Munster and Connaught alone was 37 per cent.
9. *Church of Ireland Gazette*, 26 Oct. 1923.
10. Reports of the Diocesan Board of Education, 1911–26 (Cork Diocesan Office Library).
11. These records are located in the Representative Church Body Library and in the Abbeystrewrey, Carrigrohane, Fanlobbus and Moviddy Parish Unions. I am grateful to their custodians for giving me access to them.
12. These figures include junior and adult members for Dublin, Waterford, Cork, Limerick and Sligo Districts, and are derived from the Methodist Church in Ireland Minutes of Conference, 1911–26 (Wesley Historical Society).
13. *Census of Ireland*, vol. X, pp. 46–7. Most British soldiers and sailors were unmarried and many who were, were married to Catholic women, with Catholic children.
14. *Census of Ireland*, vol. X, p. 46.
15. See W. B. Stanford, *A Recognized Church: the Church of Ireland in Eire* (1944), p. 16.
16. F. Moffett, *I Also Am Of Ireland* (London, 1985), p. 83.
17. Elizabeth, Countess of Fingall, *Seventy Years Young* (London, 1937), p. 386.
18. D. Fitzpatrick, 'The Logic of Collective Sacrifice: Ireland and the British Army, 1914–1918', *Historical Journal*, forthcoming. See also P. Codd, 'Recruiting and Responses to the War in Wexford', in D. Fitzpatrick (ed.), *Ireland and the First World War* (Dublin, 1986), pp. 18–19; T. Dooley, 'Monaghan Protestants in a Time of Crisis, 1919–22', in R. V. Comerford, M. Cullen, J. Hill and C. Lennon (eds), *Religion, Conflict and Coexistence in Ireland* (Dublin, 1990), pp. 236–7.
19. For the UVF, see B. MacGiolla Choille, *Intelligence Notes 1913–16* (Dublin, 1966), pp. 8–9, 74–5, 100–2. A few companies of Ulster Volunteers were formed in Leitrim in 1914. For Protestant vigilante groups in the 1920s, see CI Monthly Reports for Monaghan and Cavan, July 1920 (CO/904/112) and for Monaghan, Feb., Mar. 1921 (CO/904/116); H. V. Ross, 'Partition and Protestants in Monaghan 1911–26' (UCD MA, 1983), pp. 19–20.
20. J. H. Bernard to Lloyd George, 3 June 1916 (B.L., John Henry Bernard Papers, Add. Ms.52781).
21. P. Buckland, *Irish Unionism I: The Anglo-Irish and the New Ireland 1885–1922* (Dublin, 1972), pp. 18–21; D. Fitzpatrick, *Politics and Irish Life*

1913–21: Provincial Experience of War and Revolution (Dublin, 1977), pp. 57–8.

22. See J. M. Wilson's notes from a tour of Ireland in 1916 (PRONI, D989A/9/7).

23. For Albinia Brodrick, daughter of Lord Midleton and cousin of Lord Bandon, see Mark Bence-Jones, *Twilight of the Ascendency* (London, 1987), pp. 107–8, 211.

24. Royal Gloucestershire Regiment Archives, Lt R. M. Grazebrook diary, 1 Oct. 1921.

25. John Regan memoirs, pp. 157–9 (PRONI, D.3160). For a much more detailed discussion of the IRA, intelligence and informers, see P. Hart, *The Irish Republican Army and Its Enemies: Violence and Community in County Cork, 1916–1923* (forthcoming).

26. J. D. Brewer, *The Royal Irish Constabulary: An Oral History* (Belfast, 1990), p. 82.

27. GHQ Ireland, *Record of the Rebellion in Ireland in 1920–21*, ii, p. 16 (IWM, Sir Hugh Jeudwine papers).

28. *A History of the 5th Division in Ireland*, Appendix XIV (Jeudwine Papers).

29. Extracts from reports quoted in Gen. Macready to Miss Stevenson, 20 June 1921 (HLRO, Lloyd George Papers, F/36/2/19).

30. Interview with C.R., 25 Oct. 1993.

31. Interview with B.T., 9 Nov. 1994.

32. Interviews with R.G and G.D., 17, 18 April 1993.

33. Interview with W.M., 17 Apr. 1993.

34. See C. G. Bloodworth, 'Talking Past Differences: Conflict, Community and History in an Irish Parish' (Cornell University PhD, 1988), pp. 260–2.

35. Interview with R.G.

36. Interview with G.H., 17 Apr. 1993.

37. Interview with G.D.

38. Sanford, p. 16.

39. Interviews with K.O., 20 April 1993, R.G. and T.N., 17 Nov. 1994.

40. James McDougall statement (PRO, Irish Grants Committee Papers, CO/762/112).

41. O Broin, p. 177.

42. The complete files can be found in the Irish Grants Committee Papers (CO/762).

43. Interview with F. B., 6 Dec. 1993. For similar opinions, see B. Inglis, *West Briton* (London, 1962), p. 31; Moffett, pp. 102–5; Edith Somerville diary, 12–13 Dec. 1920 and 24 June 1921 (Queen's University Special Collections, Somerville and Ross Papers); E. M. Ussher, 'The True Story of a Revolution', pp. 36, 58 (TCD, Ms.9269).

44. R. Harris, *Prejudice and Tolerance in Ulster: A Study of Neighbours and 'Strangers' in a Border Community* (Manchester, 1972), pp. 188–9.

45. W. G. Neely, *Kilcooley: Land and People in Tipperary* (1983), p. 140.

46. County Inspector's Monthly Reports for Cork [East Riding], Apr.–Nov. 1918 (CO/904/105–7).

47. This and following quotations are from R.M. *précis* 1914 (CO/904/227). Not every respondent was so pessimistic: the Wexford RM reported that 'if anything, there is a disposition among Catholics to go out of their way to be fair'.

48. *Cork Constitution*, 19 Jan. 1914. See also Fitzpatrick, *Politics and Irish Life*, pp. 57–8.
49. Except possibly in Enniscorthy, where the rector dated the population decline from the Volunteer occupation during Easter week. H. C. Lyster, *An Irish Parish in Changing Days* (London, 1933), pp. 117–18. See also S. F. Glenfield, `The Protestant Population of South-East Leinster, 1834–1981' (TCD M. Litt., 1991).
50. *Cork Examiner*, 19 Dec. 1918. See also *Irish Times*, 2 Jan., 2 Apr., 30 Oct. 1919.
51. Irish Command Weekly Intelligence Survey, 11 June 1918 (IWM, Lord Loch Papers).
52. Letter from Drinagh 20 May 1918 (Censorship summaries, CO/904/169).
53. CI Monthly Report, June 1918 (CO/904/106). See also CI Monthly Reports, Wicklow, April 1918; Galway [East Riding], Cork [East Riding] and Kerry, June, July 1918; Longford, Aug. 1918 (CO/904/105–7). Also, *Irish Times*, 15 June, 21 Aug. 1918; 7 Jan. 1919.
54. Rev. Jasper Joly to Canon Jesson, 1 May 1918 (HLRO, Bonar Law Papers, 83/3/7).
55. These figures have been assembled from a wide variety of sources, most importantly the *Cork Examiner*, *Irish Times* and RIC, British, National and Irish Republican army reports. For a further discussion of sources and the nature of IRA violence, see Hart, *The Irish Republican Army and Its Enemies*.
56. See Hart, *The Irish Republican Army and Its Enemies*.
57. Interview with B. T.
58. L. Fleming, *Head or Harp* (London, 1965), p. 52.
59. Interview with G.D., 19 April 1993.
60. CI Monthly Report, Tipperary [South Riding], April 1921 (CO/904/115).
61. *Irish Times*, 4 Oct. 1921.
62. See GHQ memo on the protection of loyalists, 31 Oct. 1921 and associated correspondence in PRO, WO/35/180B.
63. *Dail Eireann Official Report: Debate on the Treaty between Great Britain and Ireland* (Dublin, n.d.), p. 146.
64. Proceedings of the House of Lords, vol. 51, col. 889 (May 11, 1922).
65. See Adj., West Mayo Bde. to Major Browne, 29 April 1922 (Dept. of Taoiseach General Files, S565).
66. Rev. T. Stirling Berrym to Min. of Home Affairs, 10 June 1922 (NA, Dept. of Justice Papers, H5/372).
67. *Church of Ireland Gazette*, 16 June 1922.
68. See *Irish Times*, 2, 4, 19, 27 May, 13, 15, 17, 22 June, 8 July 1922; *Belfast News-Letter*, 13 June 1922; *Morning Post*, 1 May 1922.
69. For a detailed reconstruction of this massacre, see Hart, *The Irish Republican Army and Its Enemies*.
70. *Belfast News-Letter*, 13 June 1922.
71. Memo: 'Land agitation in the Queen's County', n.d. (Dept. of Taoiseach General Files, S566).
72. *Irish Times*, 10 Apr. 1917.
73. CI Monthly Report, Cork [East Riding], July 1918 (CO/904/106); *Cork Examiner*, 28, 30 Oct. 1918.

74.   For Clare, see Fitzpatrick, *Politics and Irish Life*, p. 78; for Sligo, see *Irish Times*, 31 July, 27 Aug. 1920.
75.   See the Annual Reports of the Grand Lodge of Freemasons of Ireland, 1920–23; *Irish Times*, 20 May 1922.
76.   CI Monthly Reports, Leitrim, Sligo, Kerry, Tipperary [South Riding], April 1921; Cork [East and West Ridings], June 1921; King's, August 1921 (CO/904/115–16). See also *Irish Times*, 22 Oct. 1921.
77.   See *First Interim Report of the Irish Distress Committee* (HMSO, 1922) and the Report of the Irish Grants Committee, 1930 (CO/762/212).
78.   Interview with D.J., 21 April 1993.
79.   George Applebe Bryan statement (Dunedin Committee Papers, CO//905/17). See also 'Compensation for Southern Irish Loyalists: Typical Cases for the Committee of Enquiry' (SILRA Papers, D989B/2/11) and C. Albert Paine to Sec., Min. of Finance, 20 June 1922 (NA, Dept. of Finance Records, FIN 665/6).
80.   I would like to acknowledge the support of the Social Sciences and Humanities Research Council of Canada and the Institute of Social and Economic Research, Memorial University of Newfoundland, in carrying out this research.

6 The Twinge of Memory: Armistice Day and Remembrance Sunday in Dublin since 1919

Jane Leonard

The cultural historian Adrian Gregory has found that the 'silence of memory', even though it only lasted two minutes, provided a unifying refuge and a rallying point for the bereaved and demobilised of interwar Britain.[1] In Ireland, no such unity was found. A wartime uprising and intensified independence struggle meant that Irish veterans (almost 200 000 in number) came home in 1919 to find themselves suspect in the eyes of republicans for their war service.[2] Division rather than dignity surrounded the commemoration of the war in Ireland. On the streets of Dublin, 11 November was marred by noisy protests, riots and bombings while the state's attitude towards participation or abstention was frequently ambivalent and contradictory.

This twinge of memory in postwar Dublin is epitomised by the poppy-snatching that disturbed the silence of 11 November and in the confusion of those whose memories of remembering were compromised by later events. A recent interview with the daughter of an ex-soldier about Armistice Day in interwar Dublin showed how private memories can jar with contemporary public sensitivities:

They used to have poppy collections in Sandymount when I was a child. [Q: Door to door?]
No, at the church. I'm almost certain. It's like a dream to me that they did this. Poppies weren't then a forbidden thing in Sandymount. Maybe I'm wrong but it's like a dream to me that I remember going to Mass as a child in the Star of the Sea Church in Sandymount and seeing people selling poppies....I remember, in later years, feeling that the poppy wasn't the thing to wear....I don't think you could get poppies here in later years. So that's what strikes me, that the poppy was part of my

99

childhood....I suppose, maybe, with the Troubles and the IRA, you wouldn't be that keen to be wearing a poppy nowadays. You'd be aggravating the situation.[3]

There is a consensus in recent research on the impact and memory of the Great War in Ireland that it evoked only an official and popular amnesia in the southern part of the island. Keith Jeffery's absorbing survey of war commemoration in interwar Ireland concluded that there was a 'considerable degree of collective disengagement' in the Irish Free State while David Officer has suggested that public commemoration there was 'driven to the periphery as it was seen by nationalists as an unfortunate if not distasteful reminder that so many Irishmen died fighting for the British cause'. George Boyce has argued that Eamon de Valera's election in 1932 led to the elimination of both the war dead and the survivors from the Irish mind. All of these views omit conflicting evidence such as the high poppy sales and expanding British Legion network in the Free State and the large Armistice parades which continued to be held throughout the 1930s and (on a smaller scale) in the quarter-century from the ending of the Second World War until the Northern Ireland conflict halted them in 1971. Nor is Boyce's additional claim that only in Ulster were war memorials used to reaffirm political and cultural values entirely true as it omits the former home rulers and southern unionists whose gatherings at southern monuments, war graves and Legion parades equally re-dedicated old loyalties.[4]

This chapter will examine four aspects of war commemoration in Dublin to show how it evoked embarrassment and resentment rather than amnesia on the part of the southern state. It first surveys the different forms and phases of the main public ceremony held on 11 November (and, from 1945, on the Sunday nearest that date) from 1919 to the present. This is followed by an analysis of the characteristics of the anniversary and, in particular, of the tension and confrontation surrounding the November parades in the interwar and Emergency period. Thirdly, the early 1980s controversy over state and army representation is examined in the context of the ambivalence that has characterised official policy regarding the ceremony since the 1920s. In particular, the government's consistent endorsement of full external commemoration (by instructing its diplomats to attend remembrance ceremonies outside Ireland) is contrasted with its shifting policy of either minimal involvement or total boycott of the Dublin ceremony. Lastly, the impact of recent events (including the Enniskillen IRA bombing of 1987 and the paramilitary ceasefires of 1994) on official and popular attitudes within the Republic to war commemoration is assessed.

I

The first anniversary of the Armistice was marked by spontaneous gatherings in cities, towns and villages throughout the British Isles. Transport companies halted services for two minutes at 11 a.m. and work stopped in factories, offices, shops and fields.[5] In Ireland, where peacetime conditions were still unknown, the armistice was not widely observed on the streets. However, in line with a Papal decree, a Mass for the war dead was said in every Roman Catholic church. In a letter of 10 November 1919 to the archbishop of Dublin, Fr Laurence Stafford (an ex-chaplain) wrote: 'it didn't need the King's two minutes to remind some of us of the great armistice of this time last year (and the relief it brought) and of the part of the world war we happened to be in at the time'. [6]

Members of the pro-government ex-service organisation, the Comrades of the Great War, paraded alongside British soldiers and members of the Royal Irish Constabulary in town squares, barracks and railway stations. Other veterans' groups such as the Federation of Discharged and Demobilised Soldiers and Sailors and the Irish Nationalist Veterans Association (INVA) did not join in the official silence, echoing their boycott of the official Peace Day celebrations in July 1919. These abstentions were prompted by dissatisfaction with general official policy towards ex-servicemen and with the failure to provide self-government for Ireland.[7]

The INVA held a strikingly separatist commemoration in Dublin on 12 November 1919. Following Mass at the Carmelite Church in Clarendon Street (significantly chosen for its links with Daniel O'Connell and nineteenth-century nationalism), INVA members marched to the Parnell monument at the top of O'Connell Street. Alongside a banner marked with the dates 1782 and 1913 (commemorating the establishment of the Irish Volunteers) were the tattered flags of the 16th (Irish) Division preserved from the Western Front (embroidered with regimental crests, Celtic motifs and Irish phrases). The marchers wore ivy-leaf emblems (the symbol adopted by Parnellite supporters) and white flowers. This was the only specifically nationalist commemoration of the armistice in Dublin and was not repeated in subsequent years.[8] The INVA's membership largely transferred into the more powerful veterans' groups which eventually merged into the British Legion (Irish Free State Area) in 1925.

One pattern established on 11 November 1919 was the halting of traffic in central Dublin by undergraduates from Trinity College in order to enforce the two-minutes' silence. When they sang 'God Save The King', students from University College Dublin responded with the Sinn Fein anthem 'The Soldiers'Song'.[9]

Armistice Day clashes between the two colleges became a feature of interwar November in Dublin. In 1925, the British Legion parade to St Stephen's Green was disrupted by fire-bombs set off by UCD students. In a statement of regret, the college president reminded students of the five hundred from UCD who had served in the war. An ex-service graduate, Michael Gilvarry, returned his degrees in protest at the disruption, noting that for those who remembered 'other Novembers, those of '14, '15, '16, '17 and '18....the two minutes silence is as sacred as any part of a religious service'.[10]

Tensions between the two colleges continued to be inflamed by war commemoration. In 1932, TCD students thrust the muzzle of a captured German cannon through the college railings to taunt UCD students locked outside. In May 1945, Trinity students marked VE day by flying Allied flags over the college and burning the Irish tricolour. In response, two UCD students (one a future Fianna Fail Taoiseach, Charles Haughey) burnt a Union Jack in College Green. While differences in the perceived political ethos of the two universities clearly fuelled these clashes, so too did other November rituals such as Kevin Barry commemorations in UCD (an IRA student activist executed in November 1920), the colours rugby match and the TCD rag week.[11]

Student scuffles apart, Armistice Day attracted little popular reaction or press coverage in the 1919–22 period. The increased street violence and curfews of the later stages of the Anglo-Irish war and the Irish Civil War reduced the urge to mark or disrupt the anniversary. The first Armistice Day in Dublin under genuine peacetime conditions was 1923. As before, Trinity students blocked off College Green. Thousands assembled there following Mass in the Pro-Cathedral and a service in St Patrick's Church of Ireland Cathedral. A hundred and fifty thousand poppies were sold in Dublin. The same venue was used in 1924 when 20 000 veterans assembled to mark the silence in front of a crowd estimated at 50 000. The British Legion announced that almost 500 000 poppies were sold in the Dublin area that year. Fighting between republicans and ex-servicemen and the disruption to traffic resulted in the ceremony (now stewarded by the British Legion) being moved in 1926 onwards to a less central site in the Phoenix Park.[12]

The ceremony was held there until 1939 when it was moved to the newly built Irish National War Memorial Park at Islandbridge on the opposite side of the River Liffey. The mustering of ex-servicemen on Bachelor's Walk for the long march along the quays towards the Phoenix Park and (after 1939) towards Islandbridge became a feature of November in Dublin until the early 1970s. The only interruption to these parades was during the Second World War years when they were banned as constituting a violation of Irish neutrality. From 1939 to 1944 ex-servicemen assembled inside the memorial park and obeyed police restrictions on displaying emblems and on poppy sales. British Legion banners which featured a Union Jack set into the corner had to be furled during the war. The ban on parading was rescinded in November 1945 in the face of anticipated protests from Allied servicemen on leave in Dublin who were keen to mark the new peace.[13]

The parade to Islandbridge was always preceded by a Mass in the Pro-Cathedral and by an Anglican service in St Patrick's Cathedral. This pattern continued until 1970. On police advice in 1971, following a number of attacks on Legion branches and on the offices of ex-service charities, the parade was cancelled. The main Remembrance Sunday ceremony in Dublin since 1971 has consisted of an ecumenical service at St Patrick's. The preacher at the Remembrance Sunday service in St Patrick's is usually an ex-British Army chaplain. The choice of preacher rotates between Roman Catholic and Protestant clergy. The Pro-Cathedral Mass also ceased in 1970. Since 1978, a Mass organised by the central Dublin branch of the British Legion has been held in a smaller church on the Friday before Remembrance Sunday.[14]

II

A key characteristic of Armistice Day in Ireland is that observance of the two minutes' silence was not always voluntary. In the 1919–21 period, Auxiliary police cadets posted notices ordering shopkeepers to close on 11 November in memory of Crown forces killed in Ireland as well as in memory of the Great War dead. Such orders were seen as a provocation similar to closing shops on the days of military and RIC funerals. Attempts to enforce the silence in November 1919 and 1920 or to protect those wishing to remember in post-1922 Ireland equally required heavy policing.[15]

Interwar Dublin was an extremely unnerving and dangerous place to wear service medals or poppies. Parading veterans were heckled and beaten up. Legion bandsmen had their instruments stolen on the eve of parades. Poppy depots and sellers were robbed or had their stock damaged. Extremes of intimidation included bomb and arson attacks on Legion halls and poppy depots. In early November 1927, the Great Southern Railway opened a Legion hut at Inchicore for its ex-service employees. The hut was burnt down less than a week later, on the eve of

Armistice Day. Two years later, again in November, the rebuilt hall was blown up.[16]

The rituals of distributing and wearing poppies differed sharply in Ireland from in Britain. Locked doors and passwords ruled access to Irish poppy depots. Poppies were sold by women instead of by disabled veterans as it was felt that women were less likely to be attacked. One newspaper reported with satisfaction in 1924 how a poppy-seller had hit an assailant in the face with her collection box. To discourage snatching, poppy wearers inserted razor blades into the flowers.[17]

There were crude attempts by republicans to censor the popular culture of the anniversary. Newspapers were warned not to publish photos of Armistice Day parades and cinemas were boycotted if they showed war films. When the Masterpiece Cinema in Talbot Street showed *Ypres* in November 1925, the print of the film was stolen. Another print was obtained, but when screenings resumed, the cinema was bombed. Two Gardai on protective duty (one an actual veteran of Ypres) outside the cinema were injured in the attack. Shop windows displaying poppies and Union Jacks were smashed. *An Phoblacht* attacked the 'subdued jingoism' of schools such as Belvedere College and the Sacred Heart Convent in Leeson Street which observed the two-minutes silence while the Irish-American press criticised firms like Jacobs Factory (run by a 'loyalist quaker oligarchy') for stopping work at 11 a.m.[18]

Anti-war rallies and alternative Armistice Day parades were organised from the mid-1920s onwards by groups such as the Anti-Imperialist League and Republican Congress. These parades regularly highlighted the plight of unemployed ex-servicemen in Ireland and alleged the British Legion was only concerned with ceremonial functions. Leading Fianna Fail members such as Eamonn de Valera, who addressed an Anti-Imperialist rally in Dublin on 10 November 1930, urged veterans to boycott the official Armistice events.[19]

Opponents of Armistice Day in Dublin claimed it commemorated the former British presence rather than the Irish dead of the Great War. Certain aspects of the day (especially the open-air singing of 'God Save The King' which continued until the 1950s) appealed especially to southern unionists. In the area around Grafton Street and Dame Street where banks and institutions still retaining a pro-British ethos predominated, Union Jacks were flown during the week of Armistice Day. Such premises included the Kildare Street Club, the United Services Club, the Royal Irish Automobile Club and large shops such as Brown, Thomas and Switzer. Elsewhere in the Free State, war memorials were draped with Union Jacks prior to unveiling. Reporting on the 1925 Dublin Armistice Day, the

British Legion Journal praised Irish veterans for remaining 'steadfast in their faith of England and the empire'.[20]

Other political loyalties were reaffirmed on 11 November. In Wexford, the Major Willie Redmond branch of the Legion concluded its 1922 parade by laying a wreath at the grave of his brother, John. The increased display of poppies in Wexford and in the other Redmondite heartland, Waterford City, led a former nationalist politician (and ex-officer) to comment in November 1923 that 'the nationalist element in Ireland which did not like Sinn Fein and Sinn Fein's methods tends to find a rallying point in the organisation of ex-servicemen'.[21]

III

The most striking characteristic of Remembrance Sunday in Dublin in recent years is the vaccillating participation of the Irish government and defence forces. This depended on who was in power and was extensively debated in the Irish media both during the early 1980s and in the aftermath of the 1987 Remembrance Sunday bombing in Enniskillen. An outline of the extent to which the Irish state was officially represented at commemoration ceremonies prior to the 1980s is necessary to put these debates in proper context.

The first Free State government was nervous about commemorating a war fought under British rule. The cabinet ruled in 1924 that it was inopportune for the Governor-General and President of the Executive Council to be associated with Armistice Day ceremonies in Dublin. However, representatives of both attended and placed wreaths annually from 1924 to 1932. The President of the Executive Council was represented by a member of the Oireachtas. A wreath was also laid each year at the London Cenotaph by the Irish High Commissioner. President William T. Cosgrave himself declined an invitation to a Dominion Prime Ministers' ceremony at the London Cenotaph in November 1926 on the grounds that as he had been interned by the British during the war he would not be an appropriate choice. Instead he nominated his Justice Minister, Kevin O'Higgins, whose brother had been killed in the war.[22]

However, participation was sanctioned on less prominent occasions. In November 1923, Cosgrave and several cabinet colleagues attended an Armistice Day Mass in Cork city. A number of Cumann na nGaedhael and Fine Gael politicians attended Armistice parades or were patrons of British Legion branches throughout the 1920s and 1930s, among them the Kildare TD, Capt. Sidney Minch, who was also on the British Legion's national executive and the Irish Free State's delegate to the British Empire Service League.[23]

Though the Free State government was reluctant to openly endorse war commemoration and re-sited the planned Irish national war memorial from Merrion Square (opposite Government Buildings) to remoter Islandbridge, its diplomats fully participated in Armistice Day ceremonies in London and throughout the Dominions. In 1926, when a memorial to Irish regiments was dedicated in Flanders, the Free State Minister in Brussels, Count Gerald O'Kelly, an ex-British officer, carried the Irish flag and spoke at the unveiling.[24]

This policy of full external participation in war commemoration was maintained by the new Fianna Fail government after 1932. While official representation at Armistice Day in Dublin ceased after November 1933, the Irish High Commissioner continued to lay a wreath at the London Cenotaph until the Second World War. This policy of remembering the war when outside Ireland was arguably initiated by the leader of Fianna Fail, Eamon De Valera. When fundraising for Sinn Fein in the USA in 1919 and 1920, he regularly attended functions organised by war veterans at which he praised the sacrifices of Irish-American units and Irish regiments of the British Army. While Sinn Fein at home was opposing war commemoration (the IRA bombed war memorials in Cork and Kerry in 1919), its propaganda bureau in Washington encouraged donations to the Irish National War Memorial Fund (which eventually built Islandbridge) and to Cardinal Bourne's scheme to build a memorial to the Irish Catholic war dead in Westminster Cathedral. Such a memorial sited beside the British parliament would reinforce the message that Irish nationalists deserved independence, or so Sinn Fein (in America) claimed.[25]

After 1932, the Irish government distanced itself from all commemorative ceremonies inside the state. Restrictions on parading, wearing uniforms or displaying emblems and flags applied equally to the British Legionnaires in the Phoenix Park as they did to Blueshirts at Beal na mBlath or Saor Eire members at Bodenstown. Permits for the sale of poppies, previously allowed for several days in the week before 11 November, were now issued for one day only. The crisis in Europe provided the government with an excuse for postponing the official dedication of the Irish National War Memorial at Islandbridge while the policy of neutrality justified the banning of Armistice Day parades during the Second World War.

The IRA's border campaign in the mid-1950s followed by the resumed conflict in Northern Ireland after 1969 dramatically lowered the profile of both Remembrance Sunday and Legion activity generally in the Republic.

Threats, bomb-scares and actual attacks resulted in extensive branch closures and the cessation of parades, Masses and annual fund-raising events. From the early 1970s onwards, war commemoration in the Republic was largely confined to Protestant church services.[26]

The cabinet has always decided whether the President attends or is represented at the Remembrance Sunday service in St Patrick's Cathedral, just as with earlier rulings about the role of the Governor-General on 11 November. In line with a government ruling, President Patrick Hillery rejected a British Legion invitation to the 1980 Remembrance Sunday service. Ex-servicemen and relatives of Irishmen killed in both world wars particularly resented Hillery's explanation that he did not attend the ceremonies of foreign armies. Although Hillery was merely repeating the government's view of the service (as indicated in a brief he had been sent by the Taoiseach's staff), the outcry at the remark forced the Taoiseach, Charles Haughey, to send a junior minister, Sean Moore, as the government's representative. Hillery was embarrassed by this *volte-face* which he later described as having been dropped through a trap-door.[27]

A senior Fianna Fail politician, the Defence Minister, James Tully, represented the government at the 1981 service. However, the deterioration in Anglo-Irish relations following the IRA hunger-strikes that year and the Irish government's neutral stance during the Falklands War in 1982 ended this brief Fianna Fail commemoration of the Irish war dead. The government declined invitations to attend St Patrick's Cathedral in November 1982.

By the autumn of 1983, a Fine Gael and Labour coalition government was in power. Individual Fine Gael politicians had a tradition of attending Remembrance Sunday, especially those representing former garrison towns or previous Redmondite strongholds such as Waterford City. Labour TDs attending the St Patrick's Cathedral service or participating in the re-dedication of war memorials have included Emmet Stagg and Jim Kemmy whose constituencies of Kildare and East Limerick retain strong folk memories of the British garrison presence and of participation in the two world wars.

Moves towards fuller official participation in war commemoration have thus seemed more likely under Fine Gael and Labour coalition governments than under Fianna Fail. In 1983, the British Legion decided to broaden the scope of the Remembrance Sunday service to commemorate Irish casualties in all wars, including those incurred on service with the United Nations. The coalition government endorsed the Legion's accompanying decision to invite the Irish Defence Forces to play a major role in the November ceremony.

This decision prompted several weeks of controversy in the Dublin newspapers and on RTE. Commentators on the propriety of officially commemorating Irish participation in both world wars included veterans of the Great War and of the IRA, Holocaust survivors and anti-nuclear campaigners. The hostility shown towards the British Legion's existence in the Republic was refuted by comparison of its charitable role with that of the St Vincent de Paul Society. One letter-writer felt that as a British organisation, the Legion posed no more threat to Irish sovereignty than the Automobile Association.

The main objections to army involvement came from Fianna Fail and independent republicans like Neil Blaney and Kevin Boland and from some retired officers. Protest meetings were organised by the Organisation of National Ex-Servicemen (the Irish army's equivalent of the British Legion) at which fears were expressed that this involvement revealed a willingness on the part of the Irish army to join NATO. An *Irish Times* editorial on 18 October pointed out that even if NATO membership was under consideration, 'the common church worship of men in green and those who wore khaki or blue is hardly sinister'.[28]

In fact, this projected official participation simply cemented a long-standing informal involvement in commemoration. The residents of ex-British service housing schemes in Killester and Clontarf during the 1920s included a couple of serving Free State army officers, who regularly paraded with their neighbours on Armistice Day. At Killester's Armistice Day parade in 1923, two uniformed Free State army buglers sounded the Last Post while elsewhere in Dublin, press reports noted that poppies were worn by some Free State soldiers. By the mid-1920s, soldiers and police were officially instructed not to wear poppies or Great War medals while in uniform.[29]

Such displays of previous allegiances embarrassed those who sought an Irish army ethos free of British garrison echoes. However, relations between the army and the British ex-service movement have always been good. This dates from the early days of the Civil War in 1922 when the Legion of Irish Ex-Servicemen (later part of the British Legion) liaised with Michael Collins and Emmet Dalton in recruiting senior ex-British NCOs and officers for the Free State army.

Likewise during the state's next major emergency, the Second World War, the British Legion encouraged its southern Irish members to join the regular Irish army or the Local Defence Force. Relations between senior Irish officers and retired British army officers remained cordial in the postwar era. Shared United Nations peacekeeping tours and common membership of groups such as the Military History Society of Ireland strengthened these bonds. The Irish army had appreciated the British Legion and the Church of Ireland's gesture of solidarity on Remembrance Sunday in 1960 when prayers and a minute's silence in memory of Irish UN peacekeepers killed in Niemba that day were incorporated into the service.[30]

One of the striking aspects of the 1983 Remembrance Service was that the senior defence personnel participating included Brigadier James Connolly, the Air Corps commanding officer who was a grandson of the 1916 leader. The Gardai were also officially represented for the first time. The German ambassador laid a wreath in St Patrick's Cathedral and a British Embassy diplomat reciprocated at the German War Cemetery in Glencree, County Wicklow. The Irish army (which had unofficially attended the German commemorative service in previous years) also sent an official delegation to Glencree.[31]

IV

During the next three years of coalition government, the presence of ministers and army officers in St Patrick's attracted little attention. There were no fundamental policy shifts on commemoration until 1987 when Fianna Fail won the general election. One of the major criticisms levied at the Irish government in the wake of the Enniskillen IRA bombing on Remembrance Sunday 1987 was that it was not represented at the St Patrick's Cathedral service that afternoon (the bomb exploded in the morning). Had a cabinet minister attended the main ceremony in the Republic, as the *Irish Times* columnist, Mary Holland, observed afterwards, it would have helped articulate popular outrage and grief. A further opportunity for expressing southern empathy with the people of Enniskillen was lost when no government representative was sent to the town's second Remembrance Sunday service held a few weeks later or to the following year's services in both Dublin and Enniskillen.[32]

However, one legacy of Enniskillen has been a renewed interest in the Republic in the Irish who served in both wars and in the condition of the monuments and institutions that strove to perpetrate their memory. The Irish National War Memorial at Islandbridge, derelict since the Troubles caused the cancellation of all ceremonies there in 1971, was seen as an appropriate symbol of forgetfulness and the government and British Legion jointly funded a restoration programme. However, as with the opening of the original park in 1939, the Fianna Fail government in 1988 declined to attend the rededication of the park. Media interest in the reopening was high. A documentary made by Gay Byrne (son of an ex-soldier) was broadcast when the park reopened in September 1988. On subsequent programmes that autumn, Byrne pledged that he would wear a poppy in memory both of his father and of the Enniskillen dead on the *Late Late Show* in November that year.

Protest phone-calls and threats resulted in Byrne having to back down on this pledge. But poppies were worn publicly by many in the Republic in 1988. Prior to the cancellation of street sales of poppies in 1971, approximately 25 000 were sold annually in the Republic. When street sales resumed in certain parts of Counties Dublin and Wicklow in 1988, over 45 000 were sold. Poppy sales in the Republic have steadily increased since then.[33]

One of the ironies of Enniskillen has been that the bombing which aimed to obliterate those remembering in a northern Irish town subsequently propelled some southern towns into a cultural and practical reclamation of their own forgotten communities. A number of war memorials have been restored since 1987 while five British Legion branches have reopened (during the 1971–76 period, over forty Legion branches closed). Limerick city provides a useful example. Its Mayor was the only politician from the Republic to attend the Enniskillen funerals. In 1989, the reopened Limerick branch of the Legion held a Remembrance Sunday Mass and parade, and in 1992 the Labour TD and then Mayor, Jim Kemmy, officiated at the rededication of the city war memorial (blown up in 1957). Relations between this branch and the Patrick Sarsfield branch of the ONE are extremely cordial. They jointly participated in the war memorial rededication and even shared premises for a period. This new rapport is in striking contrast with the tension of the 1983 era when the ONE was strongly opposed to the Irish army participating in Remembrance Sunday. Since Enniskillen, the ONE has also been represented at Remembrance Sunday services in Dublin.[34]

Another post-Enniskillen change has been the increased interest shown by local history societies, museums and theatres in publishing books and staging exhibitions and productions on aspects of Irish involvement in both world wars. On 11 November 1988, the Eamon de Valera Library in Ennis, Co. Clare, staged an exhibition and lecture series on the Great War. Echoes of Armistice Day services during the library building's earlier life as Ennis Presbyterian Church were perhaps heard. More recently, the culture of war commemoration has been linked directly to the peace process in Northern Ireland. The Frank McGuinness play, *Observe the Sons of Ulster Marching towards the Somme*, which played to a packed Abbey Theatre in the mid-1980s, was revived there in

October 1994, as the Dublin Theatre Festival's gesture of solidarity with the ceasefires.[35]

Prior to the paramilitary ceasefires of 1994, two events signalled fundamental change in political attitudes to war commemoration in the Republic. The first was the Remembrance Sunday service of 1993. As this service particularly marked the seventy-fifth anniversary of the ending of the Great War, the Irish government permitted President Mary Robinson to attend. This was the first time that the head of state had been present. An article in the *Evening Press* entitled 'At Long Last' saw her presence as symbolically restoring the Irish nationality of previously forgotten generations who served in both world wars. Potential criticism from republicans was deflected by the fact that President Robinson had attended a similar ceremony in 1991 to mark the seventy-fifth anniversary of the Easter Rising.[36]

The second event was the final completion of the Irish National War Memorial in July 1994. In the late 1930s, Fianna Fail had ruled against an official opening ceremony. In 1994 the party's Minister for Finance, Bertie Ahern, formally declared the park open and complete. An *Irish Times* columnist, Kevin Myers, applauded Ahern's presence as signifying 'a change in attitude towards Irishness, in definitions of what it is to be Irish and how many forms of Irishness there can be without betrayal of anybody or anything.'[37]

Similar sentiments were expressed in April 1995 when the new Fine Gael Taoiseach, John Bruton, commended active Irish participation in the Second World War at a VE commemoration at Islandbridge attended by war veterans and Holocaust survivors. Also present were the Northern Ireland Secretary of State, Sir Patrick Mayhew and politicians from northern and southern parties, including Fianna Fail and the Ulster Unionist Party. The presence of the Sinn Fein chairman, Tom Hartley, was widely praised. Just as the ceasefires had prompted increased participation by nationalist politicians and Catholic clergy in Remembrance Sunday services in Northern Ireland in November 1994, they were seen as having facilitated this unified commemoration and also the long-term construction of what an *Irish Times* editorial termed 'the politics of normality'.[38]

The politics of commemoration are universally conditioned by subsequent wars, rebellions, alliances and armistices. Southern Irish veterans and war bereaved were deeply scarred by their state's reluctance to acknowledge participation in both world wars.[39] Examination of the war commemoration issue (especially in the interwar era) helps us to appreciate the significance of both the southern unionist tradition and that of constitutional nationalists who valued these rituals. It also might help to

112   *Unionism in Modern Ireland*

explain northern unionist fears in the past that all manifestations of Britishness would be severely threatened in a united Ireland. Perhaps the fractures caused in Ireland by ambivalent southern policy on commemorating 1914–18 and 1939–45 may itself condition a policy of inclusive recording and memorialising of the casualties and survivors of the 1969–94 northern conflict.[40]

NOTES

1. Adrian Gregory, *The Silence of Memory. Armistice Day 1919–46* (Oxford, 1994).
2. For participation and demobilisation statistics, see David Fitzpatrick, 'Militarism in Ireland, 1900–22', in T. Bartlett and K. Jeffery, *A Military History of Ireland* (Cambridge, 1996).
3. Interview with Marjory W., Dublin, June 1993.
4. Keith Jeffery, 'The Great War in modern Irish memory' in T. G. Fraser and K. Jeffery (eds), *Men, Women and War* (Dublin, 1993); David Officer, 'Representing war: the Somme heritage centre' in *History Ireland*, Vol. 3, No. 1, Spring 1995, 42; George Boyce, 'Ireland and the First World War' in *History Ireland*, Vol. 2, No. 3, Autumn 1994, 51, 48; for constitutional nationalists' commemoration of the war, see Terence Denman, *A Lonely Grave. The Life and Death of William Redmond* (Dublin, 1995), 128–36.
5. Gregory, ibid., 8–23.
6. Dublin Roman Catholic Diocesan Archives, Walsh papers, 386/6.
7. *Irish Times* and *Irish Independent*, 12 November 1919; *Freeman's Journal*, 17 July 1919.
8. *Dublin Evening Mail*, 11 November 1919 and *Irish News,* 12 November 1919.
9. Armistice Day 1919 as experienced by a UCD student active in the IRA is described in C.S. Andrews, *Dublin Made Me* (Dublin, 1979), 127–8.
10. *Irish Independent*, 13 November 1925.
11. *Irish Times*, 12 November 1932; Robert Fisk, *In Time of War. Ireland, Ulster and the Price of Neutrality 1939–45* (London, 1987), 535; interview with Ronald Noble, Dublin, 1990 (on TCD and Armistice Day in the 1930s and 1940s).
12. *Irish News* and *Irish Independent,* 12 November 1923; *Irish Independent,* 12 November 1924–26.
13. National Archives of Ireland, Dept of the Taoiseach, S3370 (file on Armistice Day, 1924–58).
14. See the *Irish Times* and *Irish Independent* for mid-November coverage of Remembrance Sunday since 1971; British Legion files on the cancellation of 1971 parades and other events. I am grateful to the late Capt. Terence Poulter for access to these files.

15. *Dublin Evening Herald*, 12 November 1920; for a vivid memoir of British troops enforcing Armistice Day silence among shopkeepers and students in Galway in 1920, see Frances Moffett, *I Also Am of Ireland* (London, 1985), 104–5.
16. For examples of attacks, see *Irish Times*, 10 November 1926 and *Irish Independent*, 12 November 1932; the brief operation of the Inchicore hall was reported in the *Irish Independent*, 7 November 1927 and the *Weekly Irish Times*, 19 November 1927; Tim Pat Coogan, *The IRA* (London, 1971), pp. 72–3.
17. Interviews (on poppy-wearing and snatching) with the late Private Paddy Kenny and Mrs Louisa Kenny, East Wall, Dublin, 1988–90; *Irish Times*, 12 November 1932 (on the use of razor blades); *Dublin Evening Mail*, 12 November 1924; for a recent poem on Irish poppy-snatching, see Michael Longley, 'Poppies' in *Ghost Orchid* (London, Cape, 1995), p. 40.
18. *Irish Times*, 11 November 1935; *Irish Independent*, 17, 21 and 23 November 1925; *An Phoblacht*, 9 November 1929; *Irish World*, 5 December 1925.
19. November issues of *An Phoblacht* during 1920s and 1930s; National Archives of Ireland, S3370.
20. *British Legion Journal*, January 1926.
21. *Wexford Free Press*, 18 November 1922; Stephen Gwynn, 'Ireland Week by Week', in *The Observer*, 18 November 1923.
22. NAI, S3370 includes memoranda on and charts of official representation at the Dublin and London ceremonies; Cosgrave's letter of explanation to Stanley Baldwin was reprinted in the *Irish World*, 13 November 1926; for a useful survey of state participation, see Jim Duffy, 'The dilemma over those who died in British uniform', *Irish Times*, 13 November 1991.
23. *Irish Independent*, 12 November 1923; interview with Sydney Minch (son), Dublin, June 1993.
24. NAI, S3370; profile of O'Kelly in *The Clongownian*, 1928.
25. See coverage of de Valera's visit in the *Irish World*, *Boston Pilot* and *San Francisco Leader* during 1919; for his speech to wounded veterans at the Letterman Army Hospital, see *San Francisco Leader*, 26 July 1919; war memorials were endorsed in the *Weekly Irish News Bulletin of the Friends of Irish Freedom* , 13 April 1920.
26. I am grateful to the staff of the Royal British Legion's Dublin office for access to annual reports and branch affiliation records; for additional files on branch closures and the impact of the Northern Ireland conflict on Legion work, I am grateful to the late Captain Terence Poulter, the late Captain Charles Heather and the late Major Robin Hill.
27. See *Irish Times* and *Evening Herald* of early November 1980; *Irish Times*, 3 August 1991.
28. See the news and letters pages of the *Irish Times,* 15 October–14 November 1983; the controversy was also discussed on the Gay Byrne Show, RTE Radio 1 in the same period.
29. Interviews with Killester residents, 1989–91; *Freeman's Journal*, 12 November 1923; interviews with the children and neighbours of Colonel Farrell Tully (ex-Indian Army and Irish Army) and Captain Michael Stacey (ex-Irish Guards and Irish Army), Dublin, 1989–90.

30. I am grateful to Lt Col Brian Clark of the British Legion, and Major General (retd) Vincent Savino of the Irish Army for details on the rapport between the Legion and the Irish defence forces.
31. *Irish Times, Irish Independent* and *Irish Press*, 14 November 1983.
32. Mary Holland column, *Irish Times*, November 1987 and 9 November 1988.
33. On the Byrne controversy and post-Enniskillen attitudes to war commemoration, see *Evening Press*, 11 November; *Irish Times*, 12 and 14 November; *Sunday Tribune* and *Sunday Independent*, 13 November (all 1988); *Evening Press*, 12 February 1991.
34. Restored memorials include those in Portlaoise and Bray. New memorials to Irish and Allied casualties of the Second World War have been dedicated in several counties including Dublin, Wicklow and Donegal; details on branch closures in the 1970s compiled from Legion and press files; for war commemoration in Limerick, see the *Irish Times*, 15 November 1989 and *Battlelines* (Journal of the Somme Association), 1992; I am grateful to Martin Staunton of the Western Front Association, Dublin for additional details on post-Enniskillen commemoration in Ireland.
35. Examples include James McGuinn, *Sligo Men in the Great War* (Cavan, 1994); *Times Past* (Journal of the Ballincollig Community School Local History Society, 1990–91, special issue on Cork and the Great War); *Clare Champion*, 14 November 1988; for the McGuinness revival, see the *Irish Times*, 22 October 1994.
36. *Evening Press,* 2 November 1993; *Irish Times* 12 and 15 November 1993; see the *Irish Times*, 8 September 1992 for President Robinson's visit to the restored war memorial in Enniskillen and meeting with relatives of the bomb victims.
37. *Irish Times*, 2 July 1994.
38. *Irish Times*, 29 April 1995; for the ceasefire's impact on commemoration, see the Belfast newspapers of 14 November 1994 and the *Impartial Reporter* (Enniskillen) 17 November 1994.
39. See my article, 'Facing the finger of scorn: Veterans' memories of Ireland, 1919–24' in Ken Lunn and Martin Evans (eds), *War and Memory in the Twentieth Century* (forthcoming).
40. A draft version of this chapter was read at a conference in Queen's University, Belfast in April 1995 on *Celts and Conflict, 1914–18: The Impact of the Great War on Ireland, Scotland and Wales*; I am grateful to Angela Gaffney, David Fitzpatrick, Keith Jeffery and Keith Simpson for their comments on this draft.

7 Ulster Unionism and Loyalty to the Crown of the United Kingdom, 1912–74

Thomas Hennessey

INTRODUCTION

Traditional interpretations of Ulster unionist hostility to Irish nationalism have focused upon factors such as religion and economic considerations. Steve Bruce, for example, has argued that the Northern Ireland conflict is a 'religious conflict', and that it was the fact that the competing populations in Ireland adhered, and still adhere, to competing religious traditions which 'has given the conflict its enduring and intractable quality'.[1] When scholars have focused upon the role of religion in the independent Irish state, and its impact upon Ulster Protestants, they have usually concentrated on how successive Irish governments have proclaimed Ireland to be a 'Catholic nation', and enshrined Catholic social teaching within the 1937 Constitution.[2] The economic case against Ulster unionist incorporation within an Irish unitary state has been a constant element, from the Home Rule era, with unionist fears that they would be separated from British imperial markets,[3] to the acknowledgment of the dependency of Northern Ireland upon the massive subsidies supplied by Britain since the 1970s.[4] Only relatively recently has the nature of British national identity within Ulster unionism been explored academically.[5] Indeed, studies concentrating upon the relevance of British nationalism within Ulster unionism have tended to dilute the influential argument of David Miller that Ulster unionism has had as its central political ideology a theory of social contract, which reduces political obligation to a simple matter of ethics.[6] So, as Jennifer Todd has written, for a considerable period of the recent history of Ulster unionism, there has been no conflict between British nationalism (which Miller does not recognise as a key component of unionism) and contractualism.[7] In Colin Coulter's conclusion, the most common shortcoming among the myriad of analyses of unionism has been a propensity to conceive of unionism in unidimen-

115

sional terms, thereby ignoring the significant diversity of unionist political belief and practice.[8] This chapter aims to illustrate another aspect of unionism's diverse political belief, that of loyalty to the Crown, arguing that the emphasis which Ulster unionists placed upon being British subjects, within a monarchical state, profoundly influenced their relationship with Irish republicans throughout the island of Ireland. It is argued that the form of the state itself is a cause of conflict between Ulster unionists and Irish nationalists.

THE UNIONIST PERCEPTION OF IRISH NATIONALIST LOYALTY

Since the establishment of Northern Ireland the question of cross-border bodies has been a controversial issue between unionists and nationalists. The Government of Ireland Act, in 1920, sought to set up a Council of Ireland composed of members of the Northern Ireland and Southern Ireland parliaments to make executive decisions on an all-Ireland basis. In November 1920, Sir Edward Carson, speaking in the British House of Commons, hoped

> that this Council, the liaison between North and South, is not going to be the impotent body that a number of people think it will be...I should have thought that the biggest advance towards unity in Ireland was this conception of the Council. The Council will be the representatives of the Parliament of the North and...of the representatives of the South, and they are to come together...to frame measures and suggestions for the benefit of the whole of Ireland....I am optimistic enough to hope that it is in this Council...that there is the germ of a united Ireland in future.[9]

However, the strict condition under which unionists such as Carson were prepared to accept a united Ireland was one which would 'see Ireland one and undivided, loyal to this country [Great Britain] and loyal to the Empire'.[10] The 1920 Government of Ireland Act envisaged an eventual united Ireland within the monarchical state of the United Kingdom of Great Britain and Ireland. But, by 1922, an Irish Free State outside the United Kingdom, but within the British Commonwealth of Nations, had been established, by armed rebellion against the Crown. In October 1924, Carson, surveying relations between Northern Ireland and the Free State, believed that if the latter had taken the trouble to prove its loyalty to the United Kingdom, then a very different state of affairs might have existed between North and South.[11] In his view the Free State was a Republic already, although it might not be called such. He claimed that the Free State had already gone from under the British flag, for it was forbidden to fly the Union Jack on either Parliament house or any Irish government building there. Perhaps this was a sentimental matter, said Carson, but, there was a 'great deal in sentiment regarding the country you live in and the Flag you live under'. Furthermore, the Free State had blotted the King's name out of every single proceeding that the Irish government had to take. In the United Kingdom, however, they still talked of the King's writ running through the country, but the Free State had abolished his name, as that of a foreign king, from every legal proceeding. The Free State called the people of Northern Ireland and Great Britain 'foreigners', and made it compulsory for children, including Protestant children in the Free State's territory, to learn Irish, and passed a law that nobody but Free State citizens could enter their civil service. Then, he pointed out, the Free State had its own army which did not swear allegiance to the King, so it was not the King's Army, but the Irish Republican Army; in addition they had claimed the right to send their own representatives to foreign courts. Therefore, he concluded, what was the good of being frightened by the thought that the Free State would become a Republic; a change in the name would make no difference in reality. In contrast the North was 'not prepared to go from under the flag, not prepared to wipe out the King's name from every document used in connection with the carrying on of government, and not prepared with the pensioning of murderers'.[12]

Carson was articulating what many Ulster unionists believed with regard to the Free State: that its leaders were acting in a manner disloyal to the Crown. Successive Irish Free State governments sought to illustrate their independence from Britain, particularly since a civil war had been fought, in 1922–23, between former Irish nationalist allies, on the question of allegiance to the Crown. This, as Carson's views demonstrate, coloured Ulster unionist attitudes to Irish nationalists, both within Northern Ireland, and outside it. Of particular concern to the Northern Ireland government was the employment of 'disloyalists' within the Northern administration. Northern Irish nationalists attacked the employment practices of the Northern administration as sectarian, claiming that it refused to employ Roman Catholics within the state apparatus on religious grounds, despite the fact that Catholics composed a third of the population. The phrase, used by Lord Craigavon, Northern Ireland's Prime Minister from 1921 until 1940, that Northern Ireland was a 'Protestant Parliament and a Protestant State' has been regarded as testament to this. Yet, this state-ment has to be understood in the context of the perceptions Ulster union-ists had of the Irish Free State. The Free State's provisional government, under the direction of Michael Collins, had, during the early 1920s, supported IRA attacks upon the Northern state, hoping to force it into union with the South.

This confirmed Ulster unionists in their belief that Irish nationalists had always been disloyal to the Crown, and in pursuit of an Irish Republic. During the parliamentary debate on the state employment of nationalists, in 1934, in which Craigavon used his famous phrase, he moved an amendment to state that the employment of 'disloyalists' entering Northern Ireland was prejudicial, not only to the interests of law and order, and the safety of the state, but also to the prior claims of 'loyal Ulster-born citizens' seeking employment. Although he claimed to have laid down the principle that he was the Prime Minister, not of one section of the community, but of all of it, he also admitted that he was an Orangeman first and a politician and a Member of the Northern Irish Parliament afterwards. Craigavon, in reply to the Nationalist MP who raised the matter of the state's employment of Catholics, asked him to 'remember that in the South they boasted of a Catholic State. They still boast of Southern Ireland being a Catholic State. All I boast of is that we are a Protestant Parliament and a Protestant State.' Were memories so short, enquired Craigavon, that nationalists had forgotten those who came into Northern Ireland and attempted to prevent its government from being established? Unionists would 'never forget all the turmoil, murder, and bloodshed', he said. He pointed out that in the Dominions, in Canada, New Zealand and South Africa, persons likely to endanger the safety of the state – the people he referred to in his amendment – were not admitted to its territory. He therefore thought it right to give a warning to the people that they should not employ people coming over the border who might be drifting into Northern Ireland to 'destroy the constitution and to start over the trouble which we overcame in 1920, 21, 22'. Further, he did not see why the 'loyal Ulster artisan', at a time when there were 63 000 persons unemployed, should pay contributions in order to maintain people who came from the other side of the border, and he took the opportunity to 'urge the public to employ only loyalists – I say only loyalists. I do not care what their religion may be. I say that as long as they are loyal people we will engage them and give them every chance.'[13]

Yet the state employment of 'loyalists' came, for some members of the Northern Ireland government, to mean the employment of Protestants only. Dawson Bates, at the Ministry of Home Affairs, refused to allow Catholic appointments. In 1926, John Andrews, the Minister of Labour, and later Prime Minister, found two 'Free Staters' in his ministry, and initiated a tightening of regulations to disqualify such candidates automatically. In

1927, Edward Archdale, the Minister for Agriculture, boasted that there were only four Catholics in his ministry. A storm of controversy was initiated by Sir Basil Brooke, Minister of Agriculture, in 1933, when he urged supporters at a meeting to employ only 'good Protestant lads and lasses'.[14] In his defence Brooke claimed that he had never approached this employment question from a religious point of view. He denied that the remarks he had made were an attack upon the Roman Catholic Church, asking 'What...has the difference in the principles of the Christian faith or in the various methods of worship got to do with the status of Ulster?' 'Absolutely nothing' was Brooke's answer, arguing that his comments were an attack upon the Nationalist Party, which he accused of defining all Catholics as Irish nationalists, and pointing out that it was the Nationalist Party which used the words Roman Catholic in a political as well as a religious sense. He quoted an example from a previous election where nationalist voters were instructed to vote for Irish unity and for their Catholic co-religionists, a 'definite' example of the use of the words Roman Catholic in a political sense. He told the Northern Irish House of Commons of how, when in the Ulster Special Constabulary, he was informed of a plot to kidnap his eldest son, the inference being that this was not to be carried out by members of his 'own party'. Therefore, taking every precaution he 'got rid of every man in the place who I thought might betray me'. By inference this meant every Roman Catholic/nationalist. He explained:

There is, in fact, a Catholic political party, which ranges from what I might call benevolent nationalism to the extreme of the extreme. That is true, but the one plank in their platform is the destruction of Ulster as a unit and as a constitution. That is the policy, and it simply varies in method. Directly the hon. Gentlemen [Nationalist Party MPs] are attacked politically they play the old familiar game...and hang on to religion and say 'You are treating us in a tyrannical manner; you are bigots'....May I explain what I mean by the word 'disloyalist'....A disloyal man is a man who is scheming and plotting to destroy the country in which he lives. It does not mean a man who lives in that country and lives under the constitution but is opposed to the Government....But any man who is out to break up that constitution, which has been established by Great Britain, is to my mind disloyal. That is what I mean by disloyal....These gentlemen have been questioning....my urging that Roman Catholics – political Roman Catholics – should not be employed...what they [Catholic-nationalists] like to do is to employ all their own people of the same political faith, and leave our people to employ those they cannot employ themselves. There are three reasons to my mind why disloyalists should not be employed. Those who support the constitution, whether they agree with the policy of the present Government or not, should have the benefit of that constitution. Secondly every disloyalist allowed to come in is a potential voter for the destruction of this country. And, further, there is a grave danger in employing men who at the first opportunity will betray those who employ them....I shall use all my energies and whatever powers I possess to defeat the aims of those who are out to destroy the constitution of Ulster be they Protestants or be they Roman Catholics.[15]

REFORM AND REACTION

This unionist perception of the nationalist enemy within and outside the statelet remained a core facet of the Ulster unionist sense of siege. A radical departure from this perception of the enemy within was offered by the accession of Terence O'Neill to the Northern Ireland premiership in 1963. O'Neill claimed that the defence of Northern Ireland's constitution had been the motivation of his entire political life. At all times he claimed to have kept the vital words of Section 1 (2) of the Ireland Act 1949, before him: 'It is hereby declared that Northern Ireland remains part of His Majesty's Dominions and of the United Kingdom and it is hereby affirmed that in no event will Northern Ireland or any part thereof cease to be part of His Majesty's Dominions and of the United Kingdom without the consent of the Parliament of Northern Ireland.' This meant, argued O'Neill in 1969, that it was 'we here, and our successors in time to come who will determine the constitutional destiny of this Province'. The implications of those words lay at the root of his whole domestic policy. In the Northern Ireland House of Commons he said

> I want the House to understand that I am a Unionist, a convinced Unionist, not for today, or for yesterday but for the far distant future. I want our descendants to live, as we have lived, under the Union Jack and enjoying all the benefits of the British connection. And because this is my wish, because I want to secure the Constitution not just for our time but for the foreseeable future, I want to show every citizen of Ulster, every section of Ulster the benefits of the British connection are all to share.
> I want to see a day on which anti-partitionists will only be a tiny minority of eccentrics in this House. I know there are those who feel that a community which already represents over one-third of our popu-

lation and has over 50 per cent of the children of school age can just be written off as a source of support for our Constitution and status. I believe such an attitude is defeatist. I prefer to say across the historic divide: 'This is your country too. Help us to make it all it could be'.[16]

As part of this long-term strategy O'Neill met with the Republic's Prime Minister Sean Lemass, secretly, and without prior cabinet approval in January 1965. Following this thaw in North–South relations, Eddie McAteer, leader of the Nationalist Party, after a visit to the Taoiseach in Dublin, announced that his party would become the official Opposition for the first time in Northern Ireland's history. O'Neill continued to make overtures to the Northern nationalist community, as in June 1963 with a public condolence to Cardinal Conway on the death of Pope John; and in April 1964 by visiting a Catholic school. Despite the fact that O'Neill offered no structural reform of the Northern Ireland state, hoping instead that the long-term economic improvements would lead Roman Catholics into accepting the existence of Northern Ireland, a number of loyalist groups became increasingly concerned about O'Neillism and its departure from the 'traditional unionism' of Carson and Craigavon. The Protestant fundamentalist Ian Paisley took his concern into the streets in a campaign to alert his co-religionists to the dangers he perceived from O'Neillism. Further opposition came from within the Ulster Unionist Party itself, particularly from William Craig, Northern Ireland Minister for Home Affairs in the late 1960s, who came to see the Civil Rights campaign as an IRA plot to destroy Northern Ireland's place within the United Kingdom. It was the perception that the nationalist-Catholic population desired to see a united Ireland which fuelled unionist fears, leading to the political demise of O'Neill and his successors Chichester-Clark and Faulkner. In particular, the 1973 Sunningdale Agreement, establishing a unionist–nationalist power-sharing Executive and a Council of Ireland between Northern Ireland and the Republic, following the proroguing of the Northern Parliament in 1972, led to the successful UWC strike, which wrecked the Executive. Unionists were expected to share power with a new party, the Social Democratic and Labour Party (SDLP), whose aim of a united Ireland it shared with its predecessor, the Nationalist Party. Paisley stated that his opposition to power-sharing with the SDLP was because 'they claim they want a united Irish Republic....Certainly...not...a united Ireland under the Crown, so the...party are Republicans.'[17] William Craig contrasted the idea of coalition in Britain with the Ulster case; in the latter they were not simply quibbling about bread-and-butter issues and the everyday problems of running the country, but in Northern Ireland they were quarrelling about the fundamental issues and principles that lay behind the state. The division struck at the very existence of Ulster as a British community, and the SDLP was still committed to its 'fundamental and primary' objective of creating an all-Ireland Republic.[18] For evangelical Protestants in particular, loyalty to the Crown was believed to be central in securing Protestant civil and religious liberty in Ireland from the dominance of the Roman Catholic Church. In Northern Ireland the issues of the Reformation were, for many, still relevent. As Stormont Assemblyman Ernest Baird said in October 1973, such unionists were only adhering to the fundamentals of the British Constitution, which asserted in the seventeenth-century Bill of Rights and Act of Settlement that Great Britain was a Protestant Kingdom, and that the Crown was Protestant, because in the words of the law 'It hath been found by experience that it was inconsistent with the safety and welfare of this Protestant kingdom for the Crown to go to a Roman Catholic or anyone marrying a Papist.' Should a King or Queen become Roman Catholic or marry a Roman Catholic, that King or Queen lost the Crown which then passed to the next eligible Protestant and the law of the land indicated that subjects were absolved of their allegiance to any King or Queen who was not Protestant.[19] Paisley, referring to his opposition to the Sunningdale Agreement, agreed that

the citizens of the United Kingdom are only bound by the Revolution Settlement and it is established in constitutional law as long as Her Majesty is Protestant. If she ceased to be a Protestant there is no allegiance to her and people are then relieved of their obligation. That is why the succession must be a Protestant succession. If the Monarchy of England were Roman Catholic I would not be advocating union within the United Kingdom....If you are saying...that the Queen in Parliament is that to which we have to give our loyalty, that is not upheld by any constitutional lawyer because the Queen in Parliament makes the law. You are saying that our loyalty should be to the laws of Parliament. No one ever accepted that in constitutional law. Our loyalty is to the Queen being a Protestant under the terms of the Revolution Settlement. I would ask the hon. Gentleman [Mr. Larkin, an SDLP Assemblyman] what is his loyalty to the South, because I understand he carries a Southern passport. Is he loyal to the Dail and to the laws it makes or is he loyal to the concept of a Republic of Ireland?...I simply say...that it is a strange doctrine...that you cannot be loyal to the Queen being Protestant, to the Throne being Protestant, if you reject the laws that are legislated in the sovereign Parliament of the Kingdom....I believe you have to obey those laws and submit yourself to them. If for conscience sake you protest against those laws you have to bear patiently the punishment which those laws impose upon you. The conscience of the citizens of the United Kingdom cannot be bound by the laws of Parliament although those citizens must submit to them. My conscience is bound by my loyalty to Her Majesty the Queen, which is a different thing altogether.[20]

LOYALTY TO THE CROWN AND BRITISHNESS

However, in shaping Ulster unionism, loyalty to the Crown has also had a significance beyond the religious factor, particularly in the area of national identity. The cultural significance, for Ulster unionists, of loyalty to the Crown was illustrated by the passing of the Flags and Emblems (Display) Act in 1954, which gave symbolic and legal substance to the Unionist claim that Northern Ireland was the loyal British, as well as Protestant part of Ireland. George Hanna, Minister of Home Affairs at the time, said that the Act was introduced so that loyal subjects who desired to fly the Union flag would be afforded all the protection the legislature could give them. The second clause of the Act provided for the removal, by the Royal Ulster Constabulary, of any emblem, the display of which seemed likely to lead to disturbance. Referring to the claim that this effectively banned the Republic of Ireland's flag, Eire having become a Republic in 1948, Hanna declared he had no desire to ban the flag of any state with which the United Kingdom was at peace; but the 'Republican part of the island', however, claimed jurisdiction in Northern Ireland, through its 1937 Constitution, and therefore Hanna believed that a person displaying the republican tricolour, as an indication of support for that claim, was in fact alleging the right of a foreign country to govern Northern Ireland, which he saw as 'very close to an act of treason'.[21] He explained that the Union flag was the flag of 'their country and of the Kingdom of which they were proud to be citizens'. Hanna rejected the contention that the Union flag was a party emblem 'as ridiculous'. The fact, he said, that the Nationalist Party boycotted the 'national flag' did not make it the emblem of another, for the Unionist Party made no special claim or right to it. The 'broad...fundamental and undeniable fact was that the national flag was above and outside parliamentary party politics, just as the Crown was above and outside politics'. A condition, he said, precedent to membership of the Northern Ireland Parliament was the swearing of allegiance to the Crown, an assembly whose every legislative act was prefaced with the words, 'Be it enacted by the Queen's Most Excellent Majesty', and which was called into being and prorogued by the Crown; therefore, he concluded, it was wholly paradoxical that any person should openly declare that he did not recognise Her Majesty as their Queen or the Union flag as their national flag. If any man regarded the Union Jack with hatred, or the symbol of thraldom, Hanna advised them to stay away from any part of the United Kingdom. As Brooke, now Lord Brookeborough and Prime Minister, believed, the Union Jack was 'sacred', the flag he had fought for, and fought under, in the Great War, and the reason it was revered by unionists was because it was an emblem of the Crown and Constitution,[22] and of those loyalties and traditions and of the desire to live in the British way of life; whatever the conditions, unionists would rather suffer harsh penalties then be 'members of a Republic separated from the British Commonwealth'.[23]

One Unionist backbencher, Thomas Lyons, argued at the time, that 'God Save the Queen' was a national prayer, and that the people who sang it used it to express their loyalty. As to the term nationalist, he asked if it was realised what a nationalist was; he believed that unionists opposed the Nationalist Party because 'we are British Nationalists while they are not'.[24] Therefore, as Hanna claimed, 'In the Six Counties the flying of the Union Jack on one's own property is an act of loyalty' to the Queen and to the Union flag, both of which expressed loyalty to 'our native land....the Six Counties of Northern Ireland'. The Oath of Allegiance he considered an oath that the person taking it will bear true allegiance to Her Majesty the Queen.[25] Unionists denied that men such as Sir Edward Carson had broken their Oaths of Allegiance when they threatened rebellion against the British government which sought to impose home rule upon them, during the Ulster Crisis of 1912–14. In every case, argued another backbench unionist, Archibald Wilson, they were Oaths of Allegiance to the King, and the action men like Carson took was to prevent an alien state pushing them out of the United Kingdom: in other words to 'remain faithful to the King to whom they had remained faithful'. The Oath of Allegiance was, in Wilson's opinion, one of the fundamentals of the British Constitution. Wilson argued that within the terms of the Oath of Allegiance to Queen Elizabeth II the people of Northern Ireland could vote, argue and debate the laws of their Parliament, both inside and outside that Parliament, even taking matters to the courts; but, said Wilson, if, under that Oath, force was used to break their allegiance, then unionists reserved their right to use force to resist this.[26]

This right to resist by force any attempt to break the unionist allegiance has remained a central part of Ulster unionist ideology. In 1912 Carson had defined the unionist duty (as citizens) to obey the law; but there was also a correlative government duty not to tamper with the rights of citizenship, for the subversion of political status was not government, but revolution.[27] Thus Carson declared that 'If it be treason to love your King, to try to save your Constitution, to preserve your birthright, and your civil and religious liberty, then I glory in being a traitor.'[28] This meant, said the Ulster Unionist *Belfast News Letter* in 1912, that in a 'free country men still refused to bend to the autocracy of a Monarch or a Cabinet'. The former held the high place which 'Providence had committed to his charge, that he might govern his people righteously'; to the latter office was entrusted that they might work the people's will for the welfare of all, and 'not bargain away the splendid heritage of the past at the price of a faction's vote'.[29] The *News Letter* explained how British citizenship was more than just simple social contractualism:

Unionists held...that their claim to remain under...the Imperial Parliament is an inalienable right of their citizenship which no Government of any time has the right to deprive them of. There need be no mistake about this, it is the position which Ulster has taken up all along; it is the heart and the essence of what has come to be called the Ulster Question. It goes deeper and further than any question of what Party is in power....It is indeed fundamental, for it goes right down to the principle of nationhood. In other words, Ulster's resistance to Home Rule is founded upon recognition of and loyalty to the nationhood of the United Kingdom. Our loyalty to that nationhood we hold in common with people of England...Scotland and Wales, and it cannot be denied that Ulster has given the best of her sons to its service. It makes us none the less patriotic Irishmen any more than it does Englishmen and Scotsmen to their countries. Can the same be said for Irish Nationalists? Most certainly it cannot. Their conception of nationality is opposed to ours both in object and in spirit; it is confined to Ireland alone, and it is hostile to the unity of the Kingdom, therefore it is hostile to the conception of nationhood to which we are loyal. Therein lies the right of Ulster to resist...since it would be a severance against their will of a loyal people from their nationhood, which no Government has the right to do.[30]

Carson had noted how nationalists expressed faith in the great changes which would remove Ulster's apprehensions when Home Rule became a fact; but, said Carson, nationalists should remember that 'what was offered to the North was outraging in every respect the sentiment that binds them to this country [Great Britain]...[and] to each other'.[31] To the nationalist argument that unionist opposition to Irish self-government was based upon a unionist fear that they would lose their liberty, economic position and religious rights, Ronald McNeill, an Ulster Unionist MP for Cheltenham, replied that deeper than these factors was the fact that Home Rule was the 'transference of their allegiance, a degradation of their position' within the United Kingdom. 'It is that degradation of that position', he continued, 'which they resent and which they will not allow to be perpetrated if they can help it; altogether independent of what may or may not be done in the way of specific legislation [in a home rule parliament] to their disadvantage'.[32] Carson argued that it was no answer to say to unionists 'You are all Irishmen, go and live together with Nationalists'; it was absurd, he said, because 'We consider that we are satisfied that we are one nationality with Great Britain, and we are satisfied to be.'[33]

Ulster unionists had, since the first home rule crisis of 1886, exhibited a consciousness of themselves as both British and Irish. As such, unionists, living in the geographical unit of the British Isles, psychologically thought of themselves as belonging to a British nation, alongside the British-English, British-Scots and British-Welsh.[34] Since the time when Ireland had been incorporated into the United Kingdom, and until the middle of the twentieth century, allegiance to the King had determined British nationality. English law's longstanding reliance on the rule of birthplace, to determine who was a subject or citizen, expressed an important political and historical characteristic of the nation. For centuries people have become English by settlement or by birth on the territory; in England no element of culture, except a rudimentary language test, coloured the naturalisation process. From the middle ages until the middle of the twentieth century, the concept of 'belonging' was expressed in terms of being the King's subject. Subjecthood signified a personal link. It was a vertical relationship between monarch and individual, not a horizontal one between members of a nation or citizens of a body politic. From this personal link, rights and obligations arose for each party. Originally, the allegiance of a subject served the practical end of self-defence and mutual protection in a physically insecure world. Among Celtic communities of the British Isles, and Anglo-Saxon England, personal loyalty to a king or chieftain, as military leader, required devotion, the sense of sacred duty, practical service, readiness to risk one's own life and an idea of personal affection which all came together in fealty. The military feudalism, introduced by William the Conqueror, involved an oath of homage sworn by a man to his lord, in a solemn church ceremony, whereby a contract was agreed. But it was a private contract, and if one side broke it the other was released from his obligations. Under feudal law, a person born on that lord's land was that lord's subject and owed him allegiance; from the fact of birthplace arose rights and obligations on the part of both lord and subject. By the end of the thirteenth century, the primacy of determining who was the King's subject had become established. Birth in the King's ligeance made a subject. Ligeance had the sense of allegiance, and also of geographical tract. Land and loyalty went unquestionably together. Those born outside the ligeance were aliens born. Allegiance was the work of the law of nature; the law of nature was the law of God and therefore it already existed, and statutes and the decisions of judges merely declared it; they could not invent it. Because of the emphasis on land law, it was the feudal aspect of subjecthood, rather the status of those who owed allegiance to the King's royal authority, that developed into a form of nationality. It was taken for granted that everyone in the realm came under the authority of the King-as-King. The words 'British nationality' are now commonly accepted, but are of recent origin. Common-law writers of the sixteenth and seventeenth centuries did not speak of nationality. The status of a 'subject of the King of England' was that from which modern British nationality sprang. The 'Crown of Great Britain', to which British subjects owe allegiance, came into existence in 1707, when the two distinct titles of the King of England and the King of Scotland were merged into one.[35] The significance of loyalty to the Crown in defining Ulster unionist Britishness has lapsed since the legal definition of Britishness is now defined by statute and not the personal tie between King and subject. This, however, did not occur until after the Second World War, and in the period from 1922 until 1948 the independent Irish state emphasised its non-Britishness by steadily moving from being a Dominion within the Commonwealth to a Republic. In breaking the link with the Crown, Irish nationalists were formally denying that they owed allegiance to the British King, and therefore were not British subjects, the result of which was that a psychological partition of Ireland was erected between Ulster unionists and Irish nationalists. The significance of this has not been recognised, even by the more revisionist of Irish nationalists; Dr Garret FitzGerald, for example, has written that the fact that both parts of Ireland were in the Commonwealth during the 1920s and 1930s 'never made any difference to relations between North and South'.[36]

CONCLUSION

In conclusion, one can draw together the interaction of the differing concepts of loyalty within Ulster unionist political belief. It has had three aspects – that of the Irish nationalist relationship to the Crown within the island of Ireland; the question of the Crown in defining Britishness; and the continuing religious aspect. Ulster unionist belief in their loyalty to the Crown and Irish republican disloyalty have been core elements in unionist distrust of Irish nationalist intentions. As Joshua Cardwell, a Stormont MP, said in 1972, a united Ireland would mean 'we are asked to forgo Her Gracious Majesty the Queen for a Dublin President and the National Anthem for the Soldier's Song. We are asked to forgo the Union Jack for a Tricolour and the English language for the Irish language.' This he believed would be a 'betrayal of my principles and my life's work'.[37] In contrast, his colleague, Major Hall-Thompson, was prepared to consider a united Ireland, but only on certain conditions –

> first of all we must completely eliminate the IRA....This having been achieved, the Irish Republic would return to the British Commonwealth and then become part of the United Kingdom. They would accept the Union Jack in place of the Tricolour and Her Majesty Queen Elizabeth II as Head of State.[38]

NOTES

1. Steve Bruce, *God Save Ulster: The Religion and Politics of Paisleyism* (Oxford, 1986), p. 249.
2. J. H. Whyte, *Church and State in Modern Ireland 1923–1979* (Dublin, 1980), p. 48.
3. Public Record Office of Northern Ireland, D627/436/19, Hugh de Fellenberg Montgomery Papers, 21 May 1918.
4. New Ireland Forum, *The Macroeconomic Consequences of Integrated Economic Policy, Planning and Co-ordination of Ireland* (Dublin, 1984).
5. James Loughlin, *Gladstone, Home Rule and the Ulster Question 1882–93* (Dublin, 1986); Thomas Hennessey, 'Ulster Unionist Territorial and National Identities 1886–1893: Province, Island, Kingdom and Empire', *Irish Political Studies*, 8 (1993), pp. 21–36.
6. David Miller, *Queen's Rebels: Ulster Loyalism in Historical Perspective* (Dublin 1978), p. 4.
7. Jennifer Todd, 'Unionist Political Thought 1920–72', in D. George Boyce, Robert Eccleshall and Vincent Geoghegan (eds), *Political Thought in Ireland since the Seventeenth Century* (London, 1993), p. 205.
8. Colin Coulter, 'The Character of Unionism', *Irish Political Studies*, 9 (1994), p. 20.
9. *House of Commons Debates*, Volume 134, Cols 925–7 (8 November 1920).
10. Ibid., Cols 1441–2 (11 November 1920).
11. *House of Lords Debates*, Volume 59, Col. 615 (8 October 1924).

12. Ibid., Col. 563.
13. *Northern Ireland House of Commons Debates,* Volume XVI, Col. 1090 (24 April 1934).
14. Michael Farrell, *Northern Ireland: The Orange State* (London, 1976), p. 60.
15. *Northern Ireland House of Commons Debates,* Volume XVI, Cols 1114–20 (24 April 1934).
16. Ibid., Volume 71, Cols 414–15 (29 January 1969).
17. *Northern Ireland Assembly Official Report,* Volume 2, Cols 1835–6 (19 March 1974).
18. Ibid., Volume 1, Cols 430–1 (24 October 1973).
19. Ibid., Cols 495–6.
20. Ibid., Volume 2, Cols 2087–9 (26 March 1974).
21. *Northern Ireland House of Commons Debates,* Volume XXXVIII, Cols 586–91 (10 February 1954).
22. Ibid., Cols 647–50 (11 February 1954).
23. Ibid., Col. 2766 (19 October 1954).
24. Ibid., Col. 711 (11 February 1954).
25. Ibid., Col. 722.
26. Ibid., Cols 714–15.
27. *Belfast News Letter,* 19 September 1912.
28. Ibid., 24 September 1912.
29. Ibid., 16 September 1912.
30. Ibid., 19 September 1912.
31. *House of Commons Debates,* Volume LX, Cols 1669–70 (6 April 1914).
32. Ibid., Volume LII, Col. 1514 (10 June 1913).
33. Ibid., Volume XLII, Col. 1615 (10 October 1912).
34. Thomas Hennessey, 'Ulster Unionist Territorial and National Identities 1886–1893: Province, Island, Kingdom and Empire', *Irish Political Studies,* 8 (1993), pp. 27–32.
35. Ann Dummett and Andrew Nicol, *Subjects, Citizens, Aliens and Others: Nationality and Immigration Law* (London, 1990), Chapter 2.
36. Garret FitzGerald, *Towards a New Ireland* (Dublin, 1972), p. 160
37. *Northern Ireland House of Commons Debates,* Volume 84, Col. 205 (8 February 1972).
38. Ibid., Col. 206.

8 In Search of Order, Permanence and Stability: Building Stormont, 1921–32

David Officer

Situated on an elevation overlooking the Lagan Valley, above the City of Belfast, an imposing building rises. It stamps its authority on the surrounding landscape and radiates a sense of power and order. For over fifty years the governmental complex at Stormont was the heart of devolved government in Northern Ireland, the symbolic centre from within which Unionist political control was orchestrated. Yet, since Direct Rule was imposed in 1972, the building has ceased to perform the function for which it was originally built. After that, it became the venue for a succession of failed political initiatives which various British governments had attempted to introduce. Serviced by a skeleton staff, until very recently it did not play a significant part in the formal political life of the Province.

The unfolding peace process has brought Stormont back into focus. Crossing its threshold, Sinn Fein has not only laid claim to an equality of treatment on par with other parties but signalled a break with the past by entering a building which republicans had always anathematised. For the loyalist parties their entry into Stormont was conceived as the belated inclusion of a dispossessed working class who had previously never been adequately represented by a political arrangement dominated by a ruling elite. What unites these various political groupings, the media and other observers has been a recognition of the political nature of the symbolic space which they have been invited to enter.

The practice of government at Stormont has been explored in a variety of different ways, as a prominent aspect of the general political history of Northern Ireland, through the memoirs of influential civil servants and politicians or as an important reference in any consideration of the origins of the present conflict in the North. This essay is not primarily concerned to offer yet another audit of the successes or failures in the execution of state power. Neither is it simply an account of the planning, construction or the use to which the governmental complex has been put.

What is explored here is a recognition that, despite the termination of the practical role for which the building was explicitly erected, it remains the most enduring representation of the political and social forces out of which it was born. The supreme accomplishment of Stormont is signalled by its ability to convey the partial success of the unionist project through its very existence and the communicative system which it embodies.

The continued importance of the Stormont building resides in the fact that it remains synonymous with 'Protestant Ulster' and unionist power. It has survived as an emblematic representation of the northern state as it once was, a memorial to the political movement out of which it was born and through which it was sustained.

Since the legitimacy of the state in the North has been consistently challenged not only by northern nationalists and republicans over whom jurisdiction was extended, but also by the state in the South, the very fact of Stormont has always been severely contested. It is against this background that I want to explore the discerning purpose behind the building's construction, the inscription of particular meanings in its architectural design and some of the complex ways in which the building has been put to use.

I

The partition of Ireland was formalised by the Government of Ireland Act of 1920 and the signing of the Anglo-Irish Treaty the following year; dominion status was extended to the South and a limited form of home rule granted to a newly created state in the north-east of Ireland. From the very moment of its inception, Northern Ireland, as a semi-autonomous state within the United Kingdom, was viewed by Ulster unionists as a compromise enforced by the Westminster government, which appeared intent on attempting to extricate itself from Ireland as a whole. Partition had not resulted in the desired outcome. While the unionist movement had failed to preserve the union between Ireland and the Imperial centre it had successfully enforced the exclusion of six counties within the Province of Ulster from political authority emanating from Dublin. Yet as a consequence of this process the nature of the Union between the six counties and the rest of the United Kingdom had itself been transformed, rather than simply preserved as the unionist movement had demanded. The supersession of the Act of Union, which had been in place since 1801, established a governmental structure in the North which was undesired by any of the negotiating parties in Ireland. The overwhelming sense in which in important aspects the ambition of Ulster unionism had been thwarted was compounded further by those clauses contained in the Government of Ireland Act which construed the division of Ireland as a temporary expedient. Provision had been made to facilitate the reunification of the island as a whole through an inter-parliamentary body – the Council of Ireland.

Partial victory had been won by unionists although the full reach of their ambitions had been curtailed. For them, victory remained to be secured and established on firm ground. Under these conditions the accomplished fact of partition demanded a practical and symbolic expression to the new division of Ireland. The physical paraphernalia which accompanies the erection of state borders was soon put into place, border patrols were organised and new regulations ordering and overseeing the transfer of people and materials came into force. Since the detailed drawing of the boundary appeared an arbitrary act, cutting across long-established social networks engendered by trade, commerce and employment and cutting through established communities and their hinterlands, the symbolic demarcation of difference became all the more important.

Viewed at the macro level the partition of Ireland generally conformed to historically developed fault-lines which now took a new significance. The industrialised north-east, home of the linen, engineering, shipbuilding industries and related manufacture stood in contrast to a predominantly agrarian economy in the rest of the island. Consequently, the largest concentration of industrial workers was located in and around Belfast while the social structure of the south and west was numerically dominated by a proletarianised peasantry. These dissimilarities also coincided with a distribution of the population into contending groups according to religious affiliation and a developed sense of ethnic origin. The bearers of the reformed faith marked themselves out from others as the 'other' aimed to sustain its struggle to break the Union by mobilising around the coterminous identifications of being both Gaels and Catholics.

This dense social landscape of conflicting identities, contending memories and irreconcilable aspirations was reworked under novel conditions which now found expression in the creation of two separate states. Dublin and Belfast both became the respective centres of new-found power and autonomy which not only resulted in the practical task of state-building but also its appropriate symbolic expression.

For many centuries Dublin had been at the heart of colonial power in Ireland. It was here that the English pale was centred, where the administration of the country spanned out from and the seat of military power was located. The creation of the Free State saw the wholesale transfer of those institutions bequeathed by years of Imperial rule; they were now refunctioned and took on a symbolic importance as expressions of a new-found independence. Belfast had been Ireland's second city since the early part of the nineteenth century; a city which could never challenge the political, cultural and administrative importance of the capital. Nevertheless it was a regional centre for the industrially expansive Province of Ulster with a suitably grand and imposing civic architecture to match. Commenting on the Belfast City Hall which was opened in 1906, along with other major building projects during the same period, Charles Brett has noted that 'architecturally, they constitute the corporate expression of embattled Unionism, and of an effort (perhaps largely unconscious) to convert a brash and sprawling industrial centre into a politico-religious capital city'.[1]

By 1921 this subliminal desire had been transformed into a practical necessity of establishing a functioning system of state power concentrated in the northern capital. The formal mechanisms of liberal democratic rule were rapidly put in place. Elections were called for a new parliamentary body; significantly this was scheduled to take place on 24 May – Empire Day. Under a single transferable voting system the outcome unambiguously signalled the dominance of the Unionist Party through their acquisition of 40 seats. Sinn Fein and the Nationalists secured six apiece. George V was invited formally to open the first parliamentary session and thus embody the continuing relationship between Crown and people which unionists had fought to maintain.

The venue which had been selected for this occasion was the pre-eminent public building in the North – the City Hall. The ceremony which took place on 22 June combined a solemn state occasion with a festive and celebratory atmosphere in many parts of Belfast. Union flags and bunting were conspicuously arranged along public thoroughfares, and in the back streets of protestant working-class districts, pavements and lamp-posts were painted red, white and blue. The day was turned into the most spectacular public ritual that had been seen on the streets since Armistice Day in 1919. Only the absence of Nationalist, Republican and Catholic Church representatives at the ceremony and the heavy police protection afforded to the Royal party gestured towards the illegitimacy of the new parliament in the eyes of many.

The use of City Hall for this purpose had been strenuously opposed. From the very outset the location of Parliament had become a point of contestation as a part of a wider strategy to deny the legitimacy of partition. Speaking at a council meeting, the Nationalist Alderman Harkin offered a sharp contrast between local government which was presented as offering a civic service to all, irrespective of political and religious affiliations, and the new Parliament which would only pollute this atmosphere of equity and turn the City Hall 'into an arena for the accommodation of political tricksters'.[2] The Ulster

Hall was suggested as an alternative location, a building within which many unionist rallies had been held but which had no formal association with any form of liberal democratic rule. This heightened consciousness of the importance attached to the occupation of symbolic space was nothing novel, as Alderman Harkin reminded his listeners; Nationalist councillors had opposed the use of the same venue for the signing of the Ulster Covenant in 1912.

The first meeting of the Parliament had in fact taken place before the arrival of the King. The main chamber in the City Hall had been transformed into as near a replica of Westminster as was possible. The Mayoral chair became the Speaker's chair and although the mace was not visible, a local journalist reported approvingly that 'all the other paraphernalia of the House was on view'.[3] This conscious association with the regalia and ritual of the Imperial parliament was supplemented by a pointed historical association with the last Irish Parliament held before the Act of Union. The table on which members took their oath was a relic of that assembly, made by John Foster, the last speaker of the Irish House in 1799. Yet in a vital respect the semblance of a representative and democratic institution was seriously limited by the refusal of non-unionists to attend the swearing-in of new members and adopt the role of the official opposition.

After the summer recess the new parliament relocated to the Presbyterian Assembly's College in the south of the city on the grounds that the whole building could be rented for their exclusive use. It is difficult to imagine a building less suited to an attempt to convey the separation of religious affiliation from the exercise of governmental power. The chapel provided accommodation for the Senate while the House of Commons occupied the library over which brooded the portraits of past patriarchs within the Presbyterian tradition. In the most literal sense this was 'a protestant parliament for a protestant people'.

II

The creation of a new parliamentary system is invariably fraught with severe difficulties; in this case the conditions in which this was attempted were highly unfavourable. The legitimacy and authority of these new structures were denied by a substantial minority of the population and a neighbouring state voiced a desire to extend jurisdiction over its territory. Further, the Northern Parliament was subordinate to Westminster, the Imperial centre, which retained the most important powers of defence and revenue-raising for itself while keeping a judicious distance from detailed governance of the local population.

This unfavourable situation was all the more complex since the long-term prospect of a separate parliament in the North was far from guaranteed. Provision had been made in the Government of Ireland Act for a review of the border at some future point. The political and military situation in Ireland as a whole remained extremely fluid; the possibility that civil war might engulf the North was never far from the calculations of all parties concerned.

The leadership of the Unionist Party which now controlled the legislature had other related problems which had to be addressed as a matter of urgency. The assertion of authority and legitimacy had to be extended to and maintained over recalcitrant sections of the community which they claimed to represent. On the one hand the state sought to strengthen security by either disarming protestant paramilitary groups or incorporating them into new policing organisations. On the other, the inter-class alliance mobilised against Home Rule, from which the Unionist Party derived their electoral support, had to be maintained. The fear that the development of labourist politics would draw protestant workers away from the Party demanded the creation of a red spectre which was said to hover over the North, threatening to undermine both ordered government and the continued maintenance of the border.

James Craig, the Prime Minister, addressed many of these issues in his first major speech to Parliament, stressing the importance of swiftly establishing the authority and permanence of the new institution in the face of these difficult conditions:

> There must be dignity about our Parliament and the roots of that Parliament must be deeply seated in the Ulster soil so that no opponents at any time dare come forward and say of that structure – I do not refer to the architectural structure, but the real moral structure which is combined in the Parliamentary Institution – 'that it is only a small affair, and we can easily sweep it to one side.'[4]

Despite his implicit denial that there was a connection between the moral and architectural structure of Parliament, it was precisely to an exploration of this relationship that Craig was to devote an inordinate amount of time and energy, personally overseeing the construction of Stormont. In the same speech he directly alluded to this project, giving the clear impression that he had a general conception of what the new building ought to embody in outline and the practical difficulties that would be encountered in carrying it through. He noted the problem of balancing cost with effectiveness, balancing what was deemed to be appropriate to the 'business-like community' in the North and the necessity to create something both 'stately' and 'dignified', 'of sufficient character to distinguish our Northern Parliament.'[5]

The occupation of the Assembly's College was seen as a temporary measure while the new building was being planned and constructed. By October 1921 Craig, a small group of senior Unionist parliamentarians and a team from the Board of Works visited possible sites at Belvoir Park and Orangefield but finally approved a location at Stormont. A castle and estate upon which it had been built had been purchased from Charles Allen, a director of the shipbuilding firm of Workman and Clark Ltd. The intention was to build in the grounds and hand part of the castle over to the Prime Minister as his official residence. The grateful recipient of this new home commented, rather hopefully, that it would be a residence that 'will get known in much the same way as the Americans talk about the White House'.[6]

A clause in the Government of Ireland Act had guaranteed that the cost of purchasing the land and building the Capital complex, up to a financial ceiling of £1.5m would be met by the Imperial Exchequer. In the first instance the British Board of Works invited the submissions of architectural designs from which were eventually selected the plans presented by Arnold Thornby of Liverpool and Ralph Knott of London.

The original conception of the Stormont building envisaged something very different from what eventually materialised. The principal section of what is now on that site outside Belfast was clearly present in those original designs, but much else beside. Rather than a single structure, two identically proportioned wings were to stand on each side of the main building. Slightly in advance of the front elevation of the principal building, they would nevertheless remain below its height and not thereby dwarf the centre. They were to be executed in a similar neo-classical style. The original intention was to provide suitable accommodation for various departments of the Civil Service. The original plans had also envisaged a grand domed structure crowning the centre of the main building, dramatically overarching the complex.[7] This was capital-building on a grand scale and bore a close resemblance in both size and form to similar structures which had been constructed in many countries of the Old Commonwealth. Australia, New Zealand, Canada and South Africa had employed analogous designs which sprang from a shared sense of how a parliament was to be appropriately housed.

It soon became apparent to the Board of Works in London, who were responsible for costing the project, that there was an incongruity in what was after all a regional centre of administration serving a population of one-and-a-half million occupying a Parliament fit for a whole nation. Craig's continued enthusiasm for the original design which would have unambiguously signalled both the arrival and imperishability of the Northern government was not reciprocated in Whitehall. The Northern Prime Minister and his Chancellor, Andrew Pollock, attended meetings in London on three separate occasions in 1925 and by the end of the year had conceded that substantial revisions to the original plan had to be accepted. In December Craig officially announced to the House that

> Greater efficiency and economy could be secured by doing away with the two wings of the building and housing the Senate and the Commons as well as the bulk of our Civil Service in one comprehensive building situated on the foundations already completed at Stormont. This modification has been welcomed by us so that instead of having a large building laying empty a great part of the year the enlarged building will be a busy hive of industry throughout the whole time.[8]

This rather disingenuous statement obscured the disappointment which was felt by the Northern Premier and his Cabinet. It also served to obscure a practical demonstration of the real limitation on governmental power in the North, arising from their subordination to the Imperial Parliament and its administration. Despite this attempt to present the revised plan as a willing expression of financial probity many unionists were aware of the symbolic importance of the decision. A writer in the *Belfast Telegraph* was to comment later that: 'Instead of having a building which would be a credit both to the British Government and the Ulster Government, we are to have a somewhat emaciated edifice.'[9] The same complaint was voiced in Parliament in an effusive speech by the Independent Unionist MP for North Belfast. Thomas Henderson recomposed Craig's announcement as an order for the destruction of Stormont even before it had been built. Consequently,

> We are not going to get the Parliament House that the Loyalists of Ulster anticipated they were going to get. It is only going to be a skeleton of the former structure....Speaking as one who has a little knowledge of architectural structures, may I ask you that if an artist painted an angel and took away the wings would he destroy the appearance of that angel?[10]

In reality the pared-down structure remained substantial enough to soar over the North. For other critics of the Government the project was an object of attack for precisely this reason. The Labour MP Jack Beattie and the Nationalist leader in the North, Joe Devlin, were indefatigable in their opposition to what they saw as profligate spending in the pursuit of unwarranted vanity. Every opportunity was taken to resist both the specific detail of the plan and its general conception.

The location of the government complex five miles outside Belfast was seen to debar many people from access to important ministries since the cost of transport would be prohibitive. Joe Devlin was to suggest in the course of debate that there was a clear purpose behind this, to build in 'no-man's-land' so as to be 'as far away from their constituents as possible.'[11] Without directly responding to this claim, beyond suggesting that there were no suitable sites in the city centre, Pollock later replied that the complainant 'would have preferred a government even further removed from Belfast i.e. Dublin'.[12]

Despite the Imperial Government bearing the cost of construction the considerable expense involved brought sharp and persistent complaint. The wider picture of the Northern Irish economy and society was the backdrop on which Stormont was projected. Chronic unemployment and a housing stock which was both limited and generally in poor condition were important issues around which Independent Unionists, Labourists and Nationalists mobilised. The governmental complex was easily re-symbolised in this context as a grotesque waste of money, a palladian monstrosity which overlooked the slums of East Belfast. This pointed juxtaposition was directly alluded to by Devlin. Under conditions of severe economic depression,

> All this symbolism does not count...it would be a finer monument to the administration of the Government to have 10,000 families living in happy homes, than to have a magnificent empty fabric...a fabric that is entirely unneeded as far as the community is concerned.[13]

The Nationalist opposition in Parliament (despite a previous policy of abstention some had taken their seats from 1925 onwards) cast doubt on the entire project. For others the primary concern was to ensure that suitable employment was provided for those who were currently out of work and that construction costs were kept to a minimum. Both the Labour MPs Sam Kyle and Jack Beattie and the Independent Unionist Tommy Henderson were particularly assiduous in this regard.

Despite its detractors, by May 1928 the foundation-stone for the new structure had been laid by the Governor of Northern Ireland, the Duke of Abercorn. It was on this occasion that various meanings which could be attached to Stormont were first publicly aired. For the Government, Pollock stressed that the ceremony was 'the outward and visible proof of the permanence of our institutions: that for all time we are bound indissolvably to the British Crown'.[14] A similar theme echoed through the unionist press. For the Belfast *News Letter* Stormont was emblematic of the permanent union with Britain and the established legitimacy of the state in the North. After all,

> it would be a great waste of money and of effort to erect a magnificent building as the home of a merely temporary institution. The laying of the foundation stone is a formal and public declaration that the state of Northern Ireland is firmly established, and that it will never surrender its parliament....[15]

The *Northern Whig* neatly expressed the relationship which was perceived between the proposed structure and its political importance by commenting in its editorial that: 'The building which will in a few years adorn the slopes of Stormont will be well able to withstand the fury of the wildest storms that may beat against its walls.'[16] The laying of the foundation stone was rendered here as the consummation of the victory won by the anti-Home Rule campaign and as a ceremony, which 'will rank with that one on which the Covenant was signed...'.[17]

The ceremony took place on a Saturday in order to allow those workers who wished to attend to do so. Upwards of 15 000 people gathered around the completed foundations, along with the British Home Secretary, Sir William Joynson-Hicks. The unmistakable figure of Lord Carson could also be spied on the platform but he declined to speak despite shouted requests from the assembled crowd.

The speeches that day each constructed a narrative which connected Stormont to the conditions, traits or values out of which it emerged or the future which was now promised. For the British Home Secretary, the emphasis was on the common heritage which had now been sealed and the hope 'that for all time, whatever the future may have in store, you and we may think in unison and work together in loyalty to the Throne and our Empire'. He went on to stress that the roots of this common desire were deep:

> In truth the foundations are not being laid on this day, which marks the implementing of the promise. They were laid long since in the hearts of the men on whom the gift is bestowed.[18]

Craig focused on another aspect of the building and its location in order to stress his avowed aim of fair government:

> I trust that our deliberations and the work of the Civil Service within these walls will be symbolically influenced by the vista that lies before

us, ever calling to our mind the toilers upon the land and those engaged in the shipyards and the factories.[19]

The only discordant note was struck by the Labour representative who concluded his speech to the crowd by looking forward to the day when the partition was ended and Stormont would become incorporated into an all-Ireland parliamentary system:

> I hope that the walls of this great building will re-echo to the voices of Irishmen from all parts of the country, if and when, by God's grace, the two Parliaments may have occasion to meet to decide things for the good of our common country. The surroundings of this great building should certainly give breadth of vision to the members who will take part in the proceedings of parliament, when they get here, and I sincerely trust that the beautiful view will find a sympathetic reflection in the legislation and administration that will emanate from it....[20]

Although this occasion was marked by the absence of nationalist representatives, the presence of Sam Kyle, despite the hostile content of his message, is an instructive sign that tacit legitimacy had been extended to the Northern state by some non-unionists. The Labour group had become the unofficial opposition at Stormont, a role they performed for many years to come.

The other public declarations of that day did not lapse into the explicitly imperial rhetoric which usually carried with it the echo of a distinct 'blood and soil' ideology frequently employed by many Northern unionists. This was voiced the following morning, on Empire Day. Speaking to a congregation at Hillsborough that included many prominent unionists, the Rev. Brett, Dean of Belfast, expostulated on the relationship between the unionist people of Ulster and the Empire, epitomised by Stormont:

> The dominant characteristic of Ulstermen...was a passion for liberty. Not once or twice had the Ulsterman shown that he would not subject his person or conscience to a foreign domination...neither the alien nor the priest could dictate to men whose souls were free. That was why the foundation stone was laid on Saturday, the building to be erected thereon, was regarded as a symbol of a dearly cherished possession; of an attitude of mind as well as a trait of blood. And Ulster identified with the ideal it represented. But the Imperial idea was, after all, but the idea of Ulster.[21]

The 'Ulstermen', a political community which was believed to possess a complex mix of naturalised traits, capacities and dispositions, had at last found the appropriate architectural form through which to express who they were.

The construction work had proceeded at a much slower pace than was expected, to the extent that the original contractors had been replaced in 1924. The Belfast firm of Stewart and Partners Ltd, owned by William Stewart, who became Unionist MP for South Belfast in 1929, received over £650 000 to undertake the raising of the principal structure. The site was cleared and prepared for work from March 1924 onwards, nearly one-and-a-half years after the Prime Minister had announced to Parliament that work was about to begin. Although heavy rainfall that summer affected progress, 160 000 cubic yards of boulder clay was removed as a terrace was cut into the side of the hill. Some of this material was used to create a gentle incline on which the processional road up to the building was to be laid. This was completed in early 1928. In the meantime Irish granite for the foundations and Portland stone for the first floor of the building had been put in place. These foundations were made to exacting requirements since it was intended in the original plans to include a heavy dome structure which required a substantially concrete raft to be put in place. The raising of the main body of the building was completed between 1928 and April 1931 on which date some ministries began to transfer from the city centre into their new accommodation.

As the building neared final completion the attention of some MPs began to turn towards the detail of the interior and the appropriate form its decoration was to take. The Independent Unionist MP John Nixon proposed that a framed copy of the Ulster Covenant be placed in a prominent place, 'a reminder to those who come after us of a great many things that some people do not like to think about, but that nevertheless, should be kept at the forefront'.[22] This suggestion of offering a clear, unambiguous sign of the imputed association of the building with the unionist movement was compounded by the related suggestion of hanging a portrait of King William crossing the Boyne. The building was officially opened in November 1932 by the Prince of Wales, a ceremony that amplified rather than altered the diverse meanings which had already become associated with Stormont. For the next forty years it stood at the centre of the formal political life of the North.

III

Since the building's completion both the main structure and its surrounding landscape have remained largely unaltered. A lodge-house and an ornamental stone-and-iron gateway mark the entrance to 300 acres of parkland which rises in a gradual incline for about a third of a mile towards the main building. The visitor is carried towards this point of destination by a tree-flanked processional avenue which intersects with other entrance roads at a circus dominated at its centre by a bronze statue of Lord Carson raised on a granite plinth. The monumental sculpture, executed by Merrifield, captures a familiar image of the unionist leader galvanised in rhetorical declaration. The right arm raised high above the shoulder and the left hand, palm open, held in momentary abeyance conforms to the conventional recollection frequently reiterated through a variety of media. This expressive personification of the challenge which was mounted to an ascendent Irish nationalism captures only one very public aspect of a complex if not contradictory personality but is an image which is reinforced by four panels mounted around the base of the plinth. Each depicts a stage in the progress of Ulster unionism, culminating in a panel devoted to the signing of the Covenant in 1912, a pledge to resist autonomy from the Imperial Parliament at all costs.

The processional avenue continues beyond this point and meets a flight of approach steps made of unpolished Mourne granite cut from Slieve Donard, an extension of the plinth upon which the Parliament is grounded. The main building is 367 feet long, 167 feet deep and 70 feet high, the exterior faced with Portland stone. Built in a Greek classical style, the front facade appears angular and symmetrical, thus conveying a well-proportioned simplicity. This aspect is reinforced by the plain treatment of the exterior with the exception of the public entrance bay which is centred around a grand Ionic temple front. Six colonnades dominate this portico and support a pediment which is embellished with a carving described as 'Ulster bearing the Golden Flame of Loyalty to the Crown'. An upward extension rises above this central section of the building capped with a statuesque representation of Britannia flanked by two lions. On either side of this tableau Union flags can sometimes be seen rising above the building thus demarcating the allegiance of this imposing structure if it had not been read so far.

The main entrance leads into an imposing vestibule which gives access to the Central Hall 100 feet long and almost 50 feet wide, surrounded by a gallery on either side and a flight of steps leading to the various floors of the building. Overseeing this arrangement a life-size statue of James Craig, the first Prime Minister of Northern Ireland, dressed in Imperial finery, looks down from the landing of the first flight of stairs. It is only here and in the Senate and Commons chambers which are situated to the right and left of the hall that elaborate decoration predominates in the form of marble and painted plaster.

The rest of the interior is plainly enhanced with dark wood panelling common in buildings of a similar type and period. It would be difficult to mistake this internal arrangement as anything other than originating in the late 1920s and 1930s given the occasional art deco flourishes which are periodically sighted. Damaged in a fire in 1995, the Commons chamber is modelled on its equivalent in London, replete with a Speaker's chair, dispatch boxes, and a public and press gallery. Where this chamber departs from the Imperial design is in the blue upholstery of the members' benches, unlike the green livery of Westminster, and in the arrangement of the seating, which is not in two adversarial blocks facing each other but in a horse-shoe configuration. The Senate chamber is more elaborate, decorated in gold, ivory and scarlet with a ceiling above the public gallery graced with arabesque figures. Here the internal organisation of space and structure conforms to the Westminster model. Organised on four floors, the rest of the building contains not only the various auxiliary departments normally associated with this particular form of liberal-democratic rule, committee and conference rooms, the offices of parliamentary functionaries and those of the government and opposition, but also space originally allocated to a range of ministerial departments. In the past both the Northern Ireland legislature and important elements of the executive were housed together in over 220 rooms at Stormont, the working environment of many hundreds of civil servants.

IV

It is clear that there were aspirations, values and political imperatives following partition, and the creation of a separate state in the North gave them an appropriate symbolic expression in the governmental complex outside Belfast. Stability, order, permanence, authority and judicious government were all to be exemplified in both architectural form and the location of the resulting building in the surrounding landscape.

Grand symbolic buildings employ a variety of mechanisms through which meaning is transmitted in an effectual manner. They denote, exemplify, offer themselves as metaphors and act as a mediated reference which connects with a wider constellation of values and meanings far removed from the building itself.[23] Stormont offers a wide variety of concrete examples which typify each of these representations of state power in a liberal-democratic form.

It is possible to stand in many parts of Belfast and the city's surrounding districts and catch a glimpse of Stormont's unmistakable profile in the distance. In part this is a result of the decision to dress the distinctive outline building in white Portland stone but also a consequence of the raised ground on which it rests. Grandiosity combines with visibility in such a way as to induce the calculated effect of an imposing presence – a presence analogous to that of a temple which is not dispelled by drawing closer to the site. In ancient societies the citadel was customarily positioned on elevated ground, serving to accentuate the relationship between the earthly centre and its proximity to the celestial space of the heavens. The boundary around the area marks a distinction between the space of mundane activity and that of the sublime which conjoins with a distinction between high and low ground. Buildings of this order, both ancient and modern, serve as points of contact and mediation either between God and the people on the one hand or between the central tenants of liberal democracy and the citizens on the other. They also function as places of pilgrimage, a role which Stormont has certainly performed over the years. During the 1970s mass rallies were frequently held in the grounds, most notably during the Ulster Workers' Strike of 1974.

This aspect of Stormont's form and function is also facilitated by the processional avenue which conveys the visitor, protestor or pilgrim towards the main structure. The linear force of the road and those being drawn along is gathered in at the point of terminus. The place of Stormont in the history of Northern Ireland as it is conjured up through the use of photographic images and reproduced in the mass media attests to the potency of this arrangement. The image of power moving through space has been irresistible to those who have participated in such activity and those who wish to employ visually powerful images of force, direction and purpose.

The grounds through which the avenue cuts and within which the building is situated were ordered and planted during the construction process but still retain the semblance of a natural environment.[24] The imputed timelessness of the naturalised surroundings provided an important backdrop on which to project various historical narratives associated with the area around Stormont but now united with Stormont the building. The laying of the foundation stone in 1928 had prompted the *Northern Whig* to draw attention to precisely this relationship. While the building was said to be open to criticism from a 'utilitarian point of view' there was no other location richer in 'natural beauty...or traditional and historical association'.[25] The historical association alluded to the proximity of Stormont to the ancient stronghold of Con O'Neill to which he retreated after banishment from Clandeboye. The traces of this site had been effaced, the stones used to build a recently constructed protection wall: 'Thus a strand of the gaudy artificial silk of modernity has become interwoven with the gossamer of ancient romance.' For the *Northern Whig* the presence of First World War veterans at the ceremony provided an authentic fusion of past and present, bringing together modern heroes and the ghostly warriors of Ulster.

Detractors could mobilise a countervailing historical association which did not return to the seventeenth century but to a more recent period, the ramifications of which were still being experienced. An anonymous journalist from the nationalist *Irish News* commented on the relationship of the site to the 1792 uprising. The owner of the site, who also built upon it a country house that was to become Stormont Castle, was credited with a leading role in hunting down radical Presbyterians involved in the United Irishmen movement. The Rev. John Cleland was also noted as a mean and unforgiving landlord and magistrate. The writer connected the previous owner of the estate to its present occupants: 'One cannot help wondering if the spirit of the man who built Stormont Castle and acquired the estate on which the present noble palace for politicians stands, is hovering over the place.'[26] This speculation is expressed much more categorically in the chapter-heading under which the historical sketch is presented – '"Informer" Clergyman the Progenitor of Modern Stormontism'.

With or without these historical accretions the governmental complex aims to cast as spectators those who cross into its domain. The scale of the building, the boundary which surrounds it and the civic space which it encompasses enhance a denotation of power and authority. Those who enter the precincts of the powerful do so as observers rather than participants, an experience which is intensified the further you travel to the centre of Stormont. Proximity to power reveals the paradox that drawing closer to its formalised structures and processes accentuates the distance from them of those who are cast in the role of the excluded. This relationship is reinforced through a reciprocated perception by those who identify this domain as their own and who play an active part in the life of the institution. The distinction between the active and the passive, the ruler and the ruled and the participant and observer is deeply imbued in the organisation of the building and the social space which it expresses. The internal organisation of Stormont designates a hierarchical organisation of power among those who rule and a strict division between those in positions of power and the ordinary citizen. At the heart of the building lay the Commons Chamber which was only accessible to elected members, the public only being admitted to a raised gallery from which to look down on the proceedings. The Senate chamber was similarly arranged but in itself subordinate in its position to the Commons. Each passageway and door in the rest of the building signalled a gradated organisation of power which carried the visitor through a labyrinthine system both exact and hierarchical. To proceed from the main Entrance Hall to the heart of the building would have conveyed this unmistakable impression. Turning left along one of the main corridors would involve passing an entrance to the members' Cloakroom, their Smoking Room and beyond this the Commons Committee Room. Beyond this point are located three interconnected rooms for Ministers of the Government. Having reached the south-western corner of the building a large apartment is allocated to the Prime Minister which is only accessible through an ante-room off which is located a secretarial office and private cloakroom. This route was the preserve of Members, select civil servants and honoured guests, a route that became increasingly difficult to traverse without the appropriate status.

The designation of ordered power was apparent in the formal arrangement of the internal structure but it was also expressed through the social rules and conventions which governed the appropriate behaviour of those gathered at Stormont. Convention, derived from Westminster, structured exchanges in the parliamentary chambers and allocated an appropriate role to government and opposition, to the viewing public and performer. To break these rules could be the result of a calculated assault against the prevailing structures of power, which during the course of the Stormont Parliament was not an infrequent occurrence. Informal rules also abounded; these included the hushed reverence which was considered appropriate in the proximity of Parliament when it was sitting.

Since the dissolution of a devolved Assembly at Stormont in 1986, enforced silence replaced the pursuit of hushed reverence. The foundations upon which both the local state and its Parliament had been built proved to be unstable, the avowed pursuit of judicious government had been challenged and its authority, permanence and order had been violently disrupted. The ambitions out of which the building had materialised had been undermined on the one hand and partly compromised on the other. As a new phase in the history of Northern Ireland begins to unfold Stormont has ceased to be simply a monument to the political forces out of which it was born; its future role has yet to be decided.

David Officer 147

NOTES

1. C. Brett, *The Buildings of Belfast – 1700–1914* (Belfast, 1967), p. 65.
2. *Belfast Evening Telegraph*, 1 June 1921.
3. Ibid., 8 June 1921.
4. *House of Commons Debates – Northern Ireland Parliament*, 23 September 1921, col. 174.
5. Ibid., col. 177.
6. Ibid., 4 October 1921, col. 260.
7. Very few images of this original design were circulated. One is reproduced as part of the introduction to the official programme of the Northern Irish contribution to the Empire Exhibition of 1924. An artist's impression of this complex appears in a pamphlet unremittingly hostile to the entire project by an unnamed journalist from the *Irish News* – 'QX', *The Truth About Stormont*, January 1932.
8. *House of Commons Debates – Northern Irish Parliament*, 8 December 1925, col. 1818.
9. *Belfast Telegraph,* 26 August 1926.
10. *House of Commons Debates – Northern Ireland Parliament*, 9 December 1926, col. 1891–2.
11. Ibid., 9 March 1926, col. 38.
12. Ibid., 5 May 1926, col. 1000.
13. ibid., 9 March 1926, col. 37.
14. Ibid., 21 May 1928, col. 244.
15. *Belfast News Letter*, 21 May 1928.
16. *Northern Whig*, 21 May 1928.
17. Ibid.
18. Ibid.
19. Ibid.
20. Ibid.
21. Ibid.
22. *House of Commons Debates – Northern Ireland Parliament*, 30 April 1932, col. 830.
23. Lawrence Vale, *Architecture, Power and National Indentity* (New Haven Conn.: Yale, 1992).
24. An earlier example of this configuration can be seen at Versailles on the outskirts of Paris. A processional road leads to a Central structure of power and grandeur which is set in carefully orchestrated grounds. See Sigfried Giedion, *Space, Time and Architecture – The Growth of a New Tradition* (Cambridge, Mass.: Harvard, 1941), pp. 72–5.
25. *Northern Whig*, 21 May 1928.
26. 'QX', ibid.

9 'Meddling at the Crossroads': The Decline and Fall of Terence O'Neill within the Unionist Community*

Feargal Cochrane

INTRODUCTION

The career of Captain Terence O'Neill as Prime Minister of Northern Ireland from 1963 to 1969 poses many questions about the dynamics of modern unionism. This essay does not set out to pick over the much-studied bones of O'Neill's reform programme.[1] My aim here is to look at the forces within unionism which were implacably opposed to his regime, and to explain why it was that these proved stronger than the forces of moderation. I will also attempt to draw some conclusions about how the O'Neill period fits into a wider unionist context.

My central argument is that O'Neill's background and personality, together with his inability fully to understand the political dynamics within the 'state', were responsible for his ultimate political failure. His assumption that the twin-track approach, of economic modernisation and gestures of reconciliation towards the Catholic community, would solve Northern Ireland's problems, was fundamentally misconceived. I will argue here that what O'Neill naively interpreted as a behavioural problem (low Catholic self-esteem rendering them socially inept and unemployable), was in reality a structural problem. His public articulation of a 'feel-good factor' was constantly undermined by the fact that since Northern Ireland had been created, there had been no rotation of government between unionist and nationalist parties. Indeed, from the point of view of his own party, that was one of the attractions of devolution. As the political system's cohesion (and certainly that of his party) was predicated upon the existence of the sectarian cleavage, it was inevitable that O'Neill's rhetoric would remain just that.

Before analysing the growth of opposition within the unionist community to O'Neill's premiership, it is necessary to provide some political context. What many historians now call 'O'Neillism' was distinguishable in terms of the rhetoric used, as much as the practical policies that were conducted. O'Neill announced to the Ulster Unionist Council [UUC], shortly after becoming Prime Minister, that 'our task will be literally to transform Ulster, ...to achieve it will require bold and imaginative measures'.[2] The language was designed to appeal to the Catholic minority within Northern Ireland, alienated by the exclusivist tones (and actions) of Brookeborough's premiership. Perhaps as importantly, O'Neill's announcement of a 'brave new dawn' for Northern Ireland was intended for external consumption. He was anxious to convince the British government that the Unionist Party was capable of engineering internal change and maintaining stability within Northern Ireland. O'Neill, it seems, was preoccupied with the 'image' of the region not only in Britain but on the wider world stage.

There has been a deal of academic debate concerning the depth of O'Neill's commitment to reform and whether he was in fact a 'well meaning liberal'[3] at all. Some would rather portray him as a calculating cynic who articulated the language of reform as a buffer against pressure from the British government and as a means of diluting the electoral threat to cross-class unionist solidarity presented by the Northern Ireland Labour Party [NILP].

O'Neill hoped, through his rhetoric of 'planning' and 'modernisation', to re-establish the Unionist party's hegemony over the Protestant working class. He had done absolutely nothing to counter discrimination against Catholics in Northern Ireland.[4]

While this view has considerable force, it rather overstates O'Neill's Machiavellian credentials. He undoubtedly saw the NILP as an electoral threat and was not above playing 'the Orange Card' at election time. It would be an unusual leader who did not seek to preserve the hegemony of their party and O'Neill was no different from most in this respect. It is also true that O'Neill did little in practical terms to counter discrimination against Catholics (by the time he conceded the main demands of the civil rights movement his premiership was mortally wounded). As far as O'Neill was concerned, there was no contradiction between strengthening the political position of the Unionist Party and redressing Catholic grievances. His fundamental mistake was to misperceive the reasons which underlay these grievances. When we look at the legacy of O'Neill, and compare it with the supposed goal of maintaining old-style unionist domination by eliminating the threat of working-class support for the NILP, it would be difficult to conceive of a more counter-productive policy. The legacy of O'Neill, after all, was the political disintegration of the Stormont system, the splintering of the Unionist Party and personal failure.

It could be argued that he did not specifically target discrimination against Catholics because he believed the problems in Northern Ireland to be behavioural rather than structural. As far as O'Neill was concerned, the strife in Northern Ireland did not stem from the enshrined imbalance in the political positions of unionism and nationalism, from the fact that Northern Ireland was effectively a one-party state, from discrimination in local government, and from the Unionist Party's repeated determination to maintain this situation. Because the problem emanated, in his view, from poor community relations and an era of 'bad feelings', the solution to Catholic discrimination did not require legislative change, but lay rather in combating the minority's low self-esteem. Encouraged, through gestures of friendship, to 'get their act together', the Catholic community would become more employable. This perspective illustrates not so much a devious mind, as a fundamental misconception of the problems which faced Northern Ireland and the Catholic community within it.

It would be fair to say that O'Neill's reforms were largely symbolic and piecemeal. They did little to tackle the real grievances of the Catholic community and merely raised expectations which were not fulfilled. His meetings with Sean Lemass and Jack Lynch were welcomed by the Catholic community but it quickly became apparent that these were empty gestures. O'Neill had a naive belief in the political system in Northern Ireland, believing Stormont to be far superior to the nasty bickering and class politics which took place at Westminster. Thus, if he had his photograph taken with nuns and patted enough Catholic schoolchildren on the head, they would begin to behave more like Protestants. O'Neill's plan was that through general economic revival, wealth would filter down to the Catholic community, enabling them to 'live like Protestants, because they will see neighbours with cars and television sets. ...If you treat Roman Catholics with due consideration and kindness, they will live like Protestants in spite of the authoritative nature of their Church.'[5] Austin Currie's response to these comments was typical of nationalist reaction. 'I take exception to the general tone of Capt. O'Neill's remarks. It is like a squire on his estate, talking about the treatment of his cattle.'[6] Gerry Fitt summed up the Catholic mood, with his dry observation that 'While

Craigavon and Brookeborough had walked over the Catholics with hob-
nail boots, O'Neill walked over them with carpet slippers'.[7]

ONE OF US?

Perhaps the most fundamental problem for O'Neill in his relationship
with the unionist community derived from his social background. His
early years were spent at Eton and the Irish Guards, hardly an ideal
apprenticeship for a career dealing with the gritty populism of politics in
Northern Ireland. His upbringing was, to say the least, an unusual one.
O'Neill never knew his father, who was killed very early in the First
World War. After his mother remarried (her second husband being a
British diplomat), he spent a lot of his childhood abroad, in Addis Ababa
among other places. Although many of his holidays were spent at
Shane's Castle, the historic seat of the O'Neills in County Antrim, he
never established particularly deep roots in Ulster. It was only after the
war, much of which he spent in England and Australia, that he actually
settled in Northern Ireland. To the 'natives' therefore, he always seemed
a rather exotic sort of figure, sounding more like a patrician Englishman
than an Ulsterman.

O'Neill's Anglo-Irish, 'Big House' background was compounded by his
personality. He was essentially an aloof character whose social awkward-
ness could easily be taken for arrogant detachment. 'He was Olympian, a
man of destiny who found the company of world leaders more convivial
than those [sic] of his colleagues.'[8] This concern for 'life at the high table'
did not help O'Neill's battle for acceptance within the Ulster Unionist
Party.

Speaking retrospectively about the O'Neill period, the Ulster Unionist
Party's Rev. Martin Smyth commented that he was simply 'the wrong man
for the job' who did not have enough of a common touch or sufficient
political savvy, to bring the rest of his party colleagues or the wider community with him.[9] Some who worked closely with O'Neill have stated that
his public image of aristocratic pretension and arrogance did not reflect his
private persona.

Nothing could have been further from the truth than the image he often
seemed to give of arrogance and hauteur. He was, in reality, like more
politicians than many would suppose: a fundamentally shy person,
liable when presented with an awkward customer not well known to
him to throw up his head like a nervous and very highly-bred horse.[10]

Whether or not other colleagues such as Brian Faulkner held such a sympathetic view, this was certainly not the image of O'Neill held by many working-class unionists. However impeccable his diction, O'Neill's rhetoric offended the ears of a significant and powerful minority within the Protestant community, especially against the background of the guttural violence of extremist opponents such as Ian Paisley. In February 1966, for example, after O'Neill had paid a return visit to the Irish Taoiseach Sean Lemass in Dublin, Paisley wrote an article in his Free Presbyterian paper *The Revivalist*, which fell not far short of inciting his followers to rebel against the government in general and O'Neill in particular.

> It is quite evident...that the Ecumenists, both political and ecclesiastical, are selling us. Every Ulster Protestant must unflinchingly resist these leaders and let it be known in no uncertain manner that they will not sit idly by as these modern Lundies pursue their policy of treachery. Ulster expects every Protestant in this hour of crisis to do his duty.[11]

Although O'Neill cannot be blamed for the circumstances of his upbringing, and while there were other more important factors in his political downfall, his social background and his personality undoubtedly put him at a disadvantage from the outset. Even after his resignation, extreme elements within the unionist community blamed the violence in Northern Ireland on O'Neill's arrogant determination to introduce political reform, exhibiting a proletarian outlook and populist view antithetical to the spirit of 'O'Neillism'. The loyalist *U.D.A.* magazine argued that

> O'Neill make [*sic*] the greatest blunder that any politician has made this century.... Terence O'Neill, Terence O'Neill/The Captain of Buffoonery, the paternalistic moron, made the assumption that the 'Landed Gentry' who are educated in England continually make – 'they know what is best for the Ulster Loyalist.' The one thing of any benefit that they did leave was the realisation among Ulster Loyalists that the time has come for the removal of 'Landed Gentry' from the environs of political power.[12]

A similar journal which styled itself as the 'Voice of Loyalist Political Prisoners', accused O'Neill and his colleague Roy Bradford of being 'liars, hypocrites and cowards'.

> Undoubtedly the supremo of snobs O'Neill, with his false accent, must be the first of such Traitors because it was he who first made possible the NO GO areas and it was he who first contravened the convention

that existed between the British Government and ourselves that our own house was kept in order by ourselves.[13]

Aside from his background and personality, the circumstances in which O'Neill came to power within the Unionist Party did not help him wield authority within it. It should be remembered that when Brookeborough retired in 1963, there was no electoral process to produce the leader of the party. The system was akin to that which operated within the Conservative Party at the time, namely, a leader emerged out of 'a magic circle', among the notorious 'men in grey suits'. Consequently, O'Neill came to power without being able to demonstrate that he had a mandate to lead or illustrate that he could command majority support within either the Parliamentary Party or the country.

O'Neill assumed office, therefore, with no real base in the party, a compromise candidate who prospered through the ambition of others, notably William Craig. Craig was Chief Whip and thus charged with the responsibility of 'taking soundings' within the party. It has been alleged that Craig desired that O'Neill rather than Faulkner should take over, as this would have increased his own chances of following the older man into the leadership in due course. Brian Faulkner certainly believed that the job had been 'stitched-up':

> Clearly, the three key figures involved were the Prime Minister [Brookeborough], the Governor [Lord Wakehurst], and the then Chief Whip, Bill Craig. The last did much to ensure O'Neill's appointment and the two were close allies for some years after.[14]

THE EARLY YEARS

Terence O'Neill became leader of the Unionist Party and Prime Minister on 25 March 1963. This sprightly, energetic 49-year-old took over from the ailing septuagenarian Lord Brookeborough, promising 'to make Northern Ireland economically stronger and prosperous...and to build bridges between the two traditions within our community'.[15] He was welcomed by many, not least the local media, as a breath of fresh air, and perhaps a leader more suited to the economic challenges and opportunities presented by the 1960s than his rather somnambulant predecessor.

> There is no doubt that his succession to the leadership will win general acclaim from the back-benchers. Soundings of party opinion which the Chief Whip, Mr William Craig, has carried out showed overwhelming

support for Captain O'Neill. There may be one or two MPs who take a different view, but the vigour and drive which the Minister of Finance has shown both inside and outside the House in recent months assures him of a wholehearted vote of confidence at the Party meeting today.[16]

In case there was any doubting the esteem in which the new Prime Minister was held, another headline on the front page of the 26 March 1963 edition of the *News Letter* declared O'Neill to be 'A Man of Talents'. The following day the paper gave its readers the human angle: 'O'Neill's well loved in local village'. Apparently in Ahoghill, Co. Antrim, where O'Neill lived with his family, the new Prime Minister was a 'loved and respected figure'.[17] The *Belfast Telegraph*, which was to become a major supporter of the new administration, was equally support-ive, the paper's 'Viewpoint' column providing positive editorial comment the day after he took office.

A family man who brings to each day's work 'the wine of his own tem-perament' – his background and career are practically alike to Lord Brookeborough's. In his own party he has won respect and in the House of Commons he is liked by all as a man of quiet manners; in short a good representative Ulsterman – and one well adjusted to the demands of a new era.[18]

Jack Sayers, editor of the *Belfast Telegraph* during this period, soon became O'Neill's champion in the local media. His public support for the embattled Prime Minister remained to the end, and perhaps explains why O'Neill lasted as long as he did, as moves were made against him within the party as early as 1966.

The 1960s were a decade of planning and government intervention in the economy; what O'Neill could not have known was that it was to become the decade of revolution and 'people power'. The Prime Minister duly announced his intention to provide a modern and comprehensive planning system for Northern Ireland which would provide new hospitals, better roads and more public housing. He appointed Professor Tom Wilson of the University of Glasgow as economic consultant to the Government in October 1963. A few months earlier, an Economic Council had been established under the chairmanship of the new Minister of Commerce, Brian Faulkner. This was to be a coordinating body and think-tank which could recommend strategies for furthering economic develop-ment and growth. This episode provides evidence not only of the impossibility in Northern Ireland of trying to conduct an apolitical econ-omic policy, but also of O'Neill's inability to dominate his cabinet, even at the beginning of his term of office when his authority should have been at a high. It soon became clear that in order for the Economic Council to work effectively, it would need the cooperation of the trade union movement, yet they were in dispute with the government over its refusal to recognise the Northern Committee of the Irish Congress of Trade Unions (ICTU). The reason for this was political. Quite apart from the Unionist Party's general aversion to trade unionism, it saw ICTU as a Southern Irish body and therefore alien. To recognise the Northern Committee of ICTU was considered to be an implicit acceptance that the South (or its native organisations) could have some role in the internal affairs of Northern Ireland and this was, by definition, a threat to the authority of Stormont. This had indeed been a central plank of the Unionist Party's 1962 election manifesto. 'The Unionist Party does not recognise the Irish Congress of Trade Unionists, but is prepared to recognise in N. Ireland a Committee of the British T.U.C.'[19]

One of the trade union nominees to the Economic Council, however, was William Blease, the Northern Ireland Officer of ICTU. When the government refused to accept Blease as a representative on the basis that ICTU was not a recognised trade union, the other nominees immediately boycotted the Economic Council, thereby damaging its potential effectiveness.

It took until the summer of 1964 to reach a compromise, one which involved an amendment to the ICTU constitution guaranteeing the autonomy of its Northern Ireland Committee (NIC).[20] O'Neill later remarked that getting the cabinet to agree to recognise the NIC was 'one of the most difficult hurdles I surmounted during my premiership'.[21] The fact that it took him eighteen months to do so illustrates the lack of authority he exercised within his cabinet from the earliest days of his government. Even when he did manage to get the NIC recognised, he did not bring a united party in behind the decision. By his own admission, at a party-meeting held to endorse the cabinet vote, Brian Faulkner tried to have the decision postponed, while 'the small gathering – many MPs were too frightened to attend it – endorsed the Cabinet's decision'.[22] However, Cabinet papers from the period suggest that only a matter of weeks after he became Prime Minister, O'Neill was exhibiting no positive leadership over the ICTU issue. On 17 April 1963, the Cabinet debated a request by the 'Churches' Industrial Council' for a meeting with six members of the Unionist Parliamentary Party to discuss Government recognition of ICTU and redundancy in industry.

In discussion it was pointed out that some of the members and staff of the Churches' Industrial Council were unfriendly to the Unionist point of view; that if a meeting were refused the Unionist attitude on the two matters in question could be misrepresented in the absence of an authoritative exposition of the Party's standpoint; and that if a meeting did take place and it were desired to avoid formal commitments on behalf of the Party it could always be made clear that the Members of Parliament concerned were attending in their private capacity. It was agreed that the proposal for an early meeting should be declined on the ground that the date proposed, being a Parliamentary sitting day, was unsuitable.[23]

Recently released Cabinet papers provide further evidence, both of O'Neill's absence of reforming zeal, and his lack of confidence about getting his government and party to agree to measures which might go some way towards reducing nationalist alienation. Cabinet discussions over Clause Three of the 'Ministerial and Other Offices Bill', which concerned the payment of a salary to the leader of the Opposition at Stormont, provide an interesting insight into O'Neill's attitude to the Nationalist Party and a startling lack of confidence about his leadership abilities less than a year into his premiership. The cabinet had previously agreed that payment of a salary could be approved in principle, subject to the 'emergence' of a suitable leader. O'Neill commented that, although initial soundings had indicated that Unionist Party backbenchers would favour such a payment,

> these views had probably been expressed on the assumption that the payment would in fact be made to the Labour Party leader. If, in the event, the outcome proved to be payment of a salary to the Nationalist Party leader, the reaction might differ substantially from the result of the Chief Whip's soundings. ...The Nationalists were pledged, not to form and operate an alternative Government [the basis for a payment], but to subvert the constitution under which that Government operated.[24]

From the radical unionist perspective, however, O'Neill appeared hell-bent on introducing real reforms to the detriment of the Protestant community and the very fabric of the Northern Ireland 'state'. Ian Paisley successfully tapped into this seam of resentment and fear by portraying himself as a political martyr defending the Protestant heritage in Ulster. Having been accused of an unlawful assembly likely to cause a breach of the peace in July 1966, Paisley was ordered by the court to pay a £30 bail-bond to keep the peace for two years or go to jail for three months. In the *Protestant Telegraph* of 30 July 1966, Paisley explained why he (together with two of his colleagues) chose the latter and launched a vitriolic attack on O'Neill's policies.

> The term of the present Prime Minister, Capt. Terence O'Neill, has been one sad story of appeasement with the enemies of Northern Ireland. His secret meetings with Lemass were acts of treachery. By his words and actions he has shown himself to be more interested in his political dictatorship than in keeping Northern Ireland truly Protestant. ... With the grace of God and the help of the Protestants of Ulster, the day will come when I will be in Stormont – the only way true Protestant people can deal with the ruling junta of Lundies is to have someone there to root out the nest of traitors.[25]

THE ORANGE ORDER

Paisley was not the only one articulating opposition to O'Neill, even if he was the loudest. While the Order made no secret of its ambitions to exert a political influence on unionism, Orangeism's role in O'Neill's downfall should not be overestimated. The Grand Master of the Grand Lodge of Ireland, Rev. Martin Smyth, commenting retrospectively on the period, argued that although the Order had a voice within unionism,

> Unfortunately at times, I don't think Terence listened. There are those who believe that the Orange stick was wielded and therefore people just jumped to it. In my time within the Orange Order, which is going on for the best part of fifty years now, ...I've got to say that the mythology of the Orange dictating to the Unionist Council is mythology.[26]

A pamphlet produced by the *Belfast County Grand Orange Lodge* in 1972 does not attack the substance of O'Neill's policies with the vehemence characteristic of radical loyalism, but blames the outbreak of sectarian conflict on the consequences of Catholic self-organisation.

> The immediate tragedy of Ulster is that until 1968 and the civil rights marches there had been an easily recognisable improvement in community relations in the Province and a growing prosperity which was obvious to all. ...Ulster society was moving slowly but surely towards an equalisation of opportunities and responsibilities for all its citizens. There was an increasing Roman Catholic participation in the life of the whole community when before there had been reluctance to accept life in a disagreeable political situation.[27]

The reticence of the Orange Order to respond to the rhetoric of O'Neill's government might be explained by arguing that as an organisation, it was itself on the defensive during the 1960s. Put bluntly, the Order was not extreme enough for many of the young, urban, Protestant working class. It had previously attracted recruits eager to display their distinctive identity and position of communal authority within the state; by the mid-sixties, other groups were competing for the services of Protestant cultural testosterone. In comparison to the street agitation of Ian Paisley and the sectarian agenda of paramilitary organisations such as the Ulster Protestant Volunteers (UPV) and the UVF, the Orange Order appeared to many young urban Protestants to be a stodgy, over-respectable organisation run by the unionist establishment.

The connection between the Orange Order and the Unionist Party made it difficult for them openly to attack the O'Neill regime without also condemning the party. Consequently, the Order shied away from voicing their concerns in public. Ian Paisley was not so shy and his self-appointed status as a Protestant martyr attracted support from those disillusioned by the low-key attitude adopted by the Orange Order towards the government. The comments below, by the former Attorney-General, Sir Edmond Warnock, provide supporting evidence of the relationship between the unionist establishment and the Order, and the contention that its position had weakened in the 1960s.

In the mid-sixties, the Orange Order was in the invidious position of being closely associated with the leadership of unionism, while most of its members were becoming increasingly opposed to the Government. The dilemma for the Orange hierarchy was plain to see during the 'Twelfth' celebrations. The intent of the leadership was clearly to support O'Neill. On 12 July 1966, the Grand Master of the Grand Lodge of Ireland, Sir George Clark, backed the Prime Minister and called on other Orangemen not to cooperate with his main critic, Ian Paisley.

> I think it is entirely wrong that brother Orangemen should lend their platforms to a man who uses it to mount a continuous attack upon a member of the Order, and, in this case, a member who is not only a distinguished brother, but the Prime Minister recently elected by an overwhelming majority to lead this country.[28]

Despite such endorsements from the leadership of Orangeism, it is clear that there was division in the ranks. The resolutions of the Order for the 'Twelfth' celebrations were becoming more hardline, one in particular criticising the move towards ecumenism by some Protestant Churches as 'a Romeward trend' and a 'marked departure' from the Protestant faith.[29]

An account of the 'Twelfth' celebrations at Finaghy in Belfast in 1967, illustrates the conflicting tensions being experienced by the leadership of the Orange Order with respect to their support of O'Neill.

At Finaghy it was not clear whether the resolution praising the policies of Capt. O'Neill was passed or not. Dr. E.H. Berry, Grand Master of New Zealand, proposed the resolution without once referring to the Prime Minister but simply praising the work done by the Northern Ireland Government. However, when at the end of Dr. Berry's speech the County Grand Master, Mr. John Bryans, read out the terms of the resolution, it was greeted with loud booing. Mr Bryans' voice was drowned by the continual booing and shouting. There were shouts from the crowd of 'what about O'Neill' and 'Lundy'. Mr Bryans asked the crowd to indicate if the resolution met with their approval and this was received with further shouts and boohs [sic].[30]

In sharp contrast to the official Orange support for O'Neill in July 1967, there is clear evidence that the leadership were out of touch with the mood of a sizable number of their followers.

Hundreds of leaflets condemning the resolution paying tribute to Captain O'Neill were distributed on behalf of the Orange Voice of Freedom at the 'field' in Finaghy to-day. The leaflets refer to the 'tottering leadership' of the Prime Minister and adds [sic] that no true Orangeman could have confidence in him.[31]

It was only after O'Neill had resigned that magazines such as *The Orangeman* started publicly to attack his policies. This was undoubtedly linked to increasing fears about the escalation of political conflict and the disintegration of 'law and order' in Northern Ireland. It was not until 1971 that the magazine became distinctly more political and hardline loyalist, openly criticising O'Neill under the headline, 'Six into Twenty-Six Will Never Go'.

Add a few more names [to O'Neill's] of so called moderate unionist M.P.'s [sic] and the picture clearly forms of a group within the party who are prepared to have the authority of our own Parliament undermined and would in fact risk destroying the Unionist Party if they can't change it. Surely we are assailed by enemies from within and without. ...Let this message be carried to all, even the man who claims he has been asked to be President of a new Federated All Ireland State [O'Neill], the words of the old jingle we used to chant at school. 'Though De Valera says its [sic] so Six into twenty six will Never Go.'[32]

THE BEGINNING OF THE END

O'Neill's strategy of pursuing general economic growth, accompanied by conciliatory *gestures* towards the minority community began to unravel after the publication of the Wilson report in February 1965. The plan envisaged a number of ambitious proposals, including a major new ring-road for Belfast, a new city in the centre of 'Ulster', a second university, four new motorways and a plan for the building of 64 000 houses within five years. At the centre of the Wilson Report was a 'vigorous drive to import new firms to Northern Ireland, to be enticed by tax allowances, investment grants and employment premiums'.[33] However, the practical implementation of the Report saw O'Neill's stock nose-dive within the Catholic population. Having been led to believe that they would 'get their fair share' under the new regime, their raised expectations were dashed by subsequent decisions, over both the name and location of the new town Craigavon, and the siting of Northern Ireland's second university in Coleraine rather than Derry. It appeared to many nationalists that little had changed.

Things *had* changed however, and 1965 was in many ways the turning-point of the O'Neill premiership, the year when modernising rhetoric was subsumed under more symbolic events. Specifically, his attempts to forge a more cooperative relationship with the Southern government led by Sean Lemass unleashed a welter of criticism from radical unionists, notably Ian Paisley, that O'Neill was a traitor both to Protestantism and to Ulster. Accusations that O'Neill was destroying Northern Ireland became a constant theme of fundamentalist unionism and contributed significantly to O'Neill's resignation in 1969. There can be little doubt that O'Neill underestimated Ian Paisley and saw him as little more than a bigoted loudmouth, whose extremist views appealed to a very narrow section of the Northern Ireland community. With the benefit of hindsight, it is clear that Paisley was able to tap into a more general sense of fear, frustration and anger from those within a Protestant community which did not necessarily share all of Paisley's convictions. These fears became exacerbated, of course, as Catholic self-organisation increased and they began to confront the state and its institutions. Although primarily concerned with issues such as 'one man one vote' [*sic*], the fair allocation of housing and an end to gerrymandering in local elections, the Civil Rights Movement was perceived by many Protestants as an attack on the Stormont system and an attempt to overthrow the Northern Ireland state.

The Free Presbyterian newspaper *The Revivalist* consistently linked the growth of the civil rights movement to O'Neill's appeasement of the Catholic community.

Since Capt. O'Neill came to power his policy of appeasement has done nothing but harm to this province. We are now reaping the harvest of his policies. Let our government learn that this iniquitous policy has been carried too far already and must be dis-continued forthwith. And if O'Neill refuses, then O'Neill must go![34]

With the political mobilisation of Paisleyism on the one hand and an increasingly frustrated Civil Rights movement on the other, constantly confronting each other in the streets, O'Neill's tendency to stand in the middle of the road merely saw him being knocked down by traffic coming in both directions. Competing demands from unionists and nationalists for a recognition of their tribal identities was an issue as early as 1966, a year which presented the unfortunate historical coincidence of the fiftieth anniversaries of the Battle of the Somme and the Easter Rising. Decisions allowing nationalists to commemorate the Rising whilst at the same time disallowing loyalist counter-demonstrations, were reduced by critics such as Paisley to being a barometer of the O'Neill government's loyalty.

The first serious challenge to O'Neill from within the Unionist Party came in September 1966, with the circulation of a petition among the Parliamentary Party, while the Prime Minister was on a trade visit to England. The petition was alleged to have been organised by Desmond Boal, a young backbench critic of O'Neill, later to form the Democratic Unionist Party with Ian Paisley. Contemporary accounts in the local media (which was prejudiced in O'Neill's favour) illustrate the extent of bad feeling which existed in the party at the time.

A major political crisis was brewing in Stormont today. With the Unionist Party in a state of ferment, Captain O'Neill's future as Prime Minister was increasingly in doubt....I understand the document states that the Prime Minister has failed to get the party and people behind him in his policies....Over the past few months many M.P.s have been under pressure from their constituency associations. Resentment of the fact that the government permitted the 1916 Easter Rising to be celebrated on a wide scale in Northern Ireland has not died out.[35]

It is not clear exactly what role Brian Faulkner played during this crisis ('I am not making any comment at this juncture'),[36] though he would undoubtedly have been the main beneficiary had O'Neill been forced out. Though Faulkner maintained the public performance of support for the Prime Minister, it may not have been coincidental that he postponed a planned official trip to America until it was clear that the Prime Minister's position was secure. Lord Brookeborough had apparently been approached to take over as caretaker leader of the party but declined, not because he thought O'Neill was doing a good job, but on the grounds that 'I'm too old and too square.'[37] The only signatory who was prepared to come out publicly against O'Neill was ex-Attorney General Edmond Warnock, an opponent of the Prime Minister from the beginning.

> When Captain O'Neill succeeded Lord Brookeborough the parliamentary party was united and at peace, and the constituency associations were working happily together, and the Orange Order was quietly doing its job. Today the Unionist Party is split, the constituency organisations are disturbed and the Orange Order is seriously dismayed. I don't want to see the Unionist Party destroyed, or the Orange Order destroyed – or damn near it – I am very much afraid this may happen unless there is an immediate change.[38]

There were roughly a dozen signatories to the petition and though the threat soon collapsed because none had the courage to strike, it was an important benchmark in O'Neill's loss of authority within the party. The Prime Minister subsequently won a ringing endorsement in a vote of confidence, but neither he, nor his opponents in the party, forgot the episode.

The roof caved in on the O'Neill premiership in 1968 because of a culmination of events and grievances which had begun to develop several years before. Civil rights agitation increased because O'Neill had failed to deliver on his promises.[39] This was exacerbated by clumsy management, as in retrospect it is clear that moving William Craig from the Ministry of Development to Home Affairs was unwise. Craig's brutal handling of the Civil Rights Movement was counter-productive, merely inflaming the situation and increasing internal and international support for their demands. Craig became more and more obdurate, embarrassing O'Neill and intensifying pressure from the British government to accelerate the reform programme. O'Neill's subsequent 'five point' plan, announced on 22 November 1968, was viewed by his unionist critics as a sop to the 'disloyal' nationalists and an interfering Labour government. The plan included a points system for the allocation of public housing; the abolition of the company vote in local government elections; a review of the Special Powers Act; the appointment of an ombudsman and the establishment of a development commission in Derry to replace the corrupt local authority. These reforms pushed Craig and O'Neill's other critics to even more extreme positions, as they perceived these unremarkable changes to be a capitulation to the enemies of Ulster. On 2 December 1968, Craig made an inflammatory speech which talked of impending civil war and a political temperature at boiling point: 'One of these days one of these marches is going to get a massive reaction from the population.'[40] In an attempt to overcome opposition from within his cabinet and party, O'Neill made a direct television appeal for public support, in a speech which has become his public epitaph. He pointed out that 'Ulster stands at the Crossroads':

> What kind of Ulster do you want? A happy and respected province in good standing with the rest of the United Kingdom? Or a place continually torn apart by riots and demonstrations, and regarded by the rest of Britain as a political outcast? As always in a democracy, the choice is yours.[41]

O'Neill urged unionists to recognise that Northern Ireland was not in ultimate control of its political destiny and that if reforms were not accepted, the Stormont parliament would be prorogued and the British government would intervene to introduce similar change. Buoyed up by the immense public support for this broadcast as reflected in the columns of the *Belfast Telegraph* and the signing of petitions, O'Neill felt sufficiently confident of his position to sack Craig for his open rejection of the right of Westminster to intervene in the internal affairs of Northern Ireland. Within four months of doing this, O'Neill had resigned as Prime Minister and leader of the Unionist Party. On 24 January 1969, Brian Faulkner made his move, his excuse being that the government had abdicated its responsibility to govern by appointing the Cameron Commission to investigate the violence surrounding the Derry Civil Rights march of 5 October 1968. Two days later, William Morgan, the Minister of Health and Social Services, also resigned. The Ulster Unionist Council Annual Report for 1969 demonstrates the extent to which O'Neill's authority within the party was being openly questioned. The Report carries an interesting interjection by Brian Faulkner concerning the wording of a proposed vote of confidence in Terence O'Neill by the Council. Such a public censure by one of the most senior figures in the party inevitably damaged O'Neill's position further (personal animosity between the two men was heightened by their bitter exchange of letters on Faulkner's resignation, during which O'Neill accused him of disloyalty). After the Prime Minister had addressed the delegates to the UUC, the following vote of confidence was proposed by Basil McIvor:

> This Annual meeting of the Ulster Unionist Council pledges itself at this period of our history to resist all attempts from whatever quarter aimed at usurping the authority of our Parliament and the substitution of

the rule of law. Similarly we pledge ourselves to do our utmost at all times to ensure the continued and unimpaired maintenance of the Union with Great Britain and to give full support to the efforts of the Northern Ireland Government under the Leader of the Party to achieve these ends.

The Rt. Hon. Brian Faulkner, DL MP, then said it was quite clear from the agenda that there was to be an address by the Prime Minister, followed by a vote of confidence. He assumed that this was a vote of confidence in the Prime Minister. The resolution was no such vote of confidence. Practically everybody in the room would support that resolution but everyone would not agree that it was a vote of confidence. He suggested that there should be a first vote on one single issue. That everyone should vote on that statement – after the first vote which should be on the Prime Minister. ...The vote of confidence in the Prime Minister was passed by 338 votes to 263.[42]

As O'Neill's government was crumbling beneath him, he called a general election on 24 February in an attempt to try to reassert his authority. He needed a massive vote of confidence from the electorate to resuscitate his flagging leadership. What he got, however, was a result which was at best confused and inconclusive. The resignation of James Chichester-Clark as Minister of Agriculture on 23 April – bizarrely over the issue of the timing of reforms already introduced, rather than their substance – was merely the *coup de grâce*. O'Neill's leadership was already mortally wounded by that stage.[43]

MISSION IMPOSSIBLE?

O'Neill's authority within unionism disintegrated because he failed to understand the structural limitations of his position and the implications of his rhetoric. Sectarianism was not, as he proposed, a behavioural problem but was in reality woven into the fabric of the Northern Ireland state and formed the basis of political organisation – unionist *v.* nationalist. When the Unionist and Nationalist Party leaderships became unable to control the masses and grassroots mobilisation occurred in the guise of Paisleyism and the Civil Rights Movement, the rug was effectively pulled from under O'Neill and his position became untenable. Thus while many Catholics were prepared to support O'Neill in 1966, two years later the contradictions of his reform programme had become increasingly exposed by confrontations between the Northern Ireland Civil Rights Association (NICRA) and the state. Once Catholic self-organisation had 'gone public' in the form of street protests and had come into conflict with the state through confrontation with the police, it was inevitable that the radical loyalist community would react. From this point in the middle of 1968 when the two sectarian blocs began to organise in confrontation with one another, O'Neill's fate was sealed and he became a political bystander simply reacting to a chain of events over which he had little control. The conclusions of Bew and Patterson are apposite:

> the decision to hold protest marches and not to recognise the legitimacy of sectarian territorial divisions assured the irruption of just those aspects of popular Protestant sectarianism which his whole project was designed to consign to a mute and apolitical existence. O'Neill's policies could only have succeeded if the Protestant masses had remained passive. The confrontation between civil rights marchers and the police in Derry in October 1968, the RUC's brutal dispersal of the march, and the moving of the question of reform of the state's security apparatuses to the centre of the civil rights movements' demands, changed popular Protestant conceptions of the issues at stake.[44]

O'Neill was now in the impossible position of articulating the rhetoric of liberalism while at the same time defending the security apparatus against accusations of brutality. His strategy – such as it was – of internal tranquillity and economic modernisation providing the political space for cosmetic reform which would reconcile the community to the state, became increasingly incoherent and his political demise inevitable. Regardless of the various triggers which forced his resignation – his personality/background, Protestant extremism, Catholic self-organisation, and in the end, democratic accountability (the February 1969 Stormont election fatally undermined his authority) – the main cause of O'Neill's political demise was more fundamental. It related to the dynamics within Ulster unionism which operated in the 1960s and which still (though to a lesser extent) influence the direction of unionist politics today. Ulster Unionism is an ideology which, even at its crudest, seeks to retain or regain the constitutional position of Northern Ireland within the United Kingdom. Its historical development has occurred in a generally hostile environment. The British, both at governmental and popular opinion levels, have repeatedly demonstrated their desire to – at the very least – lessen their responsibility for the region. Indeed, they were only prevented from doing so in 1972 by the threat of Protestant paramilitary violence. Unionists interpreted the Sunningdale Agreement in 1973 and Power-Sharing Executive the following year, the Anglo-Irish Agreement of November 1985 and more recent events in the lead-up to the publication of the Joint

Framework document in 1995, as similar attempts to trundle them towards a 'united Ireland'. The Free State/Republic of Ireland, meanwhile, was led for much of its early existence by Eamon de Valera, former 'terrorist' and zealous Catholic. The 1937 constitution which bears his mark made explicit, through Articles 2 and 3, what many unionists feared was already implicit, that the South viewed the six counties as part of its national territory and would seek to regain them at the earliest opportunity. This negative image of the Southern State was used by Paisley to attack O'Neill's first meeting with Sean Lemass. The Taoiseach's visit to the North was regarded by many unionists as a concession to republicanism as the previous policy conducted by Brookeborough and repeatedly endorsed by O'Neill himself, had been that no Northern Ireland Prime Minister would meet their Southern counterpart until the latter administration had recognised the legitimacy of the Northern Ireland state. By breaking this pledge and by doing it in such a surreptitious manner, O'Neill left himself open to extremist allegations that he was over-friendly to republicans.

> The past years of his disastrous premiership are strewn with his broken pledges. His word is nothing, absolutely nothing. He promised the Orangemen of Ballygowan that he would never bring Lemass to Stormont or engage in conversations with him until the Republic recognised the constitution of Northern Ireland. Then, without consulting his cabinet, the parliamentary party or the Unionist Council, he smuggled the Southern murderer into Stormont. He took Lemass's hand (stained with the blood of our kith and kin).[45]

It would be too simplistic to say that unionism suffers from a siege mentality which renders it incapable of progressive liberal attitudes and innovative political behaviour. The relationship of unionism to its external political environment is more complex. There have been times when the unionist community has felt more confident about its position, such as the immediate aftermath of the Second World War, the signing of the Ireland Act in 1949, the ending of the IRA's Border Campaign in 1962, and the security policies associated with the mid-seventies. However, the problem for unionism – and the reason why O'Neill's support evaporated so rapidly – is that 'the price of liberty is eternal vigilance'. In other words, though unionists may have allies, they ultimately have to rely on themselves, their own internal cohesion and a constant assessment of their political environment. Terence O'Neill's position – and later that of Brian Faulkner – became untenable because a sufficient number of people within the Protestant community came to the belief that he had destabilised that environment and the unionist position within both Northern Ireland and the United Kingdom. The knowledge that they cannot unilaterally sustain the Union, and thus are not ultimately in control of their own political destiny, has tended to militate against progressive thought and action. The dominant dynamic is one of retrenchment, of getting back something which has been lost (or soon will be), of returning to a time which seemed more secure. There is a simultaneous desire to find some elusive formula which will guarantee the unionist position. Ironically, perhaps, if unionism is to have any long-term future, it will have to succeed where O'Neill failed, by accommodating the Catholic community within the state. As this will only be accomplished through an institutionalised relationship with the Republic of Ireland, the price unionists will have to pay is likely to be much higher than it was in 1968–69.

NOTES

*. I would like to thank Sir Kenneth Bloomfield and Rev. Martin Smyth for their cooperation and assistance in writing this chapter.
1. See for example; Paul Bew, Peter Gibbon and Henry Patterson, *The State in Northern Ireland, 1921–1972: Political Forces and Social Classes* (Manchester, 1979); Paul Arthur, *Government and Politics of Northern Ireland* (London, 1987); David Gordon, *The O'Neill Years: Unionist Politics 1963–1969* (Belfast, 1989); Sir Kenneth Bloomfield, *Stormont in Crisis* (Belfast, 1994).
2. Jonathan Bardon, *A History of Ulster* (Belfast, 1992), p. 622.
3. Paul Arthur and Keith Jeffery, *Northern Ireland since 1968* (Oxford, 1988), p. 6.
4. Paul Bew and Henry Patterson, *The British State and the Ulster Crisis* (London, 1985), p. 11.
5. Terence O'Neill is reported as having made these remarks during a radio interview in America. *Belfast Telegraph*, 10 May 1969, p. 1.
6. Ibid.
7. Gordon (1989), p. 5.
8. Arthur (1987), p. 86.
9. Interview with the author, 4 January 1995.
10. Bloomfield (1994), p. 39.
11. Ed Moloney and Andy Pollak, *Paisley* (Dublin, 1986), p. 121.
12. *U.D.A.*, No.13, February 1972, pp. 7–8.
13. *The Orange Cross*, May 1972, p. 5.
14. Brian Faulkner, *Memoirs of a Statesman* (London, 1978), p. 28.
15. Bardon (1992), p. 622.
16. *News Letter*, 26 March 1963, p. 1.
17. *News Letter*, 27 March 1963, p. 7.

18. *Belfast Telegraph*, 26 March 1963, p. 1.
19. Gordon (1989), p. 12.
20. Ibid., p. 16.
21. Terence O'Neill, *The Autobiography of Terence O'Neill* (London, 1972), p. 63.
22. Ibid., p. 63.
23. Cabinet Minutes, 17 April 1963 (P. R.O.N.I. CAB/4/1227/1).
24. Cabinet Minutes, 30 January 1964 (P. R.O.N.I. CAB/4/1254).
25. *Protestant Telegraph*, 30 July 1966, p. 1.
26. Interview with the author, 4 January 1995.
27. S. E. Long, *The Northern Ireland Problem* (Belfast, 1972), p. 7.
28. *Belfast Telegraph*, 12 July 1966, p. 6.
29. Ibid., 6 July 1966, p. 1.
30. Ibid., 12 July 1967, p. 1.
31. Ibid.
32. *The Orangeman*, Belfast, February 1971, Vol. 2, No. 5, p. 6.
33. Bardon (1992), p. 624.
34. *The Revivalist*, Belfast, October 1968, pp. 2–3.
35. *Belfast Telegraph*, 23 September 1966, pp. 1 and 6.
36. *Belfast Telegraph*, 24 September 1966, p. 3.
37. *Belfast Telegraph*, 26 September 1966, p. 1.
38. *Belfast Telegraph*, 26 September 1966, p. 4.
39. For an account of the origins, history and demands of the Civil Rights Movements consult the following works. Paul Arthur, *The People's Democracy 1968–73* (Belfast, 1974); Bew, Gibbon and Patterson (1979); Paul Bew and Gordon Gillespie, *Northern Ireland: A Chronology of the Troubles 1968–1993* (Dublin, 1993); Bernadette Devlin, *The Price of My Soul* (London, 1969); Eamonn McCann, *War and an Irish Town* (London, 1980); Liam O'Dowd, Bill Rolston and Mike Tomlinson (eds), *Northern Ireland: Between Civil Rights and Civil War* (London, 1980); Bob Purdie, *Politics in the Streets: The Origins of the Civil Rights Movement in Northern Ireland* (Belfast, 1990).
40. Bew and Gillespie (1993), p. 8.
41. O'Neill (1972), p. 149.
42. Ulster Unionist Council Annual Report for 1969, (Belfast, 1969), p. 8.
43. O'Neill won a pyrrhic victory at the Stormont election of 24 February 1969. Thirty-nine unionists were returned, though 10 of these had stood and won on an anti-O'Neill ticket. In addition, he was returned in his own constituency of Bannside on a minority vote of 7745, with Paisley getting 6331 votes. For more detail on the 1969 Stormont election, consult Bew and Gillespie (1993), and Bloomfield (1994).
44. Bew and Patterson (1985), p. 16.
45. *Protestant Telegraph*, 8 February 1969, p. 1.

10 Direct Rule and the Unionist Middle Classes
Colin Coulter

INTRODUCTION

In March 1972, as the political climate in Northern Ireland degenerated apace, the Conservative administration in London exercised its constitutional prerogative and dissolved the devolved legislature at Stormont. The introduction of 'direct rule' from Westminster represents a significant watershed in the development of modern Northern Ireland. The operation of direct rule over the past two decades has initiated a 'passive revolution'[1] which has transformed Northern Irish society. The aspect of social change occasioned by direct rule which has preoccupied commentators most is the emergence of an enlarged and variegated Catholic middle class.[2] Rather less attention has been afforded to the more affluent elements of the unionist community. This essay seeks to begin to redress this significant imbalance within the study of contemporary Northern Irish society.

A PLACE APART

One of the abiding concerns of the British political establishment since the inception of Northern Ireland has been to maintain a discreet political distance from the province.[3] This strategic imperative of the modern British state was inscribed in the actual terms of the partition settlement. The establishment of a devolved legislature within the fledgling constitutional entity of Northern Ireland primarily reflected the ambition of the metropolis to remain aloof from the sectarian political affairs of the six counties. The anxiety of the British political class to keep the province 'at arm's length'[4] further prompted the formulation in 1923 of an agreement that Westminster would not discuss those matters which fell within the remit of the Stormont parliament.[5] The operation of this convention served to ensure that over the fifty years of devolved government at Stormont the sovereign parliament devoted on average a mere two hours per annum to the consideration of the affairs of Northern Ireland.[6] Perhaps the most eloquent expression of the active disinterest of the British political establishment in the public life of the six counties, however, may be found in the scale of bureaucratic resources which Westminster devoted to the administration of the province. In 1968, as the political climate within the six counties deteriorated rapidly, the affairs of Northern Ireland were administered by a Home Office department which employed no full-time civil servants and which counted among its numerous responsibilities the onerous tasks of regulating British summer time and issuing licences to London taxi-drivers.[7]

Regarded in this particular historical light, the decision of the sovereign parliament to dissolve the Stormont legislature and assume direct responsibility for the governance of Northern Ireland would appear to mark a radical departure. In reality, however, the advent of direct rule has signified a shift in the form but not the substance of British policy towards the six counties.[8] The strategies adopted by successive administrations of direct rulers have continued to be informed by the perennial conception of Northern Ireland as 'a place apart'.[9] The official conviction that Northern Ireland represents a region irreconcilably 'different' from the rest of the state has pervaded the conduct of public policy in the six counties over the past quarter-century. The influence of this particular abiding ideology of the modern British state has proved especially pronounced in the realm of political affairs and in the sphere of social and economic concerns. The changes within each of these crucial areas of public policy wrought by the operation of direct rule will be considered in turn.

THE POLITICS OF DIRECT RULE

The dissolution of the Stormont regime furnished Westminster with the historic opportunity to govern Northern Ireland in a manner identical to the rest of the United Kingdom. Rather than treating Northern Ireland as an integral region of the state, however, the mother of parliaments has preferred to deal with the six counties in a manner reminiscent of a distant colonial possession. The structures of authority through which direct rule has operated for more than two decades are distinctly autocratic.[10] The appreciable powers of the executive are wielded by political figures who have not been democratically elected by the residents of the six counties. Legislation pertaining exclusively to the province is formulated through the exceptional mechanism of 'Orders in Council' and

administered by public bodies comprised largely of government nominees.[11] The only public institutions which are democratically account-
able to the electorate of Northern Ireland are the 26 district councils.
Those individuals who are elected to serve as local government councillors, however, exercise political powers which are notoriously menial.[12]

The peculiarly autocratic form assumed by direct rule in part reflects
the nature of the settlement which the British political establishment
believes will resolve the present impasse. In spite of their longevity, the
authoritarian structures of direct rule are officially portrayed as provisional, expedient arrangements designed to furnish the Secretary of State
with the powers required to cajole and coerce the representatives of the
fractious residents of the six counties towards mutual accommodation.
One of the central structures which will emerge to facilitate and express
this political settlement will of course be a devolved legislature which will
appropriate many of those substantial powers presently in the possession
of the Northern Ireland Office.[13] The distinctly autocratic form assumed by
the structures of direct rule, therefore, encodes the entirely noble ambition
to effect their own demise. The vigorous and sustained pursuit of a
devolved political settlement on the part of the British political establishment reveals the status of Other which has been conferred upon Northern
Ireland. In recent times there been a resurgence of demands for the
devolution of authority to the other regions of the United Kingdom, and in
particular to Scotland. The demand for Home Rule for Scotland has been
greeted by vociferous opposition from the political establishment.
Conservative Ministers have ritually denounced the proposed creation of a
devolved assembly in Edinburgh as a violation of the integrity of the state
which threatens ultimately to sunder the Union. Hence, the representatives
of the British political class have offered vehement resistance to the introduction in Scotland of political structures long since deemed appropriate
for Northern Ireland. In so doing they have acted to underwrite the subal-
tern status of the six counties as a region of the state.[14]

The willingness of the British political class to allow the political development of Northern Ireland to diverge from that of the rest of the United
Kingdom assumes of course forms considerably more radical than the
mere promotion of different structures of government for the province.
Successive direct rule administrations have issued public guarantees of the
safety of the Union. In spite of these public declarations of constitutional
fidelity, however, the British political class has proved only too willing to
consider a future for the six counties beyond the environs of the Union. At
the heart of modern British policy is the conviction that Westminster has
no 'selfish, strategic or economic' interest in the Union with Northern

Ireland and would offer no resistance should the residents of the six counties express a democratic preference to leave the United Kingdom.[15] The official indifference to the constitutional status of Northern Ireland codified in the Anglo-Irish Agreement (1985), the Downing Street Declaration (1993) and, most recently, the Framework Document (1995) adverts to the subordinate status which Northern Ireland endures within the United Kingdom. One has only to contrast the readiness of the British political class to envisage a political destiny for Northern Ireland *without* the Union with the virtual hysteria which has greeted attempts to reformulate the terms under which Scotland should remain *within* the Union to arrive at an understanding that the province represents a rather less than cherished region of the modern British state.

The political strategies instigated under the auspices of direct rule have inevitably fostered the distrust of substantial swathes of the unionist community, its more affluent elements included. The formal indifference towards the constitutional status of the six counties articulated by the British political establishment has been typically decoded by northern unionists as a veiled expression of the desire to be rid of the troublesome territory of Northern Ireland. The abiding suspicion that the intentions of the metropolis towards the Union are less than pure has exercised a pervasive – and ultimately debilitating – influence upon the political imagination of contemporary unionism.[16] The disquiet of the unionist population has been especially aroused by the conduct of security policy over the period of direct rule. The failure to effect a conclusive military defeat of republican insurgence has been broadly interpreted by unionists as a reflection of British indifference to the plight and welfare of the Northern Irish people. The suspicion grips the unionist mind that had comparable levels of political violence occurred elsewhere within the United Kingdom the response of the repressive apparatuses of the British state would have been appreciably swifter and more vigorous.

The official construction of Northern Ireland as 'a place apart' has, therefore, exercised a tangible influence upon the political initiatives fostered under direct rule. The conception of the province as 'different' has proved politically iniquitous. The form and substance of direct rule have offered to the people of Northern Ireland political and civil rights appreciably poorer than those enjoyed by their fellow British citizens. The notion that Northern Ireland is different has also guided the hand of direct rulers in the sphere of social and economic policy, but with starkly different consequences. The particular conditions which obtain within the six counties have drawn British politicians to the belief that the social and economic policies introduced throughout the other regions of the state would be inappropriate – indeed calamitous – in the context of Northern Ireland. The British political establishment has held to the view that fiscal benevolence is required to promote those social conditions deemed conducive to the formation of a durable political settlement. Consequently, the era of direct rule from Westminster has come to be characterised by distinctly generous levels of public provision.

SOCIETY AND ECONOMY UNDER DIRECT RULE

During the lifetime of the devolved legislature at Stormont, the people of Northern Ireland endured standards of public provision considerably poorer than those enjoyed by their fellow British citizens. On the eve of the Second World War the British exchequer accepted the principle that financial resources should be provided to ensure that Northern Ireland experienced levels of public expenditure comparable to the other regions of the United Kingdom.[17] These noble sentiments of parity, however, were never fully translated into public policy. Although Unionist administrations received increasingly significant transfers from the British Treasury, public spending in Northern Ireland during the era of devolved government lagged appreciably behind the remainder of the United Kingdom.[18] Not until the dissolution of the Stormont regime would the six counties come to enjoy those relatively generous standards of public expenditure appropriate to the poorest region of the state.[19]

Over the two decades of direct rule from Westminster the funding of public services has doubled in real terms.[20] The most dramatic increases in public expenditure occurred during the 1970s, primarily under the auspices of a relatively profligate Labour administration. Given the apocalyptic political violence of the time, these increases in state expenditure were in part consumed by a grotesquely inflated security budget. Nonetheless, the period in office of the last Labour government witnessed a significant improvement in state funding of vital areas of social provision including health, housing and education.[21]

With the assumption of political office by the Conservatives in 1979, Northern Ireland came to be governed by an administration guided by the doctrine of fiscal prudence. Accordingly, the 1980s witnessed the erosion of public spending across a range of services.[22] The spending cuts introduced by the Tories were, however, neither universal nor as savage as those visited upon the other regions of the state. The people of Northern Ireland have been insulated from the full rigour of the Thatcherite assault upon the institutions and philosophy of British welfarism by the particular, volatile political conditions which obtain within the six counties. Successive Conservative administrations have chosen not to implement sweeping cuts in public provision on the grounds that such policies would foster those social conditions which ultimately prompt political violence. The readiness of Conservatives to acknowledge in Northern Ireland an association between poverty and lawlessness strenuously denied in the context of the other regions of the United Kingdom offers intriguing confirmation of the status of the province as 'a place apart'.

The majority of the funds spent by direct rulers in Northern Ireland is, of course, drawn from tax revenues generated within the province. An increasingly substantial minority of public expenditure in the six counties, however, depends upon a direct subsidy from the British exchequer. The magnitude of the British 'subvention' provides arguably the starkest index of the material dependence of Northern Ireland upon the British state under direct rule. At present the British Treasury subsidises the province annually to the tune of £3.4 billion,[23] an aggregate which translates into more than £2000 for every woman, man and child in the six counties. The existence of the subvention has become ever more vital to the economic health of Northern Ireland in recent times. Indeed, as Anderson and Goodman[24] intimate, financial transfers from London currently constitute one-third of the region's Gross Domestic Product (GDP).

The enormous increases in government spending occasioned by direct rule have facilitated a substantial expansion of employment opportunities in the public sector. At the outbreak of the present political conflict, the state offered employment to one-quarter of the Northern Irish workforce, a proportion which had remained unchanged over the preceding decade. The operation of direct rule has significantly swollen the ranks of public employees in the province.[25] Of every ten individuals in work in Northern Ireland four are employed directly by the British state and another three employed indirectly. The era of direct rule, therefore, has served to establish the British state as the absolute fulcrum of the Northern Irish economy.[26]

THE CONTENTED CLASSES

The conduct of social and economic policy since the demise of Stormont has transformed Northern Ireland virtually beyond recognition. The enormous expansion of public expenditure and employment which has attended direct rule has significantly augmented the *general* standard of living in the six counties. The material benefits of direct rule have, however, been neither universal nor evenly distributed.[27] Contemporary Northern Ireland represents a social formation rather more polarised along class lines than a generation ago.[28] The virtually unpunctuated crises which have beset the local and global economies over the past quarter-century have condemned a substantial body of workers to the poverty of unemployment and many others to poorly-paid service jobs on the margins of formal economic life. The advent of direct rule, in contrast, has heralded an era of unprecedented affluence for the northern middle classes. The focus of the discussion which follows falls primarily upon the unionist elements among the province's 'contented classes'.[29]

The extension of public employment which has accompanied direct rule has furnished occupational opportunities which have facilitated the emergence of a substantially enlarged middle class in Northern Ireland. Those individuals in the six counties who are employed by the British state typically enjoy rates of remuneration on a par with the rest of the United Kingdom. Public employees living in Northern Ireland, however, face lower living costs than their counterparts in the other regions of the state.[30] In particular, houses in the province are relatively inexpensive, presently running at only two-thirds of the United Kingdom average.[31] The coincidence of salaries comparable to the remainder of the state and relatively low house prices has afforded public employees in the six counties greater purchasing power than their counterparts 'across the water'.

The considerable affluence of the northern middle classes has been further underwritten by the industrial policies pursued by direct rule administrations. In the period since the fall of Stormont, the British political class has adopted a distinctly interventionist approach to the Northern Irish economy. This has held true even for Conservative administrations. In their dealings with the province, the Tories have largely dispensed with the free market dogma which has shaped their economic strategy throughout the rest of the United Kingdom. The essentially pragmatic approach adopted by consecutive Conservative administrations was illuminated by the comments of the former Secretary of State James Prior. In the early 1980s, with monetarism at its zenith throughout the rest of the United Kingdom, Prior intimated that the tenets of economic interventionism continued to hold sway in the context of Northern Ireland when he issued the declaration that 'we are all Keynesians here'.[32] The British state has provided substantial practical and financial assistance to both indigenous and foreign capital. Given that Protestants remain heavily overrepresented among the remnants of the local bourgeoisie,[33] the benefits of the British state's generous industrial policy have inevitably accrued primarily to elements within the unionist community. The interventionist approach adopted by Westminster towards the economic life of the province has, moreover, enabled local enterprise to generate profits which are not justified by performance. A recent report by the Northern Ireland Economic Research Council (NIERC) revealed that in the 1980s manufacturing companies in Northern Ireland declared profits 60 per cent higher than those of comparably efficient undertakings operating in other regions of the United Kingdom.[34]

The wealth which direct rule has conferred upon the professional and business classes in the six counties has inevitably found expression in the realm of consumption. While Northern Ireland exhibits more indices of poverty than any other region of the state, it also boasts more luxury cars per capita.[35] The substantial disposable income possessed by the northern middle classes has sponsored the spectacular rejuvenation of the commercial and night life of the region's capital. Over the past decade or so Belfast has witnessed the arrival of most of the major retail chains and the evolution of the 'Golden Mile', a series of bars and restaurants spanning the approximate mile between the city centre and the university district.[36] Perhaps the most lucid testimony to the burgeoning wealth of elements of northern society, however, is the recent transformation of Bangor, the North Down town invariably regarded as the citadel of middle-class Ulster.[37] Where once there existed the increasingly dilapidated frontage of a traditional British coastal resort there now stands a thriving marina which provides a forum for the grotesque hedonism of a social elite drawn from the six counties and farther afield.

THE CONTRADICTIONS OF DIRECT RULE

The conduct of public policy under direct rule has, therefore, had a peculiarly contradictory effect upon the unionist middle classes. The conception of Northern Ireland as 'different' has prompted the British political class to govern the six counties in a distinctly colonial manner. The political form and substance of direct rule have inevitably sponsored among middle-class Protestants that sullen disenchantment which pervades the entire unionist community. The construction of Northern Ireland as 'a place apart' has produced a rather different, ultimately contradictory, expression in the realm of social and economic policy. The assumption that the six counties offer an inappropriate setting for the implementation of social measures introduced elsewhere has ensured the survival in the province of a welfarism abandoned a generation ago in the other regions of the state. The fiscal benevolence of direct rule has bestowed unprecedented affluence upon the unionist middle classes. Hence, the era of direct rule presents us with a peculiar paradox. The execution of public policy over the past two decades has simultaneously nurtured the political alienation of middle-class unionists from the British state and established their increasingly rewarding instrumental dependence upon the metropolis. It is this essentially contradictory experience of direct rule which has shaped the political beliefs and practice of middle-class Protestants in modern times.

MINIMALISM

At the time of partition Ulster Unionists offered stout resistance to the endeavours of Westminster to foist a separate legislature upon the new constitutional entity of Northern Ireland. The control of the apparatuses of state afforded by the partition settlement, however, rapidly became indispensable to the Unionist political project.[38] It was entirely inevitable, therefore, that the dissolution of the Stormont parliament should be greeted with the virtually unanimous opposition of northern Unionists.[39] As the material benefits of direct rule quickly became apparent, however, much of the initial hostility of the unionist community dissipated. The more wealthy elements within the unionist fold in particular abandoned their erstwhile commitment to the restoration of a devolved assembly with almost undignified haste. The shifting interests of the Protestant professional and business classes found reflection in a political outlook defined by a characteristic conservatism. By the mid-seventies it had become readily apparent that middle-class unionists would refuse to countenance any political strategy which threatened to offend an increasingly benign Westminster. The first substantial intimation of the growing circumspection among middle-class Protestants was arguably that which occurred in the early summer of 1977, when they refused to support a loyalist strike designed to compel the government to introduce more draconian security measures.[40]

The rapidly changing interests and experience of the unionist middle classes in time found coherent ideological expression in the emergence within Unionism of a political project which is usually denoted 'integrationist' but which Bew and Patterson[41] have persuasively characterised as 'minimalist'. Advanced by influential elements within the hierarchy of the Ulster Unionist Party and associated most readily with James Molyneaux, minimalist integrationism contends that Northern Ireland is best governed directly from Westminster, not least because a revived devolved assembly would, under the terms on offer, scarcely be worth the candle.[42] The pragmatic endorsement of direct rule embodied within the integrationist position clearly articulates the specific materialist interests of the unionist middle classes. The philosophy of minimalist integrationism, moreover, bears the indelible impression of that conservatism which characterises the political approach of middle-class Protestants. Integrationists such as Molyneaux have consistently eschewed those radical political strategies which would threaten to alienate the British political class. Acknowledging that the constitutional fate of Northern Ireland lies ultimately in the hands of the sovereign parliament, Molyneaux has adopted a distinctly conciliatory approach towards the British political establishment. The health of the Union would be guaranteed not by radical demogoguery on the streets of Ulster but by 'winning friends' and courting influence within the corridors of power at Westminster.[43] Over the decade which preceded the Anglo-Irish Agreement the approach adopted by minimalist integrationism appeared relatively fruitful, not least in the late seventies when it was employed to extract concessions from an increasingly vulnerable Labour administration.[44] In reality, however, the political strategy advanced by integrationism was riven with contradictions. The shortcomings of the minimalist project would be mercilessly exposed by the advent of the Anglo-Irish Agreement.

THE ANGLO-IRISH AGREEMENT

The decade or so which preceded the Anglo-Irish Agreement witnessed the development of profound political apathy among the ranks of the unionist middle classes. The apocalyptic events which scarred the early 1970s prompted the exodus virtually *en masse* of Protestant professionals from the realm of political life.[45] The gradual improvement of the political climate in the six counties, moreover, failed to dispel the inertia of middle-class unionists. As the annual death toll tumbled and the war became increasingly segregated in both class and spatial terms, a corrosive complacency descended upon the more affluent fragments of the unionist community. Rather than reflect upon the problematic nature of their political environment the unionist middle classes preferred instead to cast their considerable energies into the rather more rewarding task of accumulating wealth. The advent of the Anglo-Irish Agreement, however, unceremoniously jolted middle-class unionists from their ideological slumber. In the charged atmosphere produced by the Hillsborough Accord many northern unionists came to reflect more fully and critically upon the nature of their political beliefs and interests. This process of ideological rumination would draw a substantial body of middle-class Protestants to a clearer understanding of the contradictory position which they had come to occupy during the era of direct rule from Westminster.

The manner of the conception and introduction of the Anglo-Irish Agreement cast into stark relief the essentially autocratic powers which the sovereign parliament had assumed under the terms of direct rule. The residents of the six counties had not been formally consulted during the negotiations which had ultimately sired the Hillsborough Accord. The British political class, moreover, exhibited scant regard for the widespread alienation which the Agreement generated among the greater number of the people of Northern Ireland. The vehement opposition articulated by northern unionists and their elected representatives proved insufficient to dissuade Westminster from the course upon which it had embarked at Hillsborough. While the circumstances surrounding the introduction of the Anglo-Irish Agreement adverted to the autocratic character of direct rule, the actual substance of the document revealed the readiness of the British political establishment to employ its considerable powers to undermine the Union. The contents of the Hillsborough Accord effected a significant dilution of the constitutional status of Northern Ireland. Under the terms of the Agreement the Irish government was afforded a formal consultative role in the affairs of the province.[46] In signing the Hillsborough Accord the British government had, therefore, ceded exclusive rights of sovereignty over Northern Ireland. The hackles of Ulster unionists were raised further by article 1 (c) of the document wherein the British and Irish governments promised that 'if in the future a majority of the people of Northern Ireland clearly wish for and formally consent to the establishment of a united Ireland, they will introduce and support in the respective Parliaments legislation to give effect to that wish'.[47] To the politically sensitive ears of northern unionists this particular provision inevitably sounded like an oblique expression of the British state's ambition to disengage from the six counties.

The advent of the Anglo-Irish Agreement, therefore, led many northern unionists to a more profound understanding of the nature and perils of the mode of government which obtained under direct rule. In the decade or so which immediately predated the Hillsborough Accord the autocracy of direct rule had conferred upon the unionist middle classes appreciable material and cultural wealth. The signing of the Agreement, however, illustrated that the sweeping powers in the hands of direct rulers could be employed as readily to subvert the interests of middle-class Protestants. In the years which preceded the Anglo-Irish Agreement the system of direct rule had assumed the appearance of benign dictatorship. In the emotional aftermath of the Hillsborough Accord, however, the political authority of Westminster appeared simply dictatorial.

The introduction of the Anglo-Irish Agreement also proved critical in the sense that it mercilessly exposed the shortcomings of minimalist integrationism. Prominent figures on the integrationist wing of the Ulster Unionist Party had for some time inferred that they 'had the ear' of influential elements within the British political establishment. The advent of the Hillsborough Accord revealed such faith for the absolute folly it was. In reality, of course, there exists little affection for Ulster unionism within the corridors of Westminster and Whitehall.[48] The indifference and indeed frequent hostility of the British political class to the unionist cause found graphic illustration in both the conception of the Anglo-Irish Agreement and the overwhelming support which the Treaty received from the parties of state in the Commons. Although their political strategy had been clearly discredited, the central players within integrationism could not be dissuaded from their adopted course. James Molyneaux, the figure most readily associated with the minimalist approach, refused to countenance those bold political and ideological departures which the gravity of the situation appeared to demand. Rather, the Ulster Unionist leader opted for a political strategy which elevated inertia to the status of philosophical principle.[49] The reason which informed the 'steady course' was the ambition to avoid those grand political gestures which would threaten to alienate further the British political establishment.[50] Faced with the most profound political crisis since the fall of Stormont, minimalist integrationists chose to cling desperately to a strategy which had rendered modern unionism decidedly impotent. The indolence which shaped the integrationist 'response' to the Anglo-Irish Agreement merely served to confirm that the minimalist approach had effectively translated the material dependence of the unionist middle classes upon the British state under direct rule into a particularly debilitating form of political dependence.

ELECTORAL INTEGRATIONISM

The appearance of the Anglo-Irish Agreement, therefore, defined a specific conjuncture in the social and political life of modern Northern Ireland. The signing of the Hillsborough Accord clarified in the minds of many middle-class unionists both the perils of the autocratic powers which Westminster has assumed under direct rule and the shortcomings of minimalist integrationism. In so doing, it established the conditions which would allow – albeit briefly – the ideal of electoral integration to flourish. The social and political philosophy of electoral integrationism rests upon the conviction that Northern Ireland should be governed as an equal and integral region of the state. Electoral integrationists hold to the view that the political iniquities which blight the six counties have arisen not out of the fact that Northern Ireland happens to be administered directly from Westminster, but rather the peculiarly autocratic form which direct rule has assumed. Hence, the advocates of electoral integration assert that the present system under which Northern Ireland is governed should be reformed in accordance with the standards of democratic practice deemed appropriate for the other regions of the United Kingdom. The various proposals for the democratic reform of direct rule advocated by electoral integrationists – the formulation of legislation for Northern Ireland by the conventional means of parliamentary bills rather than the exceptional procedure of Orders in Council,[51] the creation of a Select Committee to scrutinise legislation pertaining to the province[52] and the restoration of meaningful powers to local government in the six counties[53] – were, of course, scarcely original. Indeed, the measures advanced by the electoral integrationist movement had for some time represented the standard fare of the integrationist wing of Ulster Unionism. There was, however, one element of electoral integrationism which had not previously been articulated within the environs of the Unionist mainstream. The insistence that the British political parties should organise throughout the six counties constituted the most distinctive facet of the electoral integrationist project and served to identify it as a radical ideological departure.

The demand for electoral integration was borne out of two assumptions. Firstly, electoral integrationists asserted that the incorporation of Northern Ireland into the party political affairs of the state would inexorably rehabilitate the political life of the province. The ideologues of electoral integration noted that the refusal of the British parties to admit members from Northern Ireland has denied the people of the province access to a modern, secular political culture bounded by the strictly temporal ideals of social and economic management.[54] As a result, the residents of the six counties have been compelled to embrace ethnoreligious identities which have ensured the irretrievably sectarian character of Northern Irish political life.[55] Once admitted to the parties of state, however, the people of Northern Ireland would readily shed the fetters of communal affiliation in order to embrace rather more rational, secular political personae.[56] The advent of electoral integration would, therefore, herald the emergence of a modern, secular and pluralist political culture in the north of Ireland.

Secondly, the ideologues of electoral integration contended that the decision of the British parties to organise throughout Northern Ireland would usher in an era of genuinely democratic government in the province. Electoral integrationists offered the view that the people of Northern Ireland have been denied the accepted standards of democratic practice not because they have been governed from Westminster but they have been formally excluded from those parties which could realistically expect to secure a majority in the sovereign parliament.[57] The refusal of the British parties to stand for election in the province has enabled them to dismiss casually the wishes of Northern Irish voters. The realisation of electoral integration, however, would sound the death-knell of unaccountable government in the six counties.[58] Admission to the party-political life of the state would enable the electorate of Northern Ireland to effect those relatively small shifts in the balance of political power which can transform Government into Opposition.[59] Fearful of electoral retribution, the parties at Westminster would be forced to tailor their policies to the interests and aspirations of the northern electorate. The introduction of measures such as the Anglo-Irish Agreement which offend the democratic will of the Northern Irish people would become impossible and inconceivable. In effect Northern Ireland would come to be 'governed' rather than 'ruled' and its populace transformed from British subjects into British citizens.[60]

In the decade which preceded the Anglo-Irish Agreement electoral integrationism represented a strictly marginal political project, nurtured and propagated by the ideological zealots of the British & Irish Communist Organisation (B&ICO).[61] In the atmosphere of political flux generated by the Hillsborough Accord, however, electoral integrationism came to enjoy a rather broader and more receptive audience. The ideal of electoral integration exercised a particular resonance among the unionist middle classes. The electoral integrationist strategy proved attractive for many middle-class Protestants in part because it appeared capable of resolving those contradictions which have defined their experience of direct rule. The political philosophy of electoral integrationism clearly dovetailed with the material interests of the more affluent elements of the unionist family. Had the various measures advocated by electoral integrationists been implemented, direct rule would have become both stable and permanent. The advent of electoral integration would, therefore, have assured the longevity of a mode of government which had bestowed appreciable wealth upon the unionist middle classes. The electoral integrationist project, moreover, promised not merely to prosecute the instrumental interests of the Protestant middle classes but to do so in a manner which avoided the political impotence which had debilitated minimalist integrationism. The ideologues of electoral integration counselled that it would empower and enfranchise the people of Northern Ireland. Admission to the parties of state would enable the residents of the six counties to exercise control over the conduct of the executive. The advent of electoral integration would thereby ensure that the political powers wielded by Westminster under direct rule could be employed to pursue the interests of the unionist middle classes but not to undermine them. In sum, therefore, the electoral integrationist project appeared to offer an ideological resolution of the abiding contradictions encountered by the unionist middle classes since the demise of Stormont. The realisation of electoral integration would have purportedly allowed the unionist middle classes to continue to avail themselves of the material riches of direct rule free from the anxiety that the considerable power of the executive could be used to erode or attenuate the Union. The more affluent constituents of the unionist community could, in other words, appropriate the instrumental benefits of direct rule while avoiding its political costs.

THE RISE AND FALL OF ELECTORAL INTEGRATIONISM

Hence, the operation of direct rule established within Northern Ireland certain social and economic conditions which nurtured the electoral integrationist project. Although unanticipated even by the more astute observers of northern political life,[62] the emergence of electoral integrationism as an influential political philosophy represented, therefore, an entirely rational development. Articulated by a zealous and lucid body of political activists – who for a time found common cause within the ranks of the Campaign for Equal Citizenship (CEC) – the ideal of electoral integration exercised a palpable influence upon public discourse in the six counties during the late eighties. The typically eloquent counsel of the electoral integrationist movement proved resonant in a number of quarters, not least among the grassroots of the Conservative Party. The astute and polished campaign to persuade the Conservatives to organise in Northern Ireland initiated in earnest in 1987 had within two years borne fruit. Although deeply resistant to the principle of electoral integration, the hierarchy of the Conservative Party was forced to bow to pressure emanating from the rank and file. Consequently, at their annual conference in 1989 the Conservatives agreed – to the astonishment of most and the dismay of many[63] – to establish constituency organisations throughout the province.

The decision of the Conservative Party to admit members from Northern Ireland was understandably greeted within the electoral integrationist camp as an historic breakthrough. In reality, however, the affiliation of the Ulster Tories proved merely the high-water mark of the electoral integrationist movement. The ideal of electoral integration which flourished so brightly in the late eighties has withered with equal rapidity in the early nineties. The marginalisation of electoral integrationism has been ruthlessly exposed in the truly pitiful performance of the Northern Ireland Conservative candidate in the 1994 election to the European parliament.

The ignominious demise of electoral integrationism as a mainstream political voice owes much to the conduct of the British parties. Electoral integrationism represented a bold endeavour to reverse the approach which the British state has adopted towards Northern Ireland since partition. The advent of electoral integration would have required the parties of the modern British state to embrace the six counties as an equal and integral region of the United Kingdom. Inevitably, however, the strategic imperative of the British state to maintain Northern Ireland 'at arm's length' has prevailed. The British political parties have proved distinctly unwilling to jettison their traditional construction of Northern Ireland as 'a place apart'. The conviction that the province is irredeemably 'different' has prompted the British parties to offer profound resistance to the ideal of electoral integration. The Labour Party has flatly refused to countenance extending membership to the people of the province. The strategy of resistance adopted by the Conservatives has been rather more circuitous and disingenuous. The decision to establish constituency organisations within Northern Ireland has not altered the approach which the Conservative Party has adopted towards the six counties. Recent Conservative administrations have persisted in the pursuit of political settlements which would confirm the existence of Northern Ireland on the margins of the Union. The evident inability of the Northern Ireland Conservatives to influence the conduct of public policy has exposed as fallacious the claim that admission to the parties of state would allow the residents of the six counties to exert control over the political centre. The political impotence of the Ulster Tories has thereby served to discredit the entire electoral integrationist project.

The rapid decline in the fortunes of electoral integrationism during the nineties may be further attributed to the character of the unionist mind. The outlook of modern unionism has been defined by an abiding conviction that Westminster cares little for the health of the Union. The distrust of the British state which grips the political imagination of modern unionism has fatally undermined the electoral integrationist project. Ulster unionists have simply proved unwilling to offer electoral support to parties such as the Conservatives which they do not believe have their interests at heart. Rather, they have preferred to keep faith with the traditional belief that the longevity of the Union can only be guaranteed through the existence and operation of politically autonomous Unionist parties.

CONCLUSION: THE TWILIGHT OF UNIONISM

The emergence of electoral integrationism in the late 1980s represented a critique of those strands of unionism which had hitherto sought to articulate the beliefs and interests of the more 'respectable' elements of the unionist community. The exposure of minimalist integrationism as essentially impotent created the political space which enabled the ideal of electoral integrationism to flower briefly. As the shortcomings of the electoral integrationist project have become increasingly obvious those primarily middle-class unionists who flirted briefly with electoral integrationism have inevitably returned to the minimalist fold. The rehabilitation of minimalist integrationism was confirmed and accelerated by the events which surrounded the passage of the Maastricht Bill through the House of Commons during the summer of 1993. Faced with the prospect of defeat in parliament, the Conservative government was forced to enlist the support of the province's nine Ulster Unionist MPs. In return for voting with the government the Ulster Unionists received certain unspecified assurances concerning the future conduct of British policy towards Northern Ireland.[64] The principal casualties of the horse-trading which accompanied the ratification of the Maastricht Treaty were inevitably the Northern Ireland Conservatives. The formulation of the pact between the Conservatives and Ulster Unionists illustrated that the caprice of parliamentary arithmetic could ensure that the people of Northern Ireland were better placed to exercise political power without the parties of state rather than within. In so doing, it served to eliminate the Ulster Tories' principal reason for existence.

The advent of the parliamentary understanding between the Conservative and Ulster Unionist Parties has allowed the revival of the erstwhile minimalist strategy of seeking to court influence within the corridors of power at Westminster. The prudent parliamentarism which contrived to discredit minimalist integrationism in the decade which preceded the Anglo-Irish Agreement has inevitably proved no more successful upon reprise. Indeed, the creation of the parliamentary pact has merely served to underscore the veracity of the Marxist aphorism concerning the propensity of tragic historical events – if the invocation of 'tragic' to characterise the degeneration of unionism is not to devalue the term altogether – to replay themselves in the guise of farce. Even in the context of the slapstick which passes for political life in Northern Ireland there have been few developments as farcical as the parliamentary courtship between John Major and James Molyneaux.

The 'gentleman's agreement' forged between the Conservative and Unionist Parties appeared to have furnished the latter with the political power necessary to underwrite the health of the Union. The authority afforded to the Ulster Unionists under the terms of the parliamentary pact has proved insufficient, however, to dissuade the current Tory administration from a course of action which has nudged Northern Ireland ever futher towards the margins of the United Kingdom. The inability of Ulster Unionism to alter the conduct of the Major administration casts into bold relief the strategic concerns of the modern British state. The interests which produced the parliamentary alliance – the anxiety of an increasingly precarious Conservative administration to remain in office – were, of course, merely conjunctural. The concerns which inform the approach adopted by Westminster towards Northern Ireland – essentially the strategic ambition of the British state to disengage from the six counties – are rather more organic. It has, therefore, inevitably been the interests of state rather than those of party which have exercised a greater bearing upon the actions of the executive since the formulation of the parliamentary pact. The Conservative government has continued to pursue vigorously a political project which has qualified further the constitutional status of Northern Ireland. In so doing, the Tory administration has ensured the withdrawal of Ulster Unionist support and thereby jeopardised its very existence. The apparent readiness of the Conservatives to sacrifice the narrow interests of party in order to advance the 'peace process' – an act of principle without parallel in the contemporary political life of the United Kingdom – serves to confirm that the ambition of Westminster to maintain a political distance from Northern Ireland with a view to ultimate disengagement represents not merely a transient measure of party policy but rather an absolute strategic imperative of the British state.

The advent of the parliamentary alliance hatched between the Conservatives and Ulster Unionists appeared to herald a significant revival of the fortunes of northern unionism. It was, accordingly, greeted with euphoria by elements of the unionist community. The parliamentary pact has in fact, however, proved a poisoned chalice which has merely accelerated the debilitation of Ulster unionism.[65] Seduced by the aroma of power, the Ulster Unionists have become unwitting accomplices to an unfolding political process which has served to undermine the constitutional status of Northern Ireland within the United Kingdom. Only on the eve of the publication of the British and Irish governments' proposed parameters for the dialogue which will define the political future of the province did the painful realisation finally dawn upon the Ulster Unionists that their dalliance with the Conservative government had effectively ensured their collaboration in the erosion of the Union. While the appearance of the Framework Document evidently represents a profound crisis for unionism, it also affords an opportunity to reconstruct the ideal of the Union in terms which are modern, inclusive and progressive. It is virtually impossible, however, to identify any element within the unionist fold equal to this urgent and onerous task of ideological renewal. There appears little prospect that a body of unionists will emerge capable of proffering a defence of the Union as lucid or thoughtful as that tendered by electoral integrationists a decade ago in the aftermath of the Hillsborough Accord. A rather more plausible scenario is that unionists will retreat characteristically into that sullen, charmless introspection which has deprived the unionist cause of influence and condemned Northern Ireland to the iniquitous status of mere ante-chamber of the Union.

NOTES

1. A. Gramsci, *Selections From the Prison Notebooks* (London, 1971), pp. 105–20.
2. R. J. Cormack and R. D. Osborne, 'The Evolution of the Catholic Middle Class', pp. 65–85 in A. Guelke (ed.), *New Perspectives on the Northern Ireland Conflict* (London, 1994); E. McCann, *War and an Irish Town*, Third Edition (London, 1993), pp. 52–3; D. McKittrick, 'Catholics Find a Middle Class Oasis in Belfast', *The Independent* (11 January 1991), p. 8; F. O'Connor, *In Search of a State: Catholics in Northern Ireland* (Belfast, 1993); J. Ruane and J. Todd, 'The Social Origins of Nationalism in a Contested Region: The Case of Northern Ireland', pp. 187–211 in J. Coakley (ed.), *The Social Origins of Nationalist Movements: The Contemporary West European Experience* (London, 1992).
3. A. Aughey, '"The 'Troubles" in Northern Ireland – Twenty Years On', *Talking Politics* 3:1 (1990); M. J. Cunningham, *British Government Policy in Northern Ireland, 1969–89: Its Nature and Execution* (Manchester, 1991) pp. 105–20; B. O'Leary and J. McGarry, *The Politics of Antagonism: Understanding Northern Ireland* (London, 1993) pp. 117–19; M. Ryan, *War and Peace in Ireland: Britain and the IRA in the New World Order* (London, 1994), p. 157; S. Wichert, *Northern Ireland since 1945* (Harlow,

1991); F. Wright *Northern Ireland: A Comparative Analysis* (Dublin, 1987), pp. 185–6.

4. D. Gordon, *The O'Neill Years: Unionist Politics 1963–69* (Belfast, 1989), p. 7.
5. T. Wilson, *Ulster: Conflict and Consent* (Oxford, 1989), p. 66.
6. B. O'Leary and P. Arthur, 'Northern Ireland as the Site of State- and Nation-Building Failures', pp. 1–47 in J. McGarry and B. O'Leary (eds), *The Future of Northern Ireland* (Oxford, 1990), pp. 27–8.
7. Cunningham, op. cit., p. 9; B. Rowthorn and N. Wayne, *Northern Ireland: The Political Economy of Conflict* (Cambridge, 1988), p. 27.
8. Wright, op. cit., pp. 198–9.
9. R. Rose, 'Is the UK a State? Northern Ireland as a Test Case', pp. 100–36, in P. Madgwick and R. Rose (eds), *The Territorial Dimension in UK Politics* (London, 1982), p. 125.
10. K. Bloomfield, 'Who Runs Northern Ireland?', *Fortnight* 256 (1987), pp. 11–12; S. Livingstone and J. Morison, 'An Audit of Democracy in Northern Ireland', *Fortnight* 337, Special Supplement (1995); B. O'Leary and P. Arthur, op. cit., p. 41.
11. B. Hadfield, 'Northern Ireland Affairs and Westminster', pp. 130–50 in B. Barton and P. Roche (eds), *The Northern Ireland Question: Myth and Reality* (Aldershot, 1991).
12. Cunningham, op. cit., pp. 37–8; L. O'Dowd, B. Rolston and M. Tomlinson, *Northern Ireland: Between Civil Rights and Civil War* (London, 1980), p. 95.
13. Cunningham, op. cit.; O'Leary and Arthur, op. cit.; O'Leary and McGarry, op. cit.
14. F. Millar, 'Battle for the Union to be Held on English Soil', *The Irish Times*, 16 January 1995.
15. P. Arthur, 'The Anglo-Irish Joint Declaration: Towards a Lasting Peace?', *Government and Opposition* 29:2 (1994), pp. 218–30; Ryan, op. cit., pp. 148–9.
16. P. Bew and H. Patterson, *The British State and the Ulster Crisis: From Wilson to Thatcher* (London, 1985), p. 4.
17. P. Arthur, *Government and Politics of Northern Ireland* (Harlow, 1989), p. 32; A. Green, *Government and Public Finance: Stormont 1921 to 1971* (Glasgow, 1979); Wichert, op. cit., p. 17; Wilson, op. cit., p. 83.
18. Wichert, op. cit., pp. 19–26.
19. Ibid., p. 161.
20. V. N. Hewitt, 'The Public Sector', pp. 353–77 in R. Harris *et al.* (eds), *The Northern Ireland Economy* (Harlow, 1990), p. 366.
21. B. Rowthorn, 'Northern Ireland: An Economy in Crisis', *Cambridge Journal of Economics* 5, pp. 1–31 (1981), p. 10.
22. F. Gaffikin and M. Morrissey, *Northern Ireland: The Thatcher Years* (London, 1990), p. 47.
23. M. Tomlinson, *Twenty Years On: The Costs of War and the Dividends of Peace* (Belfast, 1994), p. 18.
24. J. Anderson and J. Goodman, 'Northern Ireland: Dependency, Class and Cross-Border Integration in the European Union', *Capital and Class* 54 (1994), pp. 13–23.

25. V. Borooah, 'Northern Ireland: Typology of a Regional Economy', pp. 1–23, in P. Teague (ed.), *The Economy of Northern Ireland* (London, 1993); J. W. McAuley, *The Politics of Identity: A Loyalist Community in Belfast* (Aldershot, 1994), p. 33.

26. A. Pollak (ed.), *A Citizens' Enquiry: The Opsahl Report on Northern Ireland* (Dublin, 1993), p. 73.

27. Ibid.

28. A. Milburn, 'Class Act', *Fortnight* 328 (1994) p. 11; Wichert, op. cit., pp. 177, 184.

29. Rolston, 'The Contented Classes', *The Irish Reporter* 9 (1993), pp. 7–9.

30. I. MacKinnon, 'Ulster Few Enjoy a Golden Age', *The Independent on Sunday,* 8 August 1993.

31. *The Independent on Sunday,* 15 January 1995.

32. Cunningham, op. cit., p. 166.

33. C. Macauley, 'Catholics Scarce on the "Movers and Shakers" List', *The Irish News,* 16 March 1994.

34. P. Teague, 'Not a Firm Basis', *Fortnight* 317 (1993), pp. 28–9.

35. S. Breen, 'Middle Classes Find a Silver Lining', *Red Pepper* 5 (October 1994), pp. 26–7; B. Rolston, op. cit.

36. M. Brennock, 'Guess Who's Coming to Belfast 9?', *The Irish Times,* 23 March 1991.

37. MacKinnon, op. cit; N. O'Faolain, 'The Discreet Charm of the Northern Bourgeoisie', *The Irish Times,* 10 July 1993.

38. P. Bew and H. Patterson, *The British State and the Ulster Crisis* (London, 1985), pp. 4–5.

39. P. Buckland, *A History of Northern Ireland* (Dublin, 1981), pp. 157–8; A. Guelke, 'Limits to Conflict and Accommodation', pp. 190–206, in A. Guelke (ed.), *New Perspectives on the Northern Ireland Conflict* (Aldershot, 1994), p. 194.

40. P. Bew and H. Patterson, *The British State and the Ulster Crisis* (London, 1985), p. 103.

41. 'Unionism: Jim Leads On', *Fortnight* 256, pp. 11–12.

42. Ibid.

43. A. Aughey, *Under Siege: Ulster Unionism and the Anglo-Irish Agreement* (Belfast, 1989), pp. 141–2.

44. P. Dixon, '"The Usual English Doubletalk": The British Political Parties and the Ulster Unionists 1974–94', *Irish Political Studies* 9 (1994), pp. 26–30.

45. The absence of the unionist middle classes from Northern Irish political life was formally acknowledged by the Ulster Unionist Party in its proposals for the government of the province published on the eve of the Framework Document. *The Irish Times,* 22 February 1995, p. 6.

46. T. Hadden and K. Boyle, *The Anglo-Irish Agreement: Commentary, Text and Official Review* (London, 1989), p. 22.

47. A. Aughey, *Under Siege* (Belfast, 1989), p. 55.

48. P. Bew and H. Patterson, 'The New Stalemate: Unionism and the Anglo-Irish Agreement', pp. 41–57, in P. Teague (ed.), *Beyond the Rhetoric* (London, 1987), p. 43.

49.	A. Aughey, *Under Siege* (Belfast, 1989), pp. 138–46; P. O'Malley, *Northern Ireland: Questions of Nuance* (Belfast, 1990), p. 37.

50.	Aughey, *Under Siege,* pp. 86–7.

51.	H. Bunting and the Northern Ireland Conservatives' Political Sub-Committee, *A Conservative Approach to the Government of Northern Ireland* (Belfast, 1990); N. Faris, 'Direct Rule and Legislation in Northern Ireland: The Orders in Council System', *The Equal Citizen* 2:3 (1989); A. J. Green, *Integration for Ulster: The Broader View* (Belfast, 1991).

52.	C. Villiers, *Reunited Kingdom* (London, 1990), p. 18.

53.	Bunting *et al.*, op. cit; A. J. Green, op. cit.

54.	B. Clifford, *The Unionist Family* (Belfast, 1987), *The Road to Nowhere* (Belfast, 1987), pp. 1–3; *The Equal Citizen* March/April 1986; Institute for Representative Government, *Ending the Political Vacuum* (Belfast, 1988), p. 5, *Representational Politics and the Implementation of the Anglo-Irish Treaty* (Belfast, 1988), pp. 6–7; R. L. McCartney, *What Must Be Done* (Belfast, 1986), p. 4; H. Roberts, 'Sound Stupidity: The British Party System and the Northern Ireland Question', *Government and Opposition* 22:3 (1987), pp. 315–35.

55.	B. Clifford, *The Politics and Economics of Fair Employment in Northern Ireland* (Belfast, 1994), pp. 10–13; K. Hoey, 'British Voters, So Why Not British Parties?', *Parliamentary Brief: A Northern Ireland Supplement* 3:1 (October 1994), p. 54; *The Northern Star*, 16 November 1991.

56.	A. Aughey, 'The Politics of Equal Citizenship' *Talking Politics* 2:1 (1989), p. 24, *Under Siege* (Belfast, 1989), pp. 155–6, 'The "Troubles" in Northern Ireland – Twenty Years On' *Talking Politics* 3:1, p. 4; B. Clifford, *Parliamentary Sovereignty and Northern Ireland* (Belfast, 1985), p. 13; McCartney, op. cit., p. 6.

57.	E. Haslett, *Devolution, Integration: Prospects for Government in Northern Ireland* (Belfast, 1987), p. 11; M. Langhammer and D. Young, 'The UDA Plan: Opening for Dialogue or Sectarian Fix?', *Fortnight* 249 (1987), pp. 14–15.

58.	J. Davidson, *Electoral Integrationism* (Belfast, 1986).

59.	B. Clifford, *Government Without Opposition* (Belfast, 1986).

60.	*The Equal Citizen*, March 1989, p. 3.

61.	Although a small Stalinist splinter of the far left, the B&ICO has cast a long shadow over the political and intellectual life of modern Northern Ireland. At the outset of the troubles the B&ICO broke with the prevailing leftist orthodoxy to propound the 'two nations theory' which identified the partition of Ireland as a legitimate acknowledgement of the ethnic divisions which exist within the island. The loyalist strikes of the mid-seventies drew the B&ICO to the understanding that the disunity of the Northern Irish working classes owed its origins primarily to the exclusion of northern workers from the British Labour Party. Thereafter, the members of the B&ICO cast their considerable energies into persuading the Labour Party to extend membership to the six counties, a demand articulated with skill and vigour through the pressure group the Campaign for Labour Representation (CLR). The key intellectual within the B&ICO fold is the prolific maverick Brendan Clifford, whose writings have exercised a palpable, although often unacknowledged, influence upon an entire generation of revisionist Marxist academics.

62. P. Bew and H. Patterson, 'The New Stalemate: Unionism and the Anglo-Irish Agreement', pp. 41–57, in P. Teague (ed.), *Beyond the Rhetoric* (London, 1987).
63. E. Pearce, 'Not Everyone Was Cheering', *Fortnight* 278, p. 8.
64. A. Bevins, 'Major's Pact with Unionists Exposed', *The Independent* 28 July 1993; E. McCann, op. cit., pp. 56–7.
65. J. W. Foster, 'Processed Peace?', *Fortnight* 326 (1994), pp. 35–7.

11 17 November 1993 – A Night to Remember?
Scott Harvie

The relationship between sport and political division within Ireland has rarely been subject to as much scrutiny, media debate, and, arguably, myth-making as focused on the ninety-plus minutes of the World Cup soccer encounter between Northern Ireland and the Republic of Ireland in Belfast on 17 November 1993. While the connoisseur of footballing excellence may have taken little from the game, its wider social and political repercussions have given rise to a wide-ranging literature stretching from a virulent correspondence in the letters column of the *Belfast Telegraph* through a variety of articles in the Irish and British press to a major feature in the top-selling American magazine/journal, *Sports Illustrated*. It has influenced questions and comments in both the Dail and the House of Commons in Westminster and provided material for a play which has toured Irish repertory theatres to considerable acclaim and may lead to an even wider audience becoming familiar with its interpretation of *A Night in November*.

In this chapter, at the risk of adding to the dramatisation of events surrounding one inevitably limited sporting encounter, the insights offered in respect of the politics of what may be loosely termed the loyalist community in Northern Ireland are assessed. First, the extent to which this particular North–South clash offers a suitable vehicle from which to garner such insights is evaluated. An outline of the footballing context within which the two parts of Ireland find themselves is then set out and a background sketch of events around this fixture presented. Analysis of the political implications focuses on four elements fundamental to our understanding of loyalism today; the divisions within its own ranks, relations with the nationalist community within Northern Ireland, external relations *vis-à-vis* the Irish Republic and developments in the relationship loyalists have with the British state.

The belief that politics can be kept out of sport, if it ever had any credible basis, has proven increasingly difficult to sustain in the modern age, particularly where popular sporting activities, national aspirations and societal divisions and/or tensions combine. In *Sport, Sectarianism and Society in a Divided Ireland* John Sugden and Alan Bairner demonstrate the depth and complexity of such relationships in the history and development of Irish sport. Association football's universal, mass appeal has made it singularly susceptible to manifestations of wider, political influence. Over recent history this has included acting as a catalyst for war between the Central American states of El Salvador and Honduras; being used as a mechanism for expressing international condemnation through the ban on Yugoslavian participation in tournaments administered by UEFA and FIFA; and providing a vehicle for a variety of political regimes and leaderships to try to sustain their position by basking in the limelight of real or anticipated success. For instance, the 1990 World Cup witnessed the active interference of President Biya of Cameroon in the operation of the national football association, the appointment by Argentinian President Carlos Menem of Diego Maradona as a consultant ambassador for sport, and the more mundane sight of English and Irish players being greeted on their return as conquering heroes by their respective prime ministers. Lincoln Allison's work, *The Politics of Sport,* illustrates how sport and politics have become intertwined in a range of settings worldwide.[1]

Closer to home, Sugden and Bairner say that

the linkage of association football and politics in Northern Ireland goes far beyond the direct impact of the troubles and resultant security considerations. The sport is played by members of both the Protestant and Catholic communities, frequently together, or at the very least, in direct competition and would appear to offer a significant channel for reconciliation. In truth, however, the sport's capacity to divide has been at least as marked during most of the 20th century as have been its integrative capabilities. Football has not simply been on the receiving end of Ireland's troubled political history. It has often reflected the divisions which have helped to create political unrest and, on occasions, has even helped to exacerbate these divisions.[2]

In short, while most mass sports in Northern Ireland have, due to the nature of their origins and historical development, been more or less the preserve of either the Protestant or Catholic community, association football, as a recent research study confirmed, is supported actively by both, which gives it a unique social and political import.

From the perspective of the loyalist community association football holds especial significance, not only because of its mass popularity and place in working-class culture but also due to the fact that it is one of the few sporting activities in which Northern Ireland is represented in its own right at national level, rather than being part of an all-Ireland structure (normally within a nine-county Ulster branch) as in rugby union or being swallowed up inside a United Kingdom organisation as with equestrian events. Research on the relationship between sport and the community in Northern Ireland confirmed the extent to which association football is an odd man out in this respect. Of the 15 most popular sports surveyed, 13 were formally organised on an all-Ireland basis.[3] Given the suggestion in recent literature, particularly the work of Steve Bruce, that loyalists perceive themselves as being increasingly embattled, feel deserted by the British state and believe that they are steadily losing ground to nationalist politicians and paramilitaries, it appears likely that symbols of Northern Irish identity distinct from those tied to Britain will take on added significance. For the reasons outlined above one of the most potent symbols of this separate identity is contained in the Northern Ireland football team.

Before analysing the significance of more recent developments, a brief outline of the historical, political context in which Irish international football is set and an account of events leading up to and surrounding the World Cup fixture with the Republic of Ireland in November 1993 follows.

THE HISTORICAL AND POLITICAL CONTEXT OF IRISH INTERNATIONAL FOOTBALL

Association football, a spin-off from the game which became known as rugby football, was introduced to Ireland in the mid-nineteenth century. Although it was initially restricted to the same upper-middle-class bastions of the English public school system as sports like rugby union and hockey, association football soon broke out of this narrow mould since, for a combination of technical and socio-economic reasons, it was adopted as the most popular game of the working classes in mainland Britain. Given this base, it is perhaps not surprising that in Ireland association football was first taken up as a mass sport in the north-east corner, the area which had advanced most in respect of urbanisation and industrialisation, spreading there from the mainland in the wake of its growing popularity, not least among Irish emigrant labour.

Following the establishment of the Football Association (FA) in 1867 and Scottish FA in 1873, the Irish Football Association (IFA) was set up in Belfast in 1880. Reports suggest that it was another five years before the game, under the established code, was played in Dublin.[4] The British upper-middle-class influence on the sport was reflected in the fact that some of the first club sides to be formed were based around regiments of the army stationed in Ireland. However, in Belfast, the dominance of urban workers in playing and watching the game and the way in which it had spread across from the west of Scotland where Rangers and Celtic were fast becoming icons for their respective Protestant and Catholic communities around Glasgow, led to clubs being founded on community bases which tended towards religious exclusivity. Linfield and Glentoran, formed during the 1880s, took their support largely from the Protestant working class of West and East Belfast respectively while Belfast Celtic, established on the model of their Glaswegian namesakes in 1891, gave Catholic workers, located for the most part in the west of the city, a football team to identify with. In Dublin, Bohemians were set up in 1890 and around the turn of the century a number of other clubs emerged both in the capital and in other parts of what is now the Republic of Ireland, although Sugden and Bairner point out that association football continued to be linked to the Anglo-Irish community there, and among nationalists was tarred with the brush of being a foreign game, which stunted its development in areas where the revival of Gaelic pursuits had been most effective.[5]

The struggle for Home Rule and the eventual partitioning of Ireland impacted on sport generally by consolidating the gulf between Gaelic games and sports associated with the British establishment. By this stage the nature and extent of the growth of association football had taken it beyond either camp, as it became one of the most popular activities among the urban working class of both Protestant and Catholic communities. In this context it is perhaps to be expected that the political tensions and upheavals of the day were transmitted to and reinforced by happenings within the sport.

While sectarian hostilities in Belfast were reflected in rioting, shots being fired and a large number of injuries being sustained at matches between Belfast Celtic and both Linfield (1912) and Glentoran (1920),[6] the process which led to the political division of Ireland was closely mirrored and possibly exacerbated by the growing distrust of and dissatisfaction with the Belfast-based administration of the game. Accusations of bias towards Belfast clubs and their players in the selection of Irish representative sides, the refusal of the IFA to allow an Irish Cup semi-final replay in 1919 between Glentoran and Dublin club Shelbourne to be staged outside Belfast and symbolic slights such as the 'bunting incident' of 1921 when IFA officials insisted that an Irish tricolour be removed from spectators attending an amateur international match between France and

Ireland in Paris, along with the fall-out from the Anglo-Irish conflict of the time, produced a split which saw Dublin clubs withdraw from the Irish Football League. As relations between Dublin and Belfast deteriorated, the split widened. The establishment of the FA of Ireland (FAI) in June 1921 set the seal on the organisational division of association football within Ireland.

During the first half-century of their dual existence, relations between the respective football authorities in Belfast and Dublin were generally frosty but workable. However, there were bones of major contention with regard to the constituency from which each could draw its international players and the name used by the respective national sides. The Belfast-based (Northern) Ireland continued to select players born in the 26 counties until 1950 but since their fixtures were largely restricted to the British home international championship and those of the Dublin-based (Republic of) Ireland to non-competitive matches against foreign opposition, a pragmatic approach allowing players (32 in all) to appear for both could be adopted. After the Second World War, with relations between the Stormont government and the administration in the fledgling Republic becoming more actively hostile, the decision of both associations to enter the qualifying process for the World Cup signalled an end to this situation. As with the 1921 split, the initiative for consolidating the division of Irish international football came from the south and this does appear to have left some longstanding sense of grievance on the part of the IFA. In the official match programme for the first full international played in Belfast between Northern Ireland and the Republic in 1979 Malcolm Brodie wrote:

> Until then [1950] we had the spectacle of players appearing for 'Ireland' on a Saturday and the next week for another 'Ireland'. Pressure, however, was brought to bear on certain Southern-born players around that period and the practice ended.[7]

Perhaps partly to demonstrate that they were innocent parties in the process of division the IFA persisted in calling its side 'Ireland' until well into the 1970s. An attempt by the FAI to have the 1954 congress of the world body (FIFA) pass a motion giving it the exclusive right to use the name 'Ireland' was successfully resisted but inevitably heightened latent antagonisms.

The next 20–25 years witnessed a slow thaw in relations between the two Irish football authorities. As far as the respective support bases were concerned, Northern Ireland appeared to be in a stronger position during this time since association football had few comparable rivals in terms of the breadth of its appeal which was reinforced by the national side's success in the 1958 World Cup and the presence of well-known and revered cross-channel stars such as Danny Blanchflower, George Best and Pat Jennings. In the Republic of Ireland soccer lagged behind Gaelic sports and rugby union in terms of popular appeal and the limited success enjoyed by the national football team could hardly have been expected to excite the imaginations of potential supporters.

As a result, although the loyalist community provided the strongest and, certainly, most vociferous backing for the Northern Ireland side, nationalists were also found among its supporters and the mixed religious composition of the players helped consolidate their allegiance. Thus, the background to Irish international football, mirroring the political setting, is one of division and, to a degree, distrust between North and South at official level but within Northern Ireland, even after the onset of the 'Troubles' which forced international fixtures to be played outside the province during the 1970s, support for the national football team remained strong and was by no means exclusive to loyalists.

The change that has occurred over recent years and the relationship between this and wider political development within Northern Ireland, particularly in respect of the loyalist community, are illustrated by means of a brief background sketch of events from the first full soccer international between the two Irelands in 1978 to the aftermath of the World Cup clash at Windsor in 1993. Underpinning the analysis here is the view that the situation in Northern Ireland prior to the paramilitary ceasefires in the autumn of 1994 could be understood as one of institutionalised guerrilla warfare on top of a polarised community structure and while the guerrilla violence may have been brought to an end, the basic social polarisation remains and the problems arising from this may prove more difficult to resolve in the longer term.

BACKGROUND TO THE EVENTS OF NOVEMBER 1993

In September 1978 the national soccer sides of the Republic of Ireland and Northern Ireland met in Dublin for the first time in a qualifying fixture for the European Championship. The game was marked by crowd disturbances between rival spectators. Almost a year later the (Northern) Irish League champions Linfield visited League of Ireland champions Dundalk in the preliminary round of the European Cup on the day 18 British soldiers were killed by a massive Provisional IRA bomb near Warrenpoint and Lord Mountbatten and members of his family assassinated in Sligo. Some of the most serious crowd disorder of the 1970s was acted out around the game, leading to the return leg being staged outside Ireland. November 1979 saw the first full international clash between North and South to be held in Belfast. The game passed off relatively peacefully with Northern Ireland winning 1–0.

After Northern Ireland's success in the home international championship of 1980 under new manager Billy Bingham, the 1981 tournament was played against the backdrop of the H-block hunger strikes with England and Wales belatedly pulling out of fixtures in Belfast. The Northern Irish side went on to unexpected success in the World Cup Finals of 1982, reaching the last 12 thanks to a one-goal victory over tournament hosts Spain. Considerable media attention was focused on the squad, their mixed religious composition and the effect of their success in crossing the community divide within Northern Ireland. However, ten days after the World Cup ended, media coverage of the carnage left by two Provisional IRA bombs in London, particularly the scenes of devastation in the wake of one bomb targeted on a cavalry division of the army, sent stark reminders of the nature of the conflict around the world.

The decision by the English and Scottish FAs to scrap the home international tournament, following Northern Ireland's win in 1984, gave rise to doubts about the future of independent international sides for the four home nations, and the criteria on which players were selected also came into question. Previously this had been based by agreement between the four home nations on the place of birth of the individual player or his parents. Elsewhere, passport eligibility was the general rule but this presented particular problems in Northern Ireland where citizens could carry either British or Irish (or both) passports.

In February 1985 Northern Ireland's preparations for a home tie with England in the qualifying stages of the 1986 World Cup were disrupted by an INLA car-bomb which exploded a short distance from the ground. The return match in November 1985 was played two days before the signing of the Anglo-Irish Agreement and saw Northern Ireland clinch their place in the finals by drawing 0–0 against an England side who were accused of taking it easy since they were already assured of qualification. The Republic of Ireland's failure to qualify for the World Cup finals led to Englishman Jack Charlton being appointed controversially as their new manager in February 1986. His side to face Scotland in the opening qualifying fixture for the 1988 European Championships included several players from top-level English club sides whose eligibility was based on one of their grandparents being born in Ireland. At the same time, after Northern Ireland's failure to progress beyond the first round of the World Cup Finals several prominent players of the previous decade, most notably goalkeeper Pat Jennings, retired. With no obvious replacements, Northern Ireland's squad resources were seriously stretched and local part-time players had to be fielded, goalkeepers George Dunlop of Linfield and Paul Kee of Ards featuring in different games against the Republic.

An unexpected win by the Scottish national football team in Bulgaria allowed the Republic of Ireland to qualify for the 1988 European Championship finals, their first major tournament. A number of supporters based in Northern Ireland followed the Republic to Germany where their side defeated England and went close to reaching the semi-finals. Some violent disturbances marred the England game, reported largely to be the work of English fans who greeted their Irish counterparts with sectarian abuse.

In September 1988 Northern Ireland met the Republic of Ireland in Belfast after being drawn together in the qualifying series for the 1990 World Cup. The IFA and FAI decided that tickets should only be made available to home supporters and that only the host-nation's anthem should be played. This game coincided with an inquest into the shooting of three Provisional IRA members by British Army undercover soldiers in Gibraltar and several songs and chants from the Northern Ireland supporters referred to this incident. Less than six months later Northern Ireland lost to Spain in Belfast, making qualification for the finals unlikely. The team's display drew criticism from large sections of the home support and the barracking of defender Anton Rogan was particularly noted. Rogan was a Catholic, originally from West Belfast, who played at the time for Celtic. He had also scored an own goal and played badly in Northern Ireland's previous match, a four-goal drubbing in Spain.

In February 1990, having been largely absent from the province's football grounds during the 1980s, serious sectarian disorder reared its head once more, disrupting a cup-tie in Belfast between Linfield and West Belfast non-league side, Donegal Celtic. A new feature, noted at the game, was for Catholic supporters to voice their preference for the Republic of Ireland over the Northern Irish side, which was the object of some derision.

Following another flashpoint match with England, the Republic of Ireland side exceeded expectations in the 1990 World Cup, eventually reaching the quarter-final stage with a squad of which less than one-third of players were born in Ireland. As the media reported on how supporters in the North were getting behind them, several letters in Belfast newspapers complained about BBC Northern Ireland showing the Republic's game against Holland in preference to the England match seen by the rest of the BBC network.

The random shooting of Catholics in a Belfast bookmakers' in February 1992 was one of the worst atrocities of recent years and indicated the serious nature of an upsurge in loyalist paramilitary violence. In the United States Father Sean McManus, president of the Irish National Caucus, called for Coca-Cola to withdraw its sponsorship of the IFA and for Northern Ireland to be banned from the 1994 World Cup finals, to be held in America, due to the sectarian practices of the club (Linfield) on whose ground their home matches are played.

In early 1993 a meeting of the four British football associations decided to adopt the 'granny rule', allowing passport eligibility to be used as the basic criterion in determining whether a player could be selected for the national side. Later that year, at a meeting of the IFA, concern was expressed about young players being encouraged to opt to make themselves eligible for the Republic of Ireland rather than Northern Ireland in the wake of the former's success.

After a Provisional IRA bomb exploded in a busy shopping-centre in Warrington, Cheshire in March 1993, media attention focusing on the children killed in the blast helped to generate a wave of revulsion. Less than two weeks later a World Cup football match between the Republic of Ireland and Northern Ireland in Dublin was preceded by a moment's silence for all victims of violence in Ireland. The Republic's easy 3–0 win proved an embarrassment to Northern Ireland and the small group of supporters who travelled south, particularly during the second half as the home supporters sang that 'There's only one team in Ireland'.

During the course of 1993 informal talks recommenced between SDLP leader John Hume and Sinn Fein president, Gerry Adams. This led to loyalist paramilitaries stepping up their activities, targeting what they called a 'pan-nationalist front'. In the media and among academics, increasing attention was paid to alienation in the loyalist community, a telephone poll indicating that 42 per cent of callers from this background were prepared to support loyalist violence.[8] The Adams–Hume talks reached a conclusion in September with a joint proposal document on the way ahead in Northern Ireland being delivered to the Irish government. Attacks by loyalist paramilitaries escalated: totals for the year to September showed that the number of murders carried out by loyalist groups was far in excess of those by republican organisations.

On the football field, while Northern Ireland's hopes of qualifying for the 1994 World Cup finals had long since been dashed, the Republic were left, by October 1993, requiring one win from two matches to guarantee a place. However, one of their poorer performances, resulting in a heavy home-defeat against Spain, made a victory in their final match in Belfast

appear essential. The Republic's supporters were expected to make strenuous efforts to obtain tickets for the game despite the fact that tickets were
only to be available in the North.

A Provisional IRA bomb attack on the Shankill Road in Belfast on a
busy Saturday afternoon in late October killed 10 people and exacted
promises of retribution from loyalist paramilitary groups. After a string of
murderous attacks, the following weekend's sporting fixtures were badly
disrupted since players and officials, particularly from the South, decided
not to travel. Doubts began to be expressed as to whether the World Cup
match between the two Irelands could go ahead in Belfast on
17 November as scheduled. The month ended with seven more people
killed in a UFF attack on a bar frequented largely by Catholics in
Greysteel, County Londonderry. The nature of this incident on top of the
Shankill bombing was reported to have left an atmosphere of fear and
tension and prompted a decision by the British and Irish governments to
meet urgently to discuss the situation.

During early November 1993 newspaper reports suggested that the
Northern Ireland–Republic game was to be moved to mainland Britain due
to the upsurge in violence. Statements by the FAI left their position on
travelling to Belfast for the match appear somewhat ambiguous and
cynical observers suggested that their doubts were motivated by a desire to
make victory on the field easier rather than by off-the-field concerns.
Ultimately, UEFA decided that the game should go ahead in Belfast but a
number of articles in the press made much of the dangers surrounding the
game and the sectarian hostility and hatred likely to be found at Windsor
Park. Anticipating developments, news media from around the world
attempted to gain access to the game. On the playing side, Northern
Ireland manager Billy Bingham, who was set to retire after the game,
seemed to relish the clash and commented with regard to the Republic's
football team, that 'at least our team is of Irish extraction and not full of
mercenaries'.[9]

A major security operation was staged on the day of the match with the
Republic of Ireland supporters who attended being segregated into a
section of one stand. After the game they related having received considerable verbal abuse; however there were no reported violent incidents and
few arrests. As he walked along the touchline, the Northern Ireland
manager was greeted with acclaim by the home crowd and responded by
waving to the supporters and gesturing to them to increase the volume of
their backing. During the match racist abuse was aimed at the Republic's
coloured players and subsequent reports in the Irish media claimed that
ugly, sectarian-motivated abuse was also heard. Northern Ireland's goal,

scored in the later stages of the second half, gave rise to scenes of wild celebration on the part of the home support, who sang that 'There's only one team in Ireland' with Bingham again gesturing to them to raise the volume. With 12 minutes remaining, the Republic equalised and the sides played out a 1–1 draw. A clear-cut result in the game being played between Spain and Denmark allowed the Republic of Ireland to qualify for the finals on goals scored but it was several moments after the match before news of Spain's win was confirmed. As the two managers left the field, Jack Charlton directed some criticism at Bingham for which he later apologised. At the post-match press conference Bingham congratulated the Republic on their success but refused to retract his 'mercenaries' charge. Ten of the 15 Irish-born players on the field were playing for Northern Ireland.

Following the Belfast match, reaction in some quarters seemed to border on the hysterical. In the Dail Fine Gael TD Austin Deasy was quoted as saying that the Northern Ireland manager should be 'indicted for incitement to national hatred' and accused Bingham of going 'out of his way to provoke a crowd who were already showing extraordinary bigotry'. IFA secretary David Bowen responded by describing the game as 'a wonderful example of sport in Northern Ireland'.[10] Articles in the Irish press and in nationalist newspapers within Northern Ireland condemned Bingham and the home supporters for the intimidatory nature of their behaviour. The *Irish News* said: 'it was a night of shame for soccer at Windsor Park last week. Most of the home supporters showed that the game is only secondary to politics and when that happens what chance have we of peace on this little island?'[11]

In the month after the game, reports of talks between the British government and the Provisional IRA gathered force despite an earlier categorical denial by the British Prime Minister. Secretary of State for Northern Ireland, Patrick Mayhew, finally admitted that there had been contacts between them, although the nature of these communications was hotly disputed. The British and Irish governments hinted at significant progress in their talks over Northern Ireland, and in December, after much raising and downplaying of expectations, the two governments unveiled their Downing Street Declaration, which offered paramilitary organisations access to talks over the future of Northern Ireland if they laid down their arms.

In January 1994 Northern Ireland and the Republic of Ireland were drawn together again in the qualifying stages for the 1996 European Championships. Neither of the two football associations were reported to be happy with the draw, the FAI revealing that they lobbied UEFA to keep the two sides apart. Retiring Northern Ireland manager Bingham was quoted as saying, 'There is no point in hiding the fact that there will always be things outside football attached to games between these teams.'[12] The Republic of Ireland began their moderately successful 1994 World Cup finals campaign with a victory over Italy in June. Catholics watching the game on television in a pub in Loughinisland, County Down, were victims of a UFF gun-attack which left six dead. This proved to be one of the last atrocities before the Provisional IRA and loyalist paramilitary organisations declared their respective ceasefires in August and October 1994.

POLITICAL IMPLICATIONS

This subjective interpretation of events on and off the field certainly seems to confirm the view that association football in Ireland holds a political currency of some significance. It also appears clear that during the last 15–20 years there has been a marked shift in the nature of allegiance towards the two Irish national football sides on the part of both major communities living in the north. Perhaps then what lies at the heart of this analysis is the wider political meaning which can be attached to the shift in allegiances, particularly where the loyalist community is concerned.

Before directly addressing the sets of relationships which are involved here, the nature and importance of the change among nationalist supporters merits some consideration. Until at least the early 1980s it appears that, despite the symbols of political union with Britain being prominent at Northern Ireland's matches and the overtly pro-loyalist sympathies of the most vocal elements of their support, nationalists did offer some form of allegiance, albeit largely passive, to the Northern Irish side. In more recent years this seems to have been cast off in favour of the Republic of Ireland. Obviously the change can partly be explained by the run of successes enjoyed by the Republic's football side which has only relatively recently awakened interest in the South and which might be expected to produce a knock-on effect among northern nationalists, particularly where the symbols used coincide with those of their own culture and where the contrast with Northern Ireland, both in respect of its decline on the field and the symbolic associations off it, is highlighted. However, this is not quite the full picture according to Sugden and Bairner:

> The association of loyalist extremism with the Northern Ireland soccer team has alienated many Catholics who now find it both psychologi-

cally and physically threatening to attend matches in Windsor Park. This Catholic exodus has been accompanied by a gradual drift away by more liberal minded Protestants who have been turned off both by their team's poor performances and by the sectarianism of sections of the crowd there.[13]

The hypotheses arising from their analysis appear to be that to the extent to which the shift in allegiance among nationalist football supporters is politically motivated, it is for the most part a reaction to what has been happening in the loyalist community and that developments within this community have led to there being an increasing division between hard-line and liberal elements, reflected in and reinforced by their attitudes to the two Irish national football sides. These can be tested with regard to the insights provided by the World Cup encounter of November 1993, concerning the four key sets of relationships affecting the loyalist community, starting with relations inside that broad grouping.

INTRA-LOYALIST RELATIONS

Divisions between the many heterogeneous elements which may be seen in some form or other as 'loyalist', defined here as holding some political or psychological affiliation to the union with Britain and/or the protection and furtherance of the interests of the Protestant community within Northern Ireland, have received increasing academic scrutiny in recent years. Jennifer Todd's distinction between 'Ulster loyalist' and 'Ulster British' has been particularly influential and has been echoed in subsequent work, such as that of Steve Bruce.

Sugden and Bairner's studies of the relationship between sport and sectarianism in Northern Ireland may also be seen as reinforcing the view that there is a such a divide, particularly with regard to the phenomenon they identify as taking place among loyalist football supporters over recent years. They consider that until then the apparent contradiction between the pro-loyalist and often overtly sectarian sympathies of substantial elements of the Northern Ireland support and the mixed religious composition of their team was resolved without alienating either Catholic or liberal Protestant supporters due to a combination of political naivety, the side's success and 'the sanguine attitude towards sectarian abuse which most Northern Irish people have tended to adopt even during the lowest points in the current Troubles'.[14] However, they suggest that latent tensions began to emerge from the mid-1980s on, reflected in the abuse directed at certain players, particularly Anton Rogan. Their explanation for this is partly that Catholic players are being made scapegoats for the decline in Northern Ireland's playing fortunes particularly *vis-à-vis* the Republic but, more significantly, they argue that it marks a general shift in loyalist popular culture away from manifestations of Britishness and towards bodies and symbols exclusive to Northern Ireland, and, if they were going to have anything to do with it, exclusive to their own community. Sugden and Bairner say:

> During the 1980s the red, white and blue scarves and union jacks were replaced on the terraces by the green and white colours which the team had always worn, and Northern Ireland flags. Windsor Park became an increasingly unfriendly place for Catholics...symbolised by the message 'Taigs Keep Out' daubed on a wall near one of the approach routes to the ground.[15]

Following Todd's categorisations, this can be interpreted as a marked shift in the direction of the 'Ulster loyalist' camp, leading to and being reinforced by the alienation of those liberal Protestant elements who previously had been happy to support Northern Ireland and who would fit into the 'Ulster British' category. In turn, as Bruce points out, there is likely to be a relatively close fit between being in the 'Ulster loyalist' grouping and coming from a working-class background and, conversely, between being considered 'Ulster British' and having middle-class associations. Thus, the implication appears to be that the phenomenon identified in more general discourse of the 'proletarianisation' of loyalist politics is matched by what is going on around the arena of international association football.

How far do the events of 17 November bear this out? First impressions based on media coverage of the match would almost certainly concur that loyalist extremists appeared to have won the day among Northern Ireland's support. Reports on the mood of the crowd and the nature and extent of the verbal abuse emanating from it suggest the worst. An account in the Belfast-based nationalist newspaper, the *Irish News*, sums up this view:

> For me it was the worst experience that I ever had at a game of any kind. Being a family newspaper I will not relate what I heard from the crowd but what I do know is that it was not a small section of the Northern Ireland fans who gave vent to their feelings. Reports from all over the ground have been the same and anyone who tries to make it appear that it was just good natured bantering needs their head examined.[16]

In the immediate aftermath of the game, a number of comments and reports, particularly in the Dublin-based media, contained various allegations of menacing behaviour on the part of spectators and, indeed, individuals associated with the official Northern Ireland party.

As far as its significance in respect of perceived political divisions within the loyalist community is concerned, a number of points can be made. First that due to FIFA's ban on standing accommodation, it is difficult to make any distinction in terms of the likely social class distribution of those attending the game and expressing the extreme views which have been reported. However, the fact that the least expensive tickets for the game were considerably above the going rate for matches in Northern Ireland and that a substantial percentage of them were tied in with a package deal involving tickets for other home games, requiring a quite substantial outlay, suggests that, if anything, people from more middle-class backgrounds were likely to be over-represented in the Windsor Park crowd. If this is the case the argument that it is the loyalist 'proles' who are setting the extreme agenda may be suspect. Personal observation of the crowd on the Spion Kop, the least expensive standing area at Winsor Park, during the previous World Cup qualifying series, would confirm the view that they were no more overtly sectarian than spectators in other sections of the ground. Indeed, bearing in mind the reports of sectarian abuse aimed at Anton Rogan given by observers in the stands, and the limited evidence I found of this on the terracings, a contrary argument in line with Sarah Nelson's observation in the 1970s that members of the Protestant middle class 'often had more extreme views on Catholics, on the Union or on economic matters than did members of the UVF and the UDA'[17] might be made.

What may also be seen as interesting and potentially significant is the reaction on the part of the IFA establishment to media criticisms of the behaviour shown by the Windsor Park crowd. A stock response on the part of football authorities to instances of unruly behaviour and/or hooliganism by spectators is to claim that those causing the trouble are a small minority and to condemn their activities out of hand while stressing that the majority are well-behaved. No attempt appears to have been made by the IFA to use such a defence, which might perhaps again be taken to suggest that the perceived hostility on the part of the crowd was relatively widespread. Also, while not condoning any intimidatory behaviour, the implication in statements such as the one by the IFA secretary calling 17 November 'a wonderful night for sport in Northern Ireland' seems to be of a blind eye being turned. Cynics might ask if this is because such behaviour not only reflects the attitudes of the so-called extremist 'proles' but also general, latent hostility which is felt equally as strongly by middle-class elements who might be expected to belong in the quasi-liberal 'Ulster British' camp.

A final point with regard to perceived divisions within the loyalist community arises from the symbolism on show at Windsor Park. Sugden and Bairner's view is that over recent years the Ulster identity of loyalist football supporters has become more pronounced at the expense of their affiliations to Britain, again suggestive of more extreme 'Ulster loyalist' elements holding sway over those categorised as 'Ulster British'. However, casual observation of the Windsor Park crowd reveals a proliferation of blue, red and white favours, Union Jack flags and smaller Union Jack motifs within red hand of Ulster flags. Also, the manner in which the British national anthem is vigorously or aggressively sung and the emphasis placed on its observation suggest that at least in symbolic terms there is still a strong identification with Britain. It may be that since the Republic of Ireland were the opponents on this occasion such associations were exaggerated, but personal observation at other Northern Ireland matches would again point to the conclusion that there is no clear-cut divide between working-class Protestant extremists draped in red hand of Ulster regalia and middle-class, liberal unionists clapping politely as a mark of respect for their British heritage.

Perhaps reflecting attitudes within the loyalist community as a whole, the supporters in the stands of Windsor Park on the night of 17 November 1993 seem to show a fair amount of pragmatism as far as the location of their political identity is concerned and there certainly appears to be little evidence either of a marked shift from 'Ulster British' to 'Ulster loyalist' sympathies or of there being any tangible liberalisation of views as their class profile rises. What does seem to be confirmed, however, from the general nature of the verbal abuse handed out and intimidatory atmosphere created around the match at Windsor, is that loyalists do display a form of unity, albeit of a negative kind, when faced with some challenge or threat from outside their own ranks. For this reason, in considering relationships between loyalists and other parties involved in the Northern Irish equation they will be treated as one, despite the many differences which undoubtedly exist between elements grouped loosely together under the 'loyalist' label.

RELATIONS BETWEEN LOYALISTS AND NATIONALISTS LIVING WITHIN NORTHERN IRELAND

What do events surrounding the World Cup clash between Northern Ireland and the Republic tell us about the nature of relations between loyalists and nationalists living inside the province? It certainly does seem that until the 1980s individuals from the nationalist community might have been found on the terracings of Windsor Park for international matches. However, accounts in the Irish media in the lead-up to the November 1993 encounter and first-hand reports from Catholic football supporters living in Belfast suggest that this was always an uncomfortable experience which, given the sectarian songs and regalia, hardly seems surprising.[18] One of the main factors in encouraging them to put up with the hostile atmosphere and to go along and offer at least passive support for the Northern Ireland team appears to have been the opportunity of seeing some of the cross-channel stars like Best, Jennings and Whiteside in the flesh. When the standard of player on show dropped, as it undoubtedly did at the end of the 1980s, the incentive to travel into an area where they were likely to feel uneasy and to endure the sectarianism displayed in various guises around each match was likely to be significantly reduced. Conversely, where players from the most popular cross-channel clubs such as Houghton, Keane and McGrath were to be seen in an environment more conducive to supporters from a nationalist background in Northern Ireland, where the team represented a constituency which those supporters had aspirations to be part of and where it was enjoying a considerable degree of success on the field, it was perhaps only to be expected that the allegiance of Catholic supporters would easily transfer to the Republic of Ireland.

The significance of this in respect of political developments affecting the loyalist community is that it suggests that the process by which any general radicalisation of views has taken place has been a reactive one. Rather than loyalist extremists taking over the terraces and driving away Catholic and moderate Protestant supporters, it may be that the shift in the allegiance of nationalists towards the Republic of Ireland was happening anyway and indeed may itself have produced a reaction on the part of loyalist supporters, already frustrated at the downturn in Northern Ireland's fortunes and the successes enjoyed by the Republic, which in turn has led to a polarisation of attitudes. In this light the sectarian taunts, abuse and hostility surrounding the match at Windsor in November 1993 can be seen as being directed less at the Republic of Ireland and supporters from across the border and more at nationalists living within the north hoping for an away success. Such a conclusion is supported by views expressed in a Linfield fanzine, likely, on the issue of the national side, to be reasonably indicative of those held generally by loyalist football supporters:

As for the bigoted element in Northern Ireland's support – sorry, but the greatest bigots in local football are those scumbags who were born in Northern Ireland but who support the Republic for reasons which have nothing to do with football, but which are solely for political and religious reasons. ... They are an embarrassment to the thousands of genuine Republic supporters (ie. those actually BORN there), most of whom have been good ambassadors for their country and who haven't used their support for the team as a political football.[19]

That there has been a polarisation of allegiance in respect of the two Irish national sides was confirmed in group discussions with supporters from either side of the main community divide. Asked to rank the five national sides from the British Isles in order of preference both sets of supporters placed Scotland, Wales and England in second, third and fourth positions respectively. However, while Protestant supporters put Northern Ireland first and the Republic last, Catholic supporters reversed these placings. A more rigorous survey of attitudes conducted a few years earlier pointed generally in the same direction.[20]

Politically, the inescapable and somewhat depressing conclusion appears to be that the gulf between Protestant and Catholic communities living within Northern Ireland has grown in recent years. This would tend to support the analysis contained in work such as that by Steve Bruce on the depth of disaffection among loyalist communities. He makes the point that loyalists feel strongly that they have been losing out in respect of the political changes which have taken place and that this in turn has increased support for more extreme attitudes such as those towards paramilitary violence. The process at work in the arena of international football; nationalists casting off any allegiance towards Northern Ireland in favour of the Republic; and the latter's success *vis-à-vis* the former, might be seen as likely to produce a similar effect, manifested in the extremism allegedly on show at Windsor Park in the November 1993 encounter. This does not augur well for attempts, however well-meaning, to bridge the sectarian divide by such means as community relations programmes. Bruce points to the problems which arise with the cultural traditions school in their emphasis that distinctions between Protestant and Catholic communities need not lead to divisions:

When the distinctions refer to competing political agendas and when the main item on those agendas – sovereignty – is indivisible and when there is an unspoken item on the agenda of many which is 'make the bastards pay for what they have done to my people' then distinctiveness does seem very obviously equivalent to divisiveness.[21]

In such a light it may be argued that loyalists have been searching less for compromise and accommodation and more for the political equivalent of Jimmy Quinn's late strike against the Republic in order to allay fears that they are moving ever closer to defeat in the long-term struggle over the future of Northern Ireland.

RELATIONS BETWEEN LOYALISTS AND THE REPUBLIC OF IRELAND

A number of emotive assessments of the attitudes of loyalists towards their neighbouring state were made in the wake of the 1993 World Cup match between Northern Ireland and the Republic. Typical of such was the report by Vincent Hogan in the *Irish Independent* which included the following account of the reactions of Northern Ireland's supporters to journalists from the south:

> Jimmy Quinn's 73rd minute thunderbolt had them thumping the glass front of our 'Fenian' press box with Islamic Jihad fervour. And we felt certain the night was closing in.[22]

The alleged hostility towards the Republic displayed around this game seems to centre on two sets of actions: those by the crowd in general and those by members of the official Northern Ireland party, particularly retiring manager, Billy Bingham. After the passage of time, two further encounters between Northern Ireland and the Republic on the field, and the declaration of paramilitary ceasefires by both loyalist and republican groups off it, how do such assessments stand up?

Firstly, examining the behaviour of the crowd, it is worth recalling reactions to the previous encounter between the two Irish national football sides in Belfast, played in September 1988. An article by a Dublin-based journalist in *Fortnight* magazine accused spectators at the match of being 'football's bigots'.[23] However, on the terracings (then open) the view was rather different, the capacity crowd being considered remarkable for its passivity:

> I expected an atmosphere of tension and hatred... but it was one of the tamest Spion Kops that I've ever stood on.[24]

It may well be the case that such completely contradictory perspectives reflect the political and/or national allegiances of the observers concerned. In a similar fashion verdicts on the behaviour of spectators at the 1993 match appear to vary according to the background of those reaching them, as the letters column in the *Belfast Telegraph* in the weeks following the game would testify.

Bearing this in mind, it is very difficult to make any objective assessment of how far the behaviour of the crowd reflects an increase in hostility towards the Republic. Perhaps a key point in this respect is that many of the more damning indictments of the Northern Ireland supporters appear to have been made by observers with little or no experience of football crowds, particularly in as highly charged a political context as the background sketch has shown this match to have been played. Two specific examples of alleged misbehaviour on the part of the Windsor Park crowd help illustrate the point. One concerns reports that a Republic of Ireland player (Andy Townsend) was greeted with particularly ugly, sectarian-motivated abuse to the effect of wishing that his mother would die of cancer.[25] While this may justifiably shock and disgust any neutral observer, it is put into perspective somewhat by the account of Scottish journalist, Ian Archer, of receiving similar abuse written on a toilet roll in response to some mild criticism of the manager of the Scottish football side in the lead-up to the 1978 World Cup.[26] Such abuse, however regrettable it may be, has become part and parcel of the soccer environment, particularly in the volatile atmosphere of a derby fixture played against the background of both longstanding and more immediate political grudges. Another factor which should not be overlooked in respect of the Northern Ireland–Republic of Ireland encounter is the extent to which the intimidatory behaviour of the crowd was a distorted form of gamesmanship based on a desire to put the opposition off their stride, in which respect it certainly does seem to have succeeded, bearing in mind both the result and the apparent gulf in the standards of the players representing Northern Ireland (generally lower English leagues) compared to those of the Republic (largely English and Scottish premier leagues).

The second example concerns the Windsor Park crowd taunting the opposition with the cry of 'There's only one team in Ireland', particularly during the short spell in which Northern Ireland were a goal ahead. This obviously harked back to the match in Dublin the previous March where the home crowd had used the same words to deride Northern Ireland, already 3–0 down, during the second half. The difference, according to the nationalist press, was in the tone of the words and the way in which they were used at Windsor. Referring to the Dublin crowd's behaviour, the *Irish News* said:

Their only guilt was to sing 'There's only one team in Ireland'. That was a little unfortunate but not in the same league as what we heard at Windsor.[27]

Once again, the views expressed are almost totally polarised on the basis of religious community background. From the perspective of Northern Ireland's largely loyalist support the complaints are written off as little more than whingeing and political mischief-making while the crowd at Windsor is seen as merely giving the Republic's supporters a taste of their own medicine. The latter view appears to be endorsed at a more official level, reflected in the comments of retiring manager, Billy Bingham, on the reception Northern Ireland encountered in Dublin that 'we were subject to intimidation both from the crowd and from the touchline'.[28]

Such comments have been refuted by observers from a nationalist background, but the argument that the Republic of Ireland supporters were singing purely in fun while the crowd at Windsor was little short of a bloodthirsty lynch mob does appear somewhat exaggerated. Bearing in mind the build-up to the match both on and off the field and also the nature of the political environment in Belfast relative to that found in Dublin, it does seem unreasonable to expect a substantial and vocal gathering of loyalist football supporters to behave as if at a Sunday school picnic. Despite this and despite the media anticipation which included screaming headlines such as 'Don't risk this game of death', the match passed off without any serious security scares. Indeed there may be some black irony in the fact that it was the other World Cup football match staged in Britain on the evening of 17 November, between Wales and Romania, which suffered a fatality as a result of crowd disorder. Given the media attention the match between the two Irelands received without any such occurrence, one wonders what reaction there would have been had this incident happened at Windsor Park.

Considering the allegations of misbehaviour on the part of members of the official Northern Ireland party, in particular manager Billy Bingham, it will hardly be a surprise to learn that opinion is once again divided along religious community lines. The basis of the competing claims are Bingham's gestures to the crowd, encouraging them to get behind his team. While the accusation of 'incitement to national hatred' made by a maverick TD in the immediate aftermath of events at Windsor Park appears something of a knee-jerk reaction, Bingham's behaviour was widely criticised in the nationalist media both north and south of the border for adding to the atmosphere of hostility and intimidation in his comments about 'mercenaries' and in gesturing for the vocal support for Northern Ireland to be increased. The *Irish News* made the following comments:

> Billy Bingham has denied that he incited the crowd with his fingering signs. Maybe he didn't mean to, but he didn't condemn the crowd's actions either and he lied when he said that the Northern Ireland team got the same reception at Lansdowne Road.[29]

The reaction of loyalist supporters to such criticisms was blunt:

> Now what did Bingham actually do? Ride onto the pitch on a white horse re-enacting the 'Battle of the Boyne' and carrying a placard reading 'F*** The Pope'? No, actually he waved to his own supporters. Wow, how offensive – lock this dangerous man up![30]

Billy Bingham's own account, though somewhat more diplomatic, takes essentially the same line:

> So when they came to Belfast I started to wind them up a bit.... . I called them mercenaries. And there was a hell of a lot of truth in that.... . I told them that my team was more Irish than theirs. That hurt them. When I walked on the field I acknowledged the cheers of the crowd. I waved back. I was afterwards called a wee Orangeman inciting violence. That was nonsense. What they were seeing was a very competitive wee man giving Jack what he gave us and encouraging the crowd to give our side the psychological boost vociferous support can give. Of course there was probably political and sectarian cat-calling but I didn't tell them to do that.[31]

While attempting to assess the various claims and counter-claims in this respect would be a futile exercise, they tend to reinforce the view of how polarised the two main communities within Northern Ireland are when issues impinging on nationality surface and take on political dimensions. It does not appear to be the case, however, that either of the examples of alleged misbehaviour reflect a major shift in terms of rising political resentment towards the Republic of Ireland. To the extent that the Republic's players, officials and spectators were targets, it seems to have been on the basis of specific grievances such as the humiliation Northern Ireland suffered in Dublin the previous March and the perceived two-facedness of the FAI in respect of moves to change the venue of the game from Windsor. Beyond this, much of the uglier abuse from the loyalist support appears to have been directed primarily at their nationalist co-habitants rather than supporters from the Republic, who were likely to be a fairly safe physical and psychological distance away from the sectarian incidents referred to.

Finally, the nature of the hostility on display at Windsor Park in November 1993 seems to be put into perspective when compared against the violent scenes both in Dublin surrounding a non-competitive fixture between the Republic of Ireland and England in February 1995 and also within Northern Ireland surrounding matches between Cliftonville, the only club with a sizable Catholic support, and Portadown, during the following month. It is interesting that the loyalist account of proceedings at the November 1993 game referred to above is fairly respectful of supporters of the Republic of Ireland born in the 26 counties. This is reinforced by what it has to say about their national side:

> the Republic qualified, and despite the fact that they scraped it and we would have loved to sicken them by knocking them out, they did so on merit and that's what matters.[32]

The profile of loyalists this suggests is far from the one of irrational bigotry, intransigence and seething resentment towards all things south of the border which is sometimes popularly depicted.

RELATIONS BETWEEN LOYALISTS AND THE BRITISH STATE

Before reaching more general conclusions, a review of relations between loyalists and the British state in the light of the World Cup encounter can be set out. As has been seen, Sugden and Bairner's analysis suggests a shift among loyalist supporters away from identification with Britain and, perhaps reflecting general disaffection with political developments which seem to be going against them, increasing emphasis on promoting Northern Ireland as a separate entity. Implicit in this process is an element of ethnic division since the Northern Ireland with which loyalists are seen to be identifying is one which holds little or no appeal to Catholics.

Doubt has already been cast on the extent to which there has been a movement within loyalism from what were described as 'Ulster British' to 'Ulster loyalist' perspectives. Interestingly one of the main distinctions Todd makes between the two typologies is in respect of their reaction to change; while the 'Ulster loyalist' camp can only change when faced with what they see as defeat and humiliation, for the 'Ulster British' change can occur either by:

following the implications of their liberal ideals or by structural changes in the British state and its relations with Northern Ireland disrupting the sense of a Great British community.[33]

The evidence of the Northern Ireland–Republic of Ireland football match at Windsor may be taken as suggesting that it is very difficult to distinguish between the two categories and, indeed, as Todd acknowledges, that many, if not most, loyalists have a foot in both camps.

Bearing in mind what has already been said about the symbolism on show at the game (the singing of the British national anthem; the display of Ulster flags and Union Jacks; the blend of blue, red and white and green and white favours), it does seem to be the case that affiliations towards both Britain and Northern Ireland are strong and are merged together with little perceived incongruence. If anything, evidence of both processes of change may also be found; the animosity shown towards the opposition and towards nationalists in general may be seen as reflecting fear of defeat and humiliation while the emphasis placed on observation of 'God Save the Queen' and the flying of the Union Jack is suggestive of insecurity with regard to the nature of changes already underway and those being further speculated upon in the relationship with the British state. Such insecurity is likely to be particularly felt at a game against the Republic of Ireland since so many fears on the part of loyalists are tied to developments seen as leading towards an all-Irish state. In this context the intensity of support for both the Northern Irish football side in taking on the Republic and for various elements of British state heritage as bulwarks against perceived Irish expansionism may be understood.

What does this tell us about developments in relations between loyalists and the British state? Sugden and Bairner point to survey evidence that almost as many Protestants, if they had to choose, would opt for an all-Irish as an all-British football team. However, in some ways, asking such a question of loyalist football supporters may be seen as facing them with a choice between the devil and the deep blue sea, so it is perhaps no surprise that opinion is fairly evenly divided. When the proliferation of British regalia at the match against the Republic (and, indeed, other matches) is taken into account it may suggest an important psychological distinction by loyalists between on the one hand the permanent features of the British state which they remain committed to and more transitory and potentially treacherous elements within that state such as governments of the day. If this is the case, then the prospects of some kind of Ulster 'Sinn Fein' approach being widely canvassed among the loyalist community, whatever the perceived sins of the British government, seem limited.

Such an analysis suggests a further distinction of note where loyalist football supporters are concerned. Critics, particularly in reference to the crowd's behaviour at the match between Northern Ireland and the Republic, have drawn attention to the apparent contradiction between the overt sectarianism displayed there and the fact that more than half the players wearing Northern Ireland shirts were likely to be from the Catholic community. However, it may be argued that by making a distinction between the heritage of the Northern Ireland side which, through local associations and its British connection, is likely to be seen as pro-loyalist, and the personnel – players, managers and officials who try to advance its interests at any particular time – the contradiction is fairly easily resolved. To this end, any individual, whatever their religious background, who does make a contribution to the success of the Northern Ireland side as a whole is likely to be welcomed. However, where, as possibly happened in the case of Anton Rogan, that contribution is in doubt, it is likely that loyalist supporters will turn first on those players whose commitment to the cause is considered suspect due to their religious background.

The conclusion here seems to be that while loyalists may have specific grievances with British politicians and administrations, there is little evidence of a fundamental shift in the nature of their relationship with the metropolitan state. In this respect, their support for the Northern Ireland football team, far from being a vehicle for aspirations towards some kind of UDI, can be seen as a symbolic representation of the way pro-British and pro-Ulster sentiments are combined together with a fair degree of pragmatism by the loyalist community.

CONCLUSION

Three hundred and sixty-four days after the original 'night in November' the Northern Irish football team again played the Republic of Ireland at Windsor Park, Belfast, in front of a (limited) capacity crowd. The circumstances surrounding the November 1994 encounter could scarcely have been different from those twelve months earlier. The match took place in the wake of the autumn's paramilitary ceasefires in an atmosphere of hope for peace and reconciliation within the province. The sense of passivity seemed to be transmitted on to the field of play where the Republic of

Ireland cruised to a four-goal win against a home side barely offering token resistance. Partly as a consequence the surrounding stands were remarkably quiet and media interest focused solely on the one-sided nature of the game.

This illustrates the dangers of reading too much into the political implications of 17 November 1993 for loyalism and indeed for the politics of Northern Ireland as a whole. However, given recent developments, particularly the resurgence of sectarian-motivated soccer violence at club level inside the province, it may be that the passivity around the North–South encounter of November 1994 will, in hindsight, prove the more unusual, made possible by the special circumstances following the lull in paramilitary violence and, arguably, unrealistic expectations of papering over deep social, cultural and political differences.

The analysis presented here suggests that the events surrounding the 1993 World Cup football match between Northern Ireland and the Republic in Belfast lay bare the extent and the increasingly polarising effect of hostilities between loyalist and nationalist communities living within the six counties. Once national football allegiance became entwined with the issue of sovereignty, as it did, for a blend of political and practical reasons during the course of the late 1970s and 1980s, it was always likely that wider social conflicts would be re-enacted around the international football arena. This bodes ill for any attempt to use support for one or other Irish national side as a channel of reconciliation. However, the analysis also suggests that much of the media reaction to events surrounding the game, particularly in respect of loyalist attitudes towards the Republic of Ireland was grossly exaggerated, perhaps for reasons which suited their own political agendas. Finally, the case for a major shift in loyalist relations with the British state is found unproven, despite the rhetoric sometimes used by unionist politicians and despite the differences which patently exist (and have existed for some time) with the Westminster government of the day.

Perhaps the final point which should be addressed is that of the appropriateness of the subject matter for quasi-academic analysis. While important in its own right as a decisive World Cup qualifier, the football match highlighted here between Northern Ireland and the Republic, as with any sporting fixture, is limited, either for good or evil, in its political significance. Nonetheless, events surrounding that fixture, it is argued here, are important if only because they are likely to have touched many people with more of a stake in the resolution of political conflict in Northern Ireland than simply its academic aesthetics.

NOTES

1. L. Allison (ed.), *The Politics of Sport* (Manchester: Manchester University Press, 1986). There is also now a second edition of this book.
2. J. Sugden and A. Bairner, *Sport, Sectarianism and Society in a Divided Ireland* (Leicester: Leicester University Press, 1993), p. 71.
3. J. Sugden, 'Sport and the Community', unpublished report for the Central Community Relations Unit, Coleraine: Centre for the Study of Conflict, 1994, p. 55.
4. J. Sugden and A. Bairner, op. cit., p. 72.
5. J. Sugden and A. Bairner, op. cit., p. 73.
6. E. Corry, *Going to America* (Dublin: Torc, n.d.), pp. 102–4.
7. Northern Ireland v Republic of Ireland, official match programme, Belfast, 21 November 1979, p. 9.
8. S. Bruce, *The Edge of the Union* (Oxford: Oxford University Press, 1994), p. 39.
9. *Belfast Telegraph*, Belfast-based daily newspaper, 15 November 1993, p. 26.
10. *Belfast Telegraph*, 18 November 1993, p. 1.
11. *Irish News*, Belfast-based daily newspaper, 24 November 1993, p. 14.
12. *Belfast Telegraph*, 24 January 1994, p. 24.
13. *Irish Times*, 16 November 1993, p. 18.
14. Sugden and Bairner, op. cit., p. 76.
15. Sugden and Bairner, ibid., pp. 77–8.
16. *Irish News*, 24 November 1993, p. 14.
17. S. Nelson, *Ulster's Uncertain Defenders: Protestant political, paramilitary and community groups and the Northern Ireland conflict* (Belfast: Appletree, 1984), p. 14.
18. *Irish Times* (Weekend Supplement), Dublin-based daily newspaper, 13 November 1993, p. 1.
19. *One Team in Ulster*, Linfield FC supporters' unofficial, occasional publication, Vol. 26, Spring 1994, p. 22.
20. N. P. McGivern, 'The Examination of Patterns of Association Football Support as a Way of Determining National Identity in Ireland', unpublished BA(Hons) dissertation, University of Ulster, 1991, pp. 59–61.
21. S. Bruce, op. cit., pp. 140–1.
22. *Irish News*, 20 November 1993, p. 9.
23. *Fortnight*, Belfast-based monthly current affairs magazine, Vol. 266, October 1988, p. 29.
24. *One Team in Ulster*, Vol. 1, January 1989, p. 5.
25. E. Corry, op. cit., p. 289.
26. *Only a Game*, BBC Scotland television production, broadcast 23 April 1993 (originally broadcast in 1986).
27. *Irish News*, 26 January 1994, p. 8.
28. *Ulster Newsletter*, Belfast-based daily newspaper, 31 January 1994, p. 16.
29. *Irish News*, 26 January 1994, p. 8.
30. *One Team in Ulster*, Vol. 26, Spring 1994, p. 21.

31. *Ulster Newsletter*, 31 January 1994, p. 17.
32. *One Team in Ulster*, Vol. 26, Spring 1994, p. 22.
33. J. Todd, 'Two Traditions in Unionist Political Culture', *Irish Political Studies*, Vol. 2, 1987, p. 19.

12 The Same People with Different Relatives? Modern Scholarship, Unionists and the Irish Nation
Richard English

I

Responding to the suggestion that there were two nations rather than one in Ireland, the eminent Irish republican Peadar O'Donnell impishly replied that he thought it 'nonsense to suggest that we are two peoples. We are the same people with different relatives.'[1] O'Donnell's socialism made him something of a dissident figure within the modern republican movement in Ireland.[2] But in his dismissal of the problem which Irish unionism posed for Irish nationalism he was, perhaps, rather typical. For within nationalist circles there has tended to be a certain complacency in regard to the question of unionist opposition to the nationalist project. The Irish nation, it has been assumed, is coextensive with the Irish island; and separatist sympathies have been taken as indicative of authentic Irishness. Coupled with the view that History (indeed, Providence) is in sympathy with the completion of the Irish nationalist agenda, these assumptions have proved powerfully resilient well into the contemporary period. Moreover, they have coloured the actions of crucial players outside the nationalist camp. As Patrick Roche has recently observed, 'The policy orientation of the British political parties is ... based on the acceptance of the intellectual coherence and practical feasibility of Irish nationalism.'[3]

Intellectually, however, there are certain difficulties with the acceptance of the views alluded to above, as indeed there are difficulties with other important features of Irish nationalist thinking. This is not to say that Irish nationalist thought must of necessity be incoherent. Rather, it is to suggest that key aspects of existing nationalist thought have been opened to intellectual scrutiny in such a way as to require serious reappraisal of the philosophy as it stands in its various guises. The assumption of one-island nationhood, of separatism as a key index of Irishness, of the harmony between progress toward peace in Ireland and progress toward nationalist goals – each of these has been so sharply challenged that the outlook which they represent may be judged to have frayed significantly. Serious modern scholarship has done múch to contribute to this process. But while a considerable amount has been written about the fierce debates character-istic of much Irish scholarship in recent years, comparatively little atten-tion has been paid in the academic literature to the triangular relationship between serious modern scholarship, Irish unionism and modern national-ist thought in Ireland. Given the vital connections in Ireland between scholarly argument and the wider political and cultural context – and given the vibrancy of contemporary scholarship on Irish unionism, as demonstrated by the essays contained in this book – it is important that this void in the literature be filled.

II

The Northern Ireland conflict has added a sharpness to Irish scholarly debates since the early 1970s. But while the inspection of traditional poli-tics and culture has been rendered both more fashionable and more urgent by the Northern Ireland violence, the momentum and dynamics of modern Irish scholarship have primarily been derived from other sources. Revulsion at the atrocities committed during the last quarter of a century has coloured the reexamination of certain pieties – on all sides in the conflict. But while a sharper focus has been achieved by means of such work, it is not possible to explain the waves of exciting new Irish research satisfactorily in this way. Indeed, one of the most conspicuous features of the scholarly literature in recent years has been the lack of scrutiny which certain subjects have received – subjects which the explosion(s) of the Northern Irish conflict might have been expected to stimulate. For example, serious treatment of Northern Irish nationalism – a phenomenon which has, after all, been at the fire-centre of the conflict – has been rarer than one might have expected, Eamon Phoenix's book only recently beginning to fill the void in our understanding.[4]

A helpful perspective is added if one recognises that the kinds of innovations and developments occurring in Irish scholarship during the last 25 years have not been unique to Ireland. The reappraisal of supposed historical verities, which has been a significant characteristic of much post-1960s scholarly writing on Ireland, has also been in evidence elsewhere. The Irish case is undoubtedly distinctive, but it none the less resembles patterns of scholarly development elsewhere. In relation to historical scholarship, perhaps the most controversial arena of all in recent years, Roy Foster has pointed out 'that historians who were any good in France or Britain or America were also deconstructing societies and mentalities, also looking for ambiguities in the 1960s in the way that historians in Ireland were'.[5] This point is echoed in the words of another leading modern Irish scholar, George Boyce: 'The notion that "revisionist" history was especially prominent in Ireland, or in Irish nationalism, is misleading.'[6] Discussions of national identity have been prominent, and sometimes ferocious, in relation to many countries in recent years.[7] Moreover, the tendency of scholars to dismantle teleological, linear readings of national experience – and to suggest instead a more complicated, contingent set of processes – is hardly confined to Ireland.[8]

Such reflections are essential if one is to avoid the danger of overly insular intellectual discussions. They are also vital, however, because they underline the fact that intellectual enquiry has a subversive quality which has the capacity to challenge all manner of orthodoxies. The overhauling of Irish assumptions in recent years has sometimes been portrayed as though it were directed unfairly in one particular direction.[9] In fact, one of the most exciting aspects about modern Irish scholarship has been precisely its refusal to be bound in this way. True, much attention has been paid to the complications and inadequacies of Irish nationalist argument and practice. But not all modern scholarship offers comfort to traditional unionist views. Alvin Jackson's superb study of unionist leader Edward Carson, for example, coolly identifies the neurosis and lack of confidence evinced by this supposedly rock-like defender of the union. Again, Jackson is piercing in his identification of 'the central paradox' of Carson's career.

Until 1910 Carson was certainly a passionate defender of the British parliamentary and judicial establishment. Until 1910 Carson was racked by the spectacle of timid government and by craven surrender to violence or to the threat of violence. Yet after 1910 Carson led a militant conspiracy to extort concession from a timid government; after 1910 Carson completely accepted what he had once defined and condemned as the strategies of Irish nationalism. The resounding irony of Carson's career is, therefore, that he is best remembered for his belligerent defence of Ulster unionism – in other words, for the complete repudiation of what had been hitherto the central purpose of his political endeavour.[10]

And, indeed, the scepticism which scholars have shown towards teleological narratives of Irish history has been as relevant when applied to the unionist as when directed at the nationalist versions of such stories of Ireland.[11] Or again, the unpicking of apologist literature has been evident in the works of scholars studying both nationalism and unionism; the fine work of Graham Walker and Alvin Jackson complement one another excellently in this regard.[12]

Behind the best of modern scholarship, in Ireland as elsewhere, has been the drive towards ever greater professionalisation. This brings us back to Professor Foster's phrase concerning scholars 'who were any good'. For at the heart of scholarly practice in recent years has been the emphasis upon rigorous, exhaustive examination of an ever-widening range of evidence; a concern with interdisciplinary dialogues which have both challenged and defined modern scholars; a commitment to originality in terms of evidence, argument, topic and theoretical approach. If popular assumptions have been targeted and exploded in a devastating way, then it is because of the unprecedented quality of the intellectual arsenal deployed during the last generation. Sceptical scholarship in Ireland owes far more to the growing professionalisation of scholarly practice than to any politically motivated reinvention of the past in accordance with current needs. It is certainly not possible to dismiss the work of large numbers of modern Irish scholars either as the product of a crude political agenda or by means of narrowly defined pigeon-holing or labelling. Attempts to confine sophisticated scholars within crude stereotypes are as unhelpful in relation to contemporary figures as they would be, for example, in relation to intellectuals from a previous age. Just as a proper understanding of W. E. H. Lecky requires an appreciation of the sinewy complexity and changing nature of his outlook, so too modern scholars working on Ireland surely deserve more space than is accorded them when they are bluntly assigned to various supposed schools or camps. One of the most influential participants in recent debates on Irish scholarship, Brendan Bradshaw, has (in the view of this author, at least) veered dangerously towards such crude stereotyping of other scholars, grouping together dramatically different work under the same disparaged banner.[13]

Much of the confusion, and much of the acrimony, can be avoided if it is recognised that professional scholarship offers an arena within which profound disagreements can be debated according to principles which produce constructive dialogue but which do not demand a bland uniformity of outlook. Most skilled Irish historians, for example, would have little difficulty in endorsing the judgements of even so thorny a practitioner as Geoffrey Elton: his concern that remedies for previous scholarly defects should not be sought in a pendulum swing toward 'new defective emphases'; his hostility to 'present-centred' history; his endorsement of the ideal of the 'professional sceptic – a scholar who cannot accept anything merely on the instruction of a faith'; and his recognition (of particular relevance, perhaps, to Ireland) that 'the demolition of comfortable myths causes pain at best and horror-struck revulsion at worst; it can lead to a dangerous over-reaction'.[14] Indeed, there are encouraging signs that scholars from various disciplines and of differing political leanings are producing work which has a healthy synergy about it. Thus, for example, people as varied in political hue as Nancy Curtin, A. T. Q. Stewart, Jim Smyth and Ian McBride are all agreed on the vital importance of understanding the British influences operating upon and moulding the United Irishmen.[15] Again, while Paul Bew's recent work on the years 1912–16 and Colm Campbell's legal treatment of the 1918–25 period grow out of different disciplines and differing perspectives, the two books can be read as simultaneously compelling accounts of their respective subjects.[16] Rigour, originality, professional scepticism, a sensitivity to and respect for evidence can all combine to constructive effect.

III

The cumulative weight of intellectual enquiry cannot, therefore, be dismissed as the product merely of crudely labelled schools of thought or of conspiratorially contrived, present-centred agendas. But it would be wrong to ignore the possibility that academic research might be able to influence wider political thinking in subtle, vital and complex ways. In particular, it is important to consider some of the implications which modern, professional scholarship dealing with Irish unionism might have for our understanding of Irish nationalist thinking. The contributors to this book have ably demonstrated the richness and diversity of current work in this field. Can we, tentatively, suggest some wider implications?

Let us look first at Ulster. Recent years have produced a greatly increased quantity and diversity of work on Ulster unionism. As noted, although this has partly been stimulated by the Northern Ireland conflict, the political and ideological implications of this work derive not so much from the ferocity of that conflict as from the intellectual weight of the professional judgements which have been reached. The emergent picture is undeniably complex. But the weight of scholarly judgement in relation to Ulster unionism commands that we should treat unionism with an historical respect and sensitivity which will lead us to view many of the current claims of both orthodox and revisionist Irish nationalists with a certain scepticism. Recent professional scholarship has emphatically demonstrated the authentic, self-supporting quality of modern Ulster unionism. In his judicious survey of the literature John Whyte recognised that, contrary to the nationalist orthodoxy that Ulster unionism was a fragile, propped-up or even artificial flower, 'On the whole, recent historians have been struck by the depth of Ulster unionist opposition to a united Ireland separate from Britain, and the independence of that opposition from British support.'[17] Nor is it just the historians: in his recent work dealing with Protestant paramilitarism the sociologist Steve Bruce has stressed the inadequacy of those explanations of the modern Ulster Volunteer Force which fail to acknowledge its origins as 'a self-recruiting, working class movement'.[18] The picture painted is of a resilient, spontaneously emergent movement far removed from the puppet creation suggested by some Irish nationalist argument. Bruce's work is, indeed, intriguing. He has repeatedly emphasised the vital role which religion has played in the modern Ulster conflict, basing this judgement on his closely researched knowledge of Ulster Protestant thinking:

> The Northern Ireland conflict is a religious conflict. ... That Paisley's brand of unionism has proved popular with such a large section of the Ulster Protestant population defies any explanation other than the obvious one: evangelicalism provides the core beliefs, values and symbols of what it means to be a Protestant. Unionism is about avoiding becoming a subordinate minority in a Catholic state.[19]

This argument has been amplified in Bruce's most recent book: 'I am arguing that the Northern Ireland conflict is an ethnic conflict and that religion plays an important part in the identity of the Protestant people.'[20]

These points are of crucial importance both for our understanding of modern Ulster unionism and for our evaluation of the arguments of Irish nationalists. For if there really is a vital ethnic and religious divide in Ireland – and the weight of evidence overwhelmingly suggests that this is so – then nationalist assumption about the supposed significance of Irish nationalism's non-sectarian, inclusive aspiration is rendered largely irrelevant. Moreover, scholarly research has underpinned this by demonstrating that even those nationalists most celebrated for their attempts to challenge the sectarian divide have so clearly failed, or have even exacerbated the problem. Let us examine the case of the eighteenth-century United Irish movement, a subject which has received considerable detailed and illuminating treatment in recent years. Jim Smyth has observed of the United Irishmen that, 'Clearly they were accurate in their identification of sectarianism as the central problem of Irish politics and society; equally clearly, they were hopelessly optimistic in their conviction that that problem was susceptible to speedy, rational and political solutions.'[21] Elsewhere Smyth observes the tension between sectarianism and secular republicanism in the United Irish movement and points out that, 'The United Irishmen never resolved this problem.'[22] Nancy Curtin's excellent study of the United Irishmen goes further. She observes that 'early Irish republicanism contained both ... a secular, democratic liberalism and a nationalism that quickly became defined in racial and religious terms'. Curtin also demonstrates the extent of the United Irish failure: 'Instead of removing religious prejudices, they exacerbated them.'

> The United Irishmen were, after all, anything but united. The class and sectarian tensions which were exacerbated by United Irish propaganda and recruitment methods and by their alliances with the lower orders and the French not only weakened the mass movement internally, but provoked mass hostility as well. Because the republicans attempted to be all things to all people, subsequent generations have been free to interpret them as they wish. The United Irishmen, it has been said, represented one link in the chain of resistance to British oppression. The United Irishmen were nationalists who united Catholics and Protestants under the common name of Irishmen. Or the union promoted by enlightened Presbyterians was betrayed by a fanatic, vengeful Catholicism which reared its ugly head in Wexford, demonstrating at last the fundamental inability of Protestant aspirations for liberty to take root in priest-ridden Catholic Ireland. The legacy of the United Irishmen, however interpreted, has proved as divisive for later generations as the practice of this so-called union did in the 1790s.[23]

For the more modern period, too, many of the assumptions held by orthodox Irish nationalists have been rather undermined by serious scholarship, and some of these points have begun to seep into popular thinking. That Irish nationalists have tended to ignore the problem posed for them by unionists has been recognised even by figures as ardently republican as Sinn Fein's Danny Morrison.[24] For in addition to the religious and ethnic points referred to above, there has emerged powerful economic argument in favour of acknowledging the difficulties with one-island/one-nation assumptions. This is true of the contemporary period,[25] and also of the partition era. As Mary Daly has put it, 'While Ireland's economic performance under the union was not the sole factor fuelling the movement for independence, it is hardly a coincidence that Ulster, the most successful province under the union, rejected independence.'[26]

Indeed, there is the force of much scholarly enquiry behind Conor Cruise O'Brien's observation that 'Nationalists are in the habit of referring to the "artifical partition" of the island. In principle, there is nothing artificial about the partition: it is a result of history, traditions and demography.'[27] Such thinking has been strengthened by the emerging stress upon the importance of understanding unionism through appreciating it firmly within a British context. Indeed, much recent scholarship has attempted to widen the angle of our vision to see Ireland's past in a British Isles framework. George Boyce has raised the vital issues in a typically sharp-sighted fashion:

is there such a thing as Irish history at all? It could be said there was before 1169 a specifically 'Irish' history. But after the Normans the histories of Great Britain and Ireland are inseparable. Ireland, though not conquered as England was, became part in some sense of the Norman empire; in the seventeenth century it became part of an English empire; in the eighteenth Ireland and Great Britain formed 'sister kingdoms'; in the nineteenth they were brought together in a political union.[28]

This plainly has implications, too, for our approach to British research. As Boyce points out elsewhere, 'the time has come for a reassessment of what constitutes British history in the first place. ... Britain in the last century was a multinational state, as she still is today. It is time that her historians began to acknowledge this, and write multinational history.'[29] As for Ireland, scholars have certainly demonstrated that from the eighteenth-century United Irishmen to the early-twentieth-century IRA, Irish experience can only fully be understood and explained if one appreciates the crucial significance of British influences and settings. This is plainly of the utmost importance in relation to Ulster unionists.

As noted, some of these scholarly reflections have begun to be echoed at a more popular level. The acknowledgement that the real obstacle to Irish unity lies in unionist objections rather than British intentions has, for example, begun to take firmer root.[30] Other points have yet, perhaps, to register in the popular view. Alvin Jackson's convincing attempt to move our understanding of unionism away from the history-of-crisis approach has, for example, yet to filter into journalistic representations of unionists.[31] Attention to unionists is too commonly reliant upon the conviction that they are in a crisis, and that their essential character is the negative one of obstructing a supposedly plausible Irish nationalist agenda. Similarly, there is some distance to go before scholarly treatment of unionist intellectuals overturns the resilient popular image of unionism as essentially anti- or non-intellectual. Or, yet again, it is unfortunate to witness the persistence, within representations of unionism, of the image of triumphalist supremacism: for scholars have powerfully demonstrated that feelings of vulnerability and even inferiority play a larger role in modern unionist thinking than do any senses of superiority or supremacism.[32]

Much of what scholars have unveiled, therefore, has still to be acknowledged at a popular ideological level; orthodox Irish nationalists have been challenged in much of their thinking, but the implications of that challenge have yet to be fully appreciated. Yet it is not merely for orthodox nationalism that modern scholarship on Irish unionism has significant implications. Much has been made in recent years of the emergence of a revisionist Irish nationalism: a more inclusive, moderate approach which seeks to understand, reassure and persuade unionists into a harmoniously united Ireland. There is indeed a striking contrast between this new nationalism and the militant, coercive approach which preceded it. To the extent that this shift has occurred, moreover, it is surely to be welcomed. Less constricting and exclusive, revisionist Irish nationalism has reflected an understandable dissatisfaction among Irish nationalists with the inadequacies of orthodox, militant irredentism and has grown out of the desire to construct a meaningful, reasonable Irish national patriotism. A telling figure in this shift has been the former Irish Taoiseach Garret FitzGerald, whose 1972 book *Towards a New Ireland* rewards consideration. In it FitzGerald went some way to acknowledging the deficiencies of existing nationalist thought. Yes, he agreed, there were indeed serious religious and economic differences underpinning partition in Ireland. But he maintained his aspiration towards Irish unity, albeit unity achieved through persuasion rather than through bullying: 'this book was written from the standpoint of a citizen of the Republic [of Ireland], who desires the political reunification of Ireland achieved with the freely given consent of a majority in Northern Ireland'.[33]

But it might be argued that the implications of modern scholarship have still to be realised even by those who have followed in these more pacific footsteps. What if unionist consent is simply not forthcoming? What if 'no' actually does mean (and continues to mean) 'no'? It is indeed preferable that Irish nationalists should argue for unification with unionist consent rather than for unification through coercion. But those nationalists who have argued for unification by consent have failed to demonstrate either, first, signs that such consent is beginning to emerge or, second, an effective explanation of how or why it should do so. Arguably, there is only marginal intellectual progress implied in the adoption of a position which accepts that unionist anti-nationalism exists, but which seeks to bypass it by means of the notion of consent. For if there appears no likelihood that unionist consent to nationalist demands is forthcoming – and the overwhelming verdict of recent scholarship would suggest that this is the case – then the notion of 'unity by consent' simply collapses into self-contradiction.

It is possible cautiously to suggest certain other refinements which might help bring about a realistic revision of nationalist thinking in accordance with modern intellectual findings. One point concerns the traditional construction put upon unionist rule in Northern Ireland between 1921 and 1972. The abuses (perceived and/or actual) perpetrated by the regime of these years have often provided the foundation for nationalist argument: unionist wrongness has compelled a sense of the need for expiation. Indeed, the sense of justification provided by these wrongs has long outlived the abuses themselves. Virtually all of the injustices protested against by the civil rights campaigners of the 1960s were addressed by the early 1970s, and those inequalities that remained were so complicated and structurally embedded as to defy easy solution or redress. But the sense of injustice justifying outrage has persisted none the less. What impact can modern scholarship have on our approach to such questions? The point is certainly not to ignore, much less to provide justification for, those aspects of unionist rule in Northern Ireland which were unjust or discriminatory. Nor is it to underplay ongoing inequalities. But recent work has tended to blur the edges of outraged nationalist certainty, and this is as relevant to revisionist as to orthodox Irish nationalists. If, as seems likely,[34] questions of discrimination were (and indeed still are) more complex than has commonly been assumed by observers with nationalist leanings, then a major prop underpinning nationalist argument is significantly weakened. Indeed, the stereotype of unionism as merely the vehicle for obstructionist intransigence is severely dented by such considerations. This is an absolutely vital point. For revisionist nationalists, like their more orthodox colleagues, hold to the view that fundamental constitutional change is required; moreover, again like orthodox nationalists, they derive a large part of their confidence on this point from their convictions, first, that unionist injustices demand that there should be change and expiation and, second, that unionism is justifiably perceived as an intransigent obstacle to be overcome on the way toward justice and peace. Such sentiments find their way even into the most intelligent of modern nationalist argument. In a sharply written and intriguing article in *Political Studies*, for example, Shane O'Neill has suggested that 'unionist blindness to otherness' is the root problem to be overcome in Northern Ireland.[35] Yet it is a matter of assumption rather than demonstration, in O'Neill's article at least, that unionist intransigence in opposing constitutional change is more central to the conflict than is Irish nationalist intransigence in demanding that such change be made, and made in a nationalist direction.

Another point which might require refinement is the increasingly prevalent assumption – common both at popular and at high political level – that unionism and nationalism are best approached in terms of their supposedly symmetrical relationship. This is reflected in United Kingdom and in Republic of Ireland pronouncements of recent years in relation to Northern Ireland.[36] But as scholars have begun to point out, there is considerable confusion in the assumption that unionism and nationalism in Ireland are somehow analogous. Arthur Aughey has perceptively pointed out, for example, that unionists and nationalists work within distinctly different frameworks: 'citizenship is the term appropriate to a doctrine concerned with the integrity of state, which unionism is, rather than self-determination, which is appropriate to the abiding concerns of nationalists'.[37] Arguably, it is the asymmetry rather than the symmetry which is striking when one pays serious consideration to unionism and nationalism in modern Ireland. Unionism does not represent an alternative ethnic or religious nationalism, but argues for the reasonableness (indeed, the necessity) of maintaining Northern Ireland's place within the multi-national, multi-faith, multi-ethnic UK state. Whatever one thinks of this unionist argument, it is vital to understand what is actually being argued. Attempts to simplify our understanding of unionism and nationalism by suggesting a crude analogy between them, reflect an intellectual confusion which surely risks negative practical consequences.

None of this, it should be stressed, implies that serious scholarship compels unionist sympathies. Rather, the aim here is to suggest that sensitivity to detail in the treatment of unionism does compel the reconsideration of certain key Irish nationalist ideas. Given the interplay between scholarly and popular thinking in Ireland, the subversive potential of such reflections is striking. The implications are certainly weighty for the Republic of Ireland state. Just as historiographical revisionism with regard to the French revolution changed not only the intellectual consensus in postwar France but also the political conception of France's place in world history,[38] so too the tremors caused by ongoing Irish scholarly reappraisals have the capacity – in the longer term – to remould political thought and assumption in the Republic of Ireland. This process has been ongoing for some time and has involved a measure of reappraisal in relation to the ideology on which the independent Irish state was founded and built. Indeed, the Sinn Fein vision which dominated the early years of independent Ireland had begun to be called into question – in relation to economics, the Irish language, the role of the Catholic church, censorship, irredentism and physical force – prior to the eruption of the modern Ulster crisis.[39] Professional scholarship has furthered this process through its rigorous examination of modern Irish experience. This has taken a number of forms. Paul Bew's compelling attempt to rescue both Ulster unionism and Redmondite constitutional nationalism of the 1912–16 period has clear consequences for the self-image of a state built on the repudiation of these two ideologies.[40] So, too, does work like that of Terence Denman which has taken seriously the experience and importance of those who have not fitted neatly into the orthodox, separatist story of Ireland.[41]

Some of the most intriguing reflections are prompted by consideration of the interaction between unionism and nationalism. Maryann Valiulis's study of leading IRA man Richard Mulcahy offers material for just such consideration. Her assertion, for example, that Richard Mulcahy's Irish nationalist 'vision was of a free, united, Christian, Irish-speaking Ireland – virtuous and prosperous'[42] requires serious scrutiny. If Ireland was to be 'united' then presumably – and nationalists did presume this – all the people of the island were deemed to be part of the national parcel. But then what of Ireland being 'free'? What attraction could there be for unionists in being 'free' from the state (the United Kingdom) of which they keenly wished to remain a part? 'Christian'? In practice this implied 'Catholic' as far as the revolutionaries were concerned; so what of the island's many Protestants? 'Irish-speaking'? Once again, there was a divisive as well as a unifying quality to this emblem of national identity. The unravelling could go on. 'Prosperous'? The most recent of economic historians has demonstrated that, for example, 'average incomes in Ireland almost trebled between 1845 and 1914', that 'a whole series of proxies for living standards – wages, consumption, literacy, life-span, height, birth weight – argue for betterment between the Famine and the First World War', and that the notion that Irish industries declined as a consequence of the union with Britain at the start of the nineteenth century is in fact mistaken.[43] Thus prosperity was actually increasing in the period prior to Irish independence from Britain. Moreover, Irish experience under the union did not justify the nationalist belief that industry had been stifled as a consequence of that union, and (as post-independence performance was to demonstrate) there was equally little ground for the nationalist conviction that once independence had been achieved economic success would follow.

The intellectual reappraisal necessitated by such scholarship is echoed by practical, political implications. Scholars have noted the complications of Southern political attitudes to the North,[44] and also the potentially disastrous effects should the Republic's formal irredentism be satisfied. As Tom Garvin has pointed out, were a serious and public offer of a united Ireland to be made by the UK government,

> it would turn Northern Ireland upside-down. However, it would have devastating, and possibly destabilising effects on the Republic as well. The structure of the Dublin state is predicated on the unspoken assumption of indefinite continuance of partition, as is its party system.[45]

Yet irredentist rhetoric and assumption does form a significant part of the ideology of independent Irish statehood. The Republic's formal and imaginative claim to Northern Ireland has had a powerful impact on politics north and south of the border, and the significance of adjusting or abandoning this stance is weighty both in ideological and in practical terms. If intellectual argument questions the seamlessness, viability and even the desirability of Irish national unity then new (perhaps more thoroughly honest) self-descriptions and self-perceptions will be required for the Republic of Ireland. Thus the implications of scholarly research – that which has taken unionism seriously, no less than that which has searchingly scrutinised Irish nationalist culture – are yet to be fully realised.

IV

There is a certain bland relativism to such arguments as Kerby Miller's (in an essay on the writing of Irish history) that, 'For statesmanship to be constructive ... the equal validity of the cultures, traditions and interests of all parties must be acknowledged.'[46] It is difficult, for example, seriously to sustain the argument that traditional nationalist and traditional unionist readings of the history of Northern Ireland between 1921 and 1972 are both simultaneously valid, given that the intellectual coherence of each view depends centrally on the argument that the other is fundamentally misconceived. Conflict has been too pronounced and too important for such relativism to be plausible or helpful. But this chapter and, indeed, this book have argued the need both for serious, sensitive treatment of unionism in Ireland, and for sustained reflection on the implications which that treatment might have in relation to Irish politics more broadly. Such an approach demands that unionism be interrogated respectfully but not uncritically, and that those who study unionism are also committed to the study of its rivals in an equally respectful and serious fashion. Intellectual life draws strength from disagreement and debate, but it is to be hoped that a certain synergy can be achieved in the study of such topics as have been addressed in this volume. It would be naive and mistaken to look in all this for overly programmatic direction on practical political questions. But it is reasonable to hope that a sensitive, wide-ranging appreciation of unionism in modern Ireland can challenge cliché and can contribute to a more profound understanding of Irish politics and culture.

NOTES

1. M. McInerney, *Peadar O'Donnell: Irish Social Rebel* (Dublin, 1974), p. 201.
2. For sustained consideration of O'Donnell's politics, see R. English, *Radicals and the Republic: Socialist Republicanism in the Irish Free State 1925–1937* (Oxford, 1994).
3. P. J. Roche, 'Northern Ireland and Irish Nationalism: A Unionist Perspective', *Irish Review*, 15 (1994), p. 70.
4. E. Phoenix, *Northern Nationalism: Nationalist Politics, Partition and the Catholic Minority in Northern Ireland 1890–1940* (Belfast, 1994).
5. R. Foster, *The Late Show*, BBC2, 12 January 1994.
6. D. G. Boyce, *Nationalism in Ireland*, 2nd edn (London, 1991), p. 393.
7. B. Parekh, 'Discourses on National Identity', *Political Studies*, 42, 3 (Sept. 1994).
8. See, for example, D. Eastwood, *Governing Rural England: Tradition and Transformation in Local Government 1780–1840* (Oxford, 1994) and A. Adonis, *Making Aristocracy Work: the Peerage and the Political System in Britain 1884–1914* (Oxford, 1993).
9. See, for example, K. A. Miller, 'Revising Revisionism: Comments and Reflections', in D. Keogh and M. H. Haltzel (eds), *Northern Ireland and the Politics of Reconciliation* (Cambridge, 1993), p. 53.
10. A. Jackson, *Sir Edward Carson* (Dublin, 1993), pp. 8, 28.
11. For compelling treatment of this theme, see R. Foster, 'The Lovely Magic of its Dawn: Reading Irish History as a Story', *The Times Literary Supplement*, 16 December 1994.
12. A. Jackson, 'Unionist History' (i, ii), *Irish Review*, 7 (1989), 8 (1990); G. Walker, '"The Irish Dr Goebbels": Frank Gallagher and Irish Republican Propaganda', *Journal of Contemporary History*, 27 (1992).
13. B. Bradshaw, 'Nationalism and Historical Scholarship in Modern Ireland', *Irish Historical Studies*, 26, 104 (1989).
14. G. R. Elton, *Return to Essentials: Some Reflections on the Present State of Historical Study* (Cambridge, 1991), pp. 5, 9, 23–4, 45–6.
15. N. J. Curtin, *The United Irishmen: Popular Politics in Ulster and Dublin 1791–1798* (Oxford, 1994); A. T. Q. Stewart, *A Deeper Silence: the Hidden Origins of the United Irishmen* (London, 1993); J. Smyth, *The Men of No Property: Irish Radicals and Popular Politics in the Late Eighteenth Century* (Dublin, 1992); I. McBride, 'The School of Virtue: Francis

234   *Unionism in Modern Ireland*

Hutcheson, Irish Presbyterians and the Scottish Enlightenment', in D. G. Boyce, R. Eccleshall and V. Geoghegan (eds), *Political Thought in Ireland since the Seventeenth Century* (London, 1993).

16. P. Bew, *Ideology and the Irish Question: Ulster Unionism and Irish Nationalism 1912–1916* (Oxford, 1994); C. Campbell, *Emergency Law in Ireland 1918–1925* (Oxford, 1994).
17. J. Whyte, *Interpreting Northern Ireland* (Oxford, 1990), p.125.
18. S. Bruce, *The Red Hand: Protestant Paramilitaries in Northern Ireland* (Oxford, 1992), pp. 24–6.
19. S. Bruce, *God Save Ulster! The Religion and Politics of Paisleyism* (Oxford, 1986), pp. 249, 264.
20. S. Bruce, *The Edge of the Union: The Ulster Loyalist Political Vision* (Oxford, 1994), p. 30.
21. J. Smyth, *Saothar*, 18 (1993), p.75.
22. Smyth, *The Men of No Property*, pp. 182–3.
23. Curtin, *The United Irishmen*, pp. 9, 10, 288–9.
24. *Andersonstown News*, 12 October 1991.
25. Whyte, *Interpreting Northern Ireland*, pp. 159–61.
26. M. E. Daly, *Industrial Development and Irish National Identity 1922–1939* (Dublin, 1992), p. 3.
27. C. C. O'Brien, *Ancestral Voices: Religion and Nationalism in Ireland* (Dublin, 1994), p. 152.
28. D. G. Boyce, 'Brahmins and Carnivores: the Irish Historian in Great Britain', *Irish Historical Studies*, 25, 99 (1987), p. 227.
29. D. G. Boyce, *The Irish Question and British Politics 1868–1986* (London, 1988), pp. 16–17.
30. A. Pollak (ed.), *A Citizens' Inquiry: The Opsahl Report on Northern Ireland* (Dublin, 1993), p. 53.
31. A. Jackson, *The Ulster Party: Irish Unionists in the House of Commons 1884–1911* (Oxford, 1989).
32. Bruce, *The Edge of the Union*, p. 62; S. Nelson, *Ulster's Uncertain Defenders: Loyalists and the Northern Ireland Conflict* (Belfast, 1984), pp. 12–13; G. Walker, 'Old History: Protestant Ulster in Lee's *Ireland*', *Irish Review*, 12 (1992), pp. 68–9.
33. G. FitzGerald, *Towards a New Ireland*, 2nd edn (Dublin, 1973), pp. viii, 3–9.
34. C. Hewitt, 'The Roots of Violence: Catholic Grievances and Irish Nationalism during the Civil Rights Period' and P. A. Compton, 'Employment Differentials in Northern Ireland and Job Discrimination: A Critique', in P. J. Roche and B. Barton (eds), *The Northern Ireland Question: Myth and Reality* (Aldershot, 1991).
35. S. O'Neill, 'Pluralist Justice and its Limits: the Case of Northern Ireland', *Political Studies*, 42, 3 (1994), p. 372.
36. R. English, '"Cultural Traditions" and Political Ambiguity', *Irish Review*, 15 (1994).
37. A. Aughey, 'Unionism and Self-determination', in Roche and Barton (eds), *The Northern Ireland Question: Myth and Reality*, p. 14.
38. S. Khilnani, *Arguing Revolution: the Intellectual Left in Postwar France* (New Haven, 1993).

39. S. O'Faolain, *De Valera* (Harmondsworth, 1939), pp. 155–6.
40. Bew, *Ideology and the Irish Question*.
41. T. Denman, *Ireland's Unknown Soldiers: the 16th (Irish) Division in the Great War* (Blackrock, 1992).
42. M. G. Valiulis, *Portrait of a Revolutionary: General Richard Mulcahy and the Founding of the Irish Free State* (Blackrock, 1992), p. 239.
43. C. O Grada, *Ireland: A New Economic History 1780–1939* (Oxford, 1994), pp. 242, 250, 307.
44. D. G. Boyce, '"Can Anyone Here Imagine ... ?": Southern Irish Political Parties and the Northern Ireland Problem', in Roche and Barton (eds), *The Northern Ireland Question: Myth and Reality*.
45. T. Garvin, 'The North and the Rest: the Politics of the Republic of Ireland', in C. Townshend (ed.), *Consensus in Ireland: Approaches and Recessions* (Oxford, 1988), p. 109.
46. Miller, 'Revising Revisionism', p. 53.

Index

Adams, G.   200
Adamson, I.   12–13
Allen, C.   136
Allen, W.   49, 51–2, 54–5
Allison, L.   193
Anderson, J.   174, 188
Andrews, J. M.   118
Andrews, T.   28, 30–1, 44
Anglo-Irish Agreement (1985)   14,
    172, 178–80, 182, 185, 187,
    198
Anglo-Irish Treaty (1921)   131
Anglo-Scottish Union (1707)   5–6
Archdale, E.   119
Armour, J. B.   27
Aughey, A.   xii, 230

Baird, E.   122
Bairner, A.   193, 195, 203–5, 207,
    214–15
Balfour, A.   xi, 46, 51, 54, 61
Barr, G.   12
Bates, R. D.   118
Beattie, J.   137, 138
Beckett, J. C.   4, 7, 11
Best, G.   197, 208
Bew, P.   xii, 165, 177, 224, 231
Bingham, B.   198, 201–3, 210,
    212–13
Blanchflower, D.   197
Blease, W.   155
Boal, D.   161
Boyce, D. G.   100, 222, 227
Bradford, R.   152
Bradshaw, B.   223
Brett, C.   13, 133
Bright, J.   26
British and Irish Communist
    Organisation [B&ICO]   182
British Legion   100–10
Brody, M.   196
Brooke, B. [Lord Brookeborough]
    11, 119, 124, 149, 153–4, 161–2,
    166

Bruce, S.   xii, 115, 194, 204–5, 209,
    225
Bryce, J.   6
Bullock, S.   66–71, 75–6

Campaign for Equal Citizenship
    [CEC]   183
Campbell, C.   224
Cardwell, J.   128
Carson, E. H.   36, 65, 72–3, 116–17,
    121, 124–6, 139, 142, 222
Chalmers, T.   22–3
Chamberlain, J.   26, 30, 43–4, 46, 58
Charlton, J.   198, 202, 213
Chichester-Clark, J.   121, 164
Church of Ireland   5, 20–1, 27, 81–4,
    86, 88, 91, 103, 109
Clark, G.   158
Collins, M.   118
Colley, L.   x, 4–5, 14
Conservative Party (in Ireland)
    24–5, 27, 34, 36, 54, 183–5
Constitution, 1937 (Irish)   115, 123,
    166
Coulter, C.   115
Craig, J. [Lord Craigavon]   66, 75,
    117–18, 121, 135–7, 139, 142
Craig, W.   121, 153, 162–3
Currie, A.   150
Curtin, N. J.   224, 226

Daly, M. E.   226
Dane, R. M.   43–5
Deasy, A.   202
Democratic Unionist Party [DUP]
    161
Denman, T.   231
De Valera, E.   73, 100, 104, 106,
    110, 159, 166
Devlin, J.   138
Dicey, A. V.   xi
Downing Street Declaration (1993)
    202

Elton, G. R. 223
Ervine, D. xi
Ervine, St John 13, 32, 67, 71–6
European Community/Union xi, 3, 12, 14

Faulkner, B. 121, 152–5, 161, 163–4, 166–7
Fianna Fail 102, 106–9, 111
Fine Gael 106–8, 111
Fitt, G. 150
FitzGerald, G. 127, 228
Flags and Emblems Act (1954) 123
Foster, J. 134
Foster, R. F. 222–3
Framework Document (1995) xi, 14, 166, 172, 187

Garvin, T. 232
Gibbon, P. xii, 7, 42–3
Gladstone, W. E. 20–1, 24–30, 44–5
Goodman, J. 174
Government of Ireland Act (1920) x, 116, 131–2, 135–6

Hanna, C. 8
Hanna, G. 123–4
Harrison, J. 8
Haughey, C. 102, 107
Henderson, T. 137–8
Hewitt, J. 11
Hogan, V. 210
Houghton, R. 208
Hume, J. 200
Hutcheson, F. 13

Ireland Act (1949) 120
Irish Home Rule ix, 2, 8–10, 19, 22, 24–30, 32–7, 41–2, 47–8, 55–7, 63, 65–6, 68, 70, 72–3, 76, 85, 87, 115, 125, 135, 139
Irish National Liberation Army [INLA] 198
Irish Republican Army [IRA] 82, 84–94, 100, 102, 106, 108, 112, 117–18, 121, 128, 166, 197–203, 227, 231

Jackson, A. ix, xii, 222–3, 227

Jeffery, K. 100
Jennings, P. 197, 199, 208
Johnstone, T. 9–10
Joynson-Hicks, W. 139

Keane, R. 208
Knott, R. 136
Kyle, S. 138, 140

Latimer, W. T. 8–9
Lecky, W. E. H. 223
Lemass, S. 121, 150, 152, 157, 160, 166
Liberal Party (in Ireland) 7–8, 20–37
Long, S. E. 168
Long, W. 55–6, 61
Loughlin, J. 128
Lynch, J. 150
Lynd, R. 9–10
Lyons, T. 124

Major, J. 186
Mayhew, P. 202
McAteer, E. 121
McBride, I. 224
McCartney, R. 13
McCosh, J. 22–3
McGrath, P. 208
McIvor, B. 163
MacKnight, T. 2, 7
McManus, S. 200
McMichael, G. xi
McNeill, R. 126
Methodist Church 83
Miller, D. 2, 115
Miller, K. 232
Molyneaux, J. 177–8, 186
Montgomery, H de Fellenberg 43–7, 57
Moore, F. Frankfort 7, 64–7, 69, 75–6
Moore, W. 55–6, 61
Morgan, W. 163
Morrill, J. 4
Morrison, D. 226
Mulcahy, R. 231

Nairn, T. 2

Nelson, S.   10, 206
Nixon, J.   141
Northern Ireland Economic Research
    Council [NIERC]   176
Northern Ireland Labour Party [NILP]
    149–50

O'Brien, C. C.   xi, 227
O'Donnell, P.   220
Oliver, J.   13
O'Neill, S.   229
O'Neill, T.   x, 120–1, 148–68
Orange Order/Orangeism   xii, 2,
    12–13, 20–1, 23, 27, 34, 37, 41,
    49–50, 56, 63, 67–8, 71–3, 93,
    118, 149, 157–9, 162
Orr, J.   48, 51, 61

Paisley, I.   121, 152, 156, 158,
    160–1, 166, 168, 225
Parnell, C. S.   25–6, 65, 74, 101
Patterson, H.   xii, 165, 177
Phoenix, E.   221
Plunkett, H.   31–2, 52, 70, 73
Pocock, J.   2–3
Pollock, A.   137–8
Presbyterian Church   8, 10, 19–37
Presbyterian Historical Society   8
Prior, J.   175
Progressive Unionist Party [PUP]   xi

Redmond, J.   105
Robinson, M.   111
Roche, P.   220
Rogan, A.   199, 205–6, 216
Roman Catholic Church   11, 20–2,
    29–30, 32–7, 101, 103, 119, 122,
    133
Royal Ulster Constabulary [RUC]
    123
Russell, T. W.   30, 45–6, 48, 53–5,
    58

Saunderson, E.   7–8, 26, 48, 51–4,
    56, 61
Scottish Enlightenment   5, 22
Shaw, G. B.   72, 75
Sinclair, T.   8, 19–40, 44–6, 56–7, 59

Sinn Fein   66, 82, 84–5, 88, 101,
    104, 106, 111, 130, 133, 200,
    215, 230
Sloan, T.   48, 52–3, 55
Smyth, J.   224–6
Smyth, M.   151, 157, 167
Social Democratic and Labour Party
    [SDLP]   14, 121–2, 200
Solemn League and Covenant (1643)
    5, 9, 35
Solemn League and Covenant (1912)
    9, 19, 35, 57, 134, 139, 141–2
Stewart, A. T. Q.   14, 224
Stewart, W.   141
Stopford, D.   81–2, 85
Sugden, J.   193, 195, 203–5, 207,
    214–15
Sunningdale Agreement (1973)
    121–2, 165

Townsend, A.   211
Thornby, A.   136
Todd, J.   xii, 13, 115, 204–5, 214–15
Tomlinson, M.   168

Ulster Defence Association [UDA]
    12
Ulster Democratic Party [UDP]   xi
Ulster Freedom Fighters [UFF]   201,
    203
Ulster Liberal Unionist Association
    [ULUA]   25–37, 42–7, 54, 56
Ulster Revival (1859)   19–20, 64
'Ulster-Scot' mythology   8–9,
    12–13, 34–6, 56
Ulster Society   12
Ulster Special Constabulary   60, 84,
    119
Ulster Unionist Council [UUC]
    54–6, 149, 163
Ulster Unionist Party [UUP]   121,
    148–67, 177, 180, 185–6
Ulster Volunteer Force [UVF]   57,
    66, 84, 95, 158, 225
Union, Act of (1800)   6, 131, 134

Valiulis, M. G.   231
Vanguard movement   12

Walker, G.   223
Wallace, R. H.   56
Warnock, E.   158, 162
Whiteside, N.   208

Whyte, J. H.   225
Wilson, A.   124
Wilson, T.   154
Woodburn, J. B.   7–9